THE LATER ROMAN EMPIRE

An Archaeology AD 150-600

THE LATER ROMAN EMPIRE

An Archaeology AD 150-600

Richard Reece

TEMPUS

First published 1999

PUBLISHED IN THE UNITED KINGDOM BY:

Tempus Publishing Ltd
The Mill, Brimscombe Port
Stroud, Gloucestershire GL5 2QG

PUBLISHED IN THE UNITED STATES OF AMERICA BY:

Tempus Publishing Inc.
2A Cumberland Street
Charleston, SC 29401

Tempus books are available in France, Germany and Belgium
from the following addresses:

Tempus Publishing Group	Tempus Publishing Group	Tempus Publishing Group
21 Avenue de la République	Gustav-Adolf-Straße 3	Place de L'Alma 4/5
37300 Joué-lès-Tours	99084 Erfurt	1200 Brussels
FRANCE	GERMANY	BELGIUM

British Library Cataloguing in Publication Data.
A catalogue record for this book is available from the British Library.

ISBN 0 7524 1449 6

Typesetting and origination by Tempus Publishing.
PRINTED AND BOUND IN GREAT BRITAIN.

Contents

Acknowledgements

The process of writing the main body of the text was done in complete isolation, which meant that it had a greater than usual crop of errors and infelicities. Kenneth Painter very kindly agreed to read through the text and he made suggestions that either saved me from a number of major blunders or added important points which had been missed out. Where I have persisted in blundering he should clearly not be blamed. My neighbours Jo and John Salfeld worked meticulously through the text to try to remove the major and minor infelicities (and errors) to try to bring it up to the standard which their earlier careers in writing and publishing suggested. In most cases I, most untypically, accepted their corrections. At this point the text was in reasonable shape but illustrations were needed. When I realised this the whole project would have ground to a halt had not Ellen Swift agreed to shoulder the infuriating job of chasing pictures, their owners and their prices. Left to myself I would have finished the job by simply photocopying the text to use as hand-outs in the last Later Roman Empire lecture series. That the text took final shape as a book is therefore due to her help.

The book itself must act as thanks to all the students who supported the course and appeared to enjoy it over the years it was taught.

Preface

This book has grown out of a course that I taught between 1973 and 1999 at the Institute of Archaeology, University College London. I have left out of the book many subjects that had to be included in the course to aim at decent coverage, but of which my knowledge is totally second hand. Here I have been able to restrict myself to subjects in which I am particularly interested and material I have tried to see for myself.

The main subjects that readers might find missing are discussions of towns, and examination of individual examples, the army, cemeteries, sarcophagi and ivory carving. Sarcophagi and ivories form for me a blind spot, even a dislike. Few examples in either category are firmly dated, in the rather harsh way that I use the term, and both seem to have developed a mystique, rather like sailing or riding, of which I am not an initiate. Towns, cemeteries and the army are rather similar topics. Their subject matter is enormous but each example, a text, a site or a category of object, belongs very much in its own time and place. The later history and archaeology of a once-Imperial capital like Trier is very different from that of Athens. In the course this was brought out year by year as different students took individual towns and we compared and contrasted them in a seminar. Here the subject is only touched upon briefly.

The reasons for writing the book are the same as the reasons for teaching the course: that the period from about AD 150–600 has an interest all of its own, and that needs to be put forward. The subject has for many years been neglected, but interest in it is now growing. It might be objected that I cover the same ground as the excellent books by Averil Cameron on the Later Roman Empire, and Late Antiquity. The period is the same, but the subject matter is different in itself and approached in a different way. I would hope that readers would first get to grips with the history and thought of the period through Dr Cameron's books (and others), so as to negotiate more surely the material and archaeological minefield I have carefully laid for them. For those who have this book and do not want to read any others, I have included a brief introduction and, at the end, two appendices. The first is a personal historical summary, the second a glossary of Early Christian ideas and terms.

My last set of excuses concerns my selection of material. I clearly stand convicted of concentration on choice examples. For Early Christian painting I choose the catacombs. But not only do I restrict myself to Rome, I home in on one particular catacomb out of a whole series of possible others. I move almost straight from that to the mosaics of Ravenna, when a comparable suite of less well-known mosaics of similar date could be collected from many different sites around the Empire.

The reason grows from teaching the course. That was very much an introduction, which means to me two things. It should include the main features of the period and it should examine them in such a way that listeners or readers can go on to consider and understand other examples for themselves. The Via Latina Catacomb brings out the basic set of questions and observations in an accessible form. The Ravenna mosaics form the backbone for dating and discussion from 450–680. Other examples that have been included, which do not match these high standards, are the result of personal preference.

Introduction: the Later Roman Empire or Late Antiquity

Why does the Later Roman Empire need special treatment? Why the capital letters and the book to itself? The Roman Empire is an episode in world history and, as such, it has a beginning and an end. But that is not how many people think history works. Everyone at school has been told that the Middle Ages did not stop on the first of January, or 25th of March if we are being careful, 1475. In the same way it is impossible to put an exact date on the end of the Roman Empire with which everyone will agree. This is partly because we cannot agree on what the end of the Roman Empire means. So the easiest way to deal with the matter is to study the beginnings of the Roman Empire from the Republic onwards, and then to leave it before anyone claims An End. The next period of study can be called Late Antiquity or the Early Middle Ages, and can be a study in transition. By leaving the Roman Empire well before any of its ends, it becomes a study in stability. A moment's thought will remind us that no period can be only stability or transition. Change is always happening, so the main characteristic that had been picked out is the rate of change. In the core period of the Roman Empire the rate of change is slow, perhaps even too slow, so that inevitable evolutionary change is suppressed. In the Later Empire the rate of change is faster, perhaps as the inevitable works itself out. The Byzantine Empire, the eastern continuation of the Later Roman Empire, is renowned for a stability which is sometimes called fossilisation.

Since the study of the Roman Empire usually fades away around the year 200, and the Later Empire is changed drastically by the Arab expansions of the seventh century, the core of the Later Empire must be somewhere between AD 150–600, and that is the period on which I will concentrate.

History

Interest in the Early Empire fades with its sources. The historian, by definition, studies written sources, and where the sources are good the history can be detailed and exact. Where the sources are poor the resulting formal history cannot be much better.

This is a very particular view and definition of historical sources. It is a classical view based on the great Roman historians like Livy, Pliny and Tacitus, who were also great literary stylists. These writers no doubt had their likes and dislikes — Tacitus on Domitian springs to mind — but they generally recorded facts.

Apart from Ammianus Marcellinus in the later fourth century the supply of objective factual historians dried up by about 230. Third-century historians are virtually non-

1 Delphi. The base of serpent column originally erected in 479BC after the Greek victory in the battele of Plataea. The column was removed by Constantine the Great in the fourth century. Copyright Richard Reece

existent, and by the fourth century there are either explicitly Christian story tellers such as Eusebius of Caesarea, or the one-line judgements on people and events written by the epitomators. To the likes of Eusebius there was one clear purpose of history, the unfolding of the Christian message. The epitomators, such as Aurelius Victor, reduced the record of each emperor to a single paragraph. History, in the first-century, classical sense, cannot be written from sources such as these.

There are many other documents. In fact there may well be more written records from the Later Empire than from the earlier empire. But the classical type of history cannot be written from venomous letters like some of those sent out by St Jerome from his cave at Bethlehem, or the works of St Augustine, devoted to the minute dissection of points of doctrine, or helpful illustrated anonymous pamphlets such as the *De Rebus Bellicis*.

At this point it has to be admitted that there are different types of history and different types of sources, none of which can probably be called either objective or factual. What is a fact to Tacitus is quite different from the fact of Eusebius, and neither may satisfy the modern historian. Perhaps the most obtrusive difference between the sources, and the history, of the early and later empires is the difference in fixed points. The early empire is the time of Consuls, Emperors, and 'things done'. The coinage reflects this. The coinage of AD 110 (Trajan, 98–117) is different from the coinage of 125 (Hadrian, 117–38). The portrait of the emperor is different, the titles are different, and the reverse types have different themes: Trajan made much of his buildings, Hadrian advertised the provinces.

2   Constantinople. The serpent column from Delphi as placed by Constantine the Great in the Circus of his new capital, Constantinople, after the dedication of the city in 330 AD Copyright Richard Reece

By the fourth century the coinage is not divided up by the reigns of emperors. Portraits are almost banished in an effort to portray the institution rather than the man, and the reverse types are greatly reduced in number and rarely, if ever, directly refer to the 'things done' by the emperor.

Even worse than the decline of facts and events is the rise of magic, superstition, and religion, sometimes difficult to tell apart. There is plenty of superstition in the early empire, Pliny talking about the protective uses of gemstones for example, but it gives the impression of being low key, usually benign, and under control. To some people the later empire is a time of State Superstition. A regime of belief, derived not from the comforting stylish writings of the Greek philosophers but from the uneducated essays of fishermen or the ungrammatical ravings of mystics, moves towards being imposed on the Roman world. In less benign mode Peter Brown has pointed to this case of the remedy increasing the illness. When there is no cure only those who cannot avoid it will have the illness. When there is a cure the illness becomes almost fashionable to have. With the arrival of the white magician, the Christian Holy Man, comes power over evil spirits, black witchcraft and demonic possession. In the fast-changing times of the fourth century, battle is joined and everyone is on one side or the other. How can an objective historian deal with such a period? Better to avoid it.

Administration

If the Christian God rules the world of the Later Empire, and the emperor is the vice-regent on earth, then the chain of command has altered. The army still needs detailed commanding, the civil service still needs direction, the provinces grouped into dioceses need administrators, but the importance of the earthly supreme ruler becomes uncertain. I suspect that Constantine the Great, the first emperor under whom Christianity was tolerated and encouraged, would have pushed for a heavenly philosophy of collegiality: one ruler for heaven, another for earth. Perhaps Theodosius the Great and Justinian (why not the great?) followed in this same line. Others had far less practical influence, yet their status at the centre of the empire became much higher. Hadrian visited many provinces on foot in rain and wind, so his biographer says, and no doubt he talked to those who got near him, shook hands and exchanged greetings with all who were introduced to him, and generally behaved like a human being. Such behaviour is unthinkable around the year 400. The emperor is *sacer*, set apart, and this is a physical matter as well as spiritual. In a sense the ineffective emperor is little more than a symbol who needs to be kept alive, taken out and dusted every so often, and paraded on the appropriate occasions for all to wonder at. He should, if possible produce offspring who will be future emperors, but if this does not happen his wife develops the ability to hand on his power to a chosen second husband after his death. She does not usually reign in her own right, but can certainly be Full Empress mother or Full Empress wife. Full Empress daughter is by definition impossible since it implies the survival of the Emperor father. If he dies the power must be transmitted to another male.

Towns and trade

At a local level the emperor was little more than a remote concept. What mattered was the unit to which you belonged. That was the civitas which held your records, probably the place of your birth. St Augustine in his *City of God (De civitate Dei)* points out that it is better to concentrate on your eternal, heavenly, home rather than your earthly, temporary, home. But home here has an official rather than a cosy connotation; perhaps domicile would be a better, if less attractive, rendering. There is a nice reminder here of the vulgar freedman Trimalchio, from the *Satyricon* of Petronius, who warns that it is far better to spend money on your tomb where you will be for ever, than your dining room, where your days are numbered.

In some cases you could be technically free, that is not a slave but yet tied to your home and also your job. Legislation which enforced this grew in the fourth century. Old divisions had changed. St Paul could reduce a centurion to a state of extreme anxiety by declaring that he was a Roman citizen. The same soldier in the fourth century would either have said 'so is everyone else; so what?', or he would have tried to find out if Paul was one of the honestiores or simply one of the humiliores. The best explanations of these terms are 'those who had contacts and could get things done' and 'the rest'. Higher up the social scale racking uncertainty had set in over exact gradation. New categories had come in, for example Constantine's manufacture of the grade Patrician from the long-disused

3 Side, Turkey. The town gateway, blocked in the later Roman period when the size of towns was reduced and access was restricted. Copyright Richard Reece

republican class term. How did this rank with the old titles of Consul and Senator? A whole section of the fifth-century law code deals with this important point.

Let us return to the city, which had been changing from the prosperous times of the early empire. The fortunes of the city were closely tied to the general fortunes of the community. In turn, the fortunes of the community were tied to trade. The most obvious characteristic of the later city is the reduction in its size from the second-century maximum. In some areas of the empire towns had pre-Imperial walls, perhaps from Hellenistic days. In others, they developed in the years of general peace of the first and second century and did not need defences. The most obvious signs of reduction come when large sprawling cities have much smaller areas within them newly walled. This happens at different times from the third to the fifth century. Where we know what is happening from archaeology the area left outside the defences withers away and becomes derelict, while inside the walls life continues. The most obvious signs come from burials outside the late walls, as is proper, but among the buildings of the earlier town, which is clearly no longer considered a full part of the city **(3)**.

Who, or what, caused the shrinkage? And is shrinkage the same as walling? In other words did the walls cause the shrinkage by only making part of the area safe, or did the walls make safe the already reduced area needed? Fragmentary historical sources tell us about raids on towns by groups of people who had broken through the frontier and caused death and destruction. Late walls, such as those of Athens, were built to repel any further attacks. This happened commonly in Gaul and perhaps the best studied-example is Tours. But the question we have to examine is whether a town like Tours which seems to have adapted almost immediately to a 'shrunken' life underwent a major change in population numbers and activities at the building of the walls, or whether the size of the circuit merely reflects the already shrunken numbers and activities of the town.

If cities were smaller than they had been, even before they were surrounded by walls, what had caused this? Above, I mentioned the link I see between towns and trade. Towns by definition are parasitic on the landscape because they have a greater population than can produce its own food from the surrounding area. Towns consist mainly of consumers who try to justify their existence by providing services for the surrounding countryside. People in the countryside, produce food, clothing, building materials and materials for furnishings, and if they want goods or services from the town they can buy them with their produce. Either the farmer sells directly to the town or puts his goods on the market that provides for the town.

One of the services the town gives is the provision of the range of goods that the farmer cannot produce at home: pepper, pottery, scarlet dye, bronze ornaments and glass beads might do for a start. If the farmer wants some of these goods and is willing to exchange produce for them then trade is established and both sides will make a profit. The shopkeeper will improve his premises and contribute towards the cost of keeping the town clean and safe, the farmer will buy seed corn and pay his taxes. Every so often his family may insist on improving, or adding to, the farmhouse.

The town exists for as long as a group of people want to live together as parasites and as long as a life parasitic on the countryside is viable. If the farmer, the producer, loses interest in pepper, pottery, scarlet dye, bronze ornaments and beads, then the shopkeepers will only have one another to sell to, and the equality of demand is lost. The producers of materials necessary for living have the edge over the sellers of knick-knacks. The town, and the only meaning of the word must be the parasitic tradesmen, is likely to de-aggregate, thin out, drop in population density, to the level where they can grow enough in their back gardens to keep themselves alive. Without potatoes this may be difficult. In other words in the absence of intensive production of carbohydrates which the potato provides corn may be essential and this needs more than a back garden for survival. If trade diminishes, either because supply drops or demand drops, or both, the revenue of the individuals who live together to form the town drops and their continued co-habitation is threatened.

We have few literary references to the rise or fall of demand for goods, perhaps because the writers of texts which have survived were either socially, or spiritually, above such things. There are a few references to supply changing, and archaeology can comment on the volume of goods supplied, used and discarded, and where they came from. The origin of goods which reached rubbish deposits in the fourth century is more restricted than for goods of the second century. The most common discarded rubbish to survive is broken pottery, and there the distance that goods have travelled between production and discard is substantially less in the fourth century than it is earlier in the empire. If this is a reliable index, then provinces have become more self-sufficient in the later empire, in pottery at least, and inter-provincial trade has declined. We can at least say that the defended area of a town decreases at roughly the same time that inter-provincial trade in pottery declines.

This very guarded statement illustrates the limitations of interpreting archaeological evidence, and perhaps explains why so many historians wonder whether it is all worth the trouble. The statement the historian wants to make is that towns declined because of the failure of long-distance trade. Even then, this is only a rather basic building block to some more interesting discussion of life in towns and countryside, failure of regimes, or deep seated political changes. But the amount of work to change the guarded statement into the desired statement is enormous and this gulf between the evidence we have and the interpretation we want has to be kept in mind all through any discussion which tries to bring together written sources and material remains.

Belief

Perhaps this is the point to leave the down to earth and consider the ethereal. This might take two forms, the spiritual and the artistic. Religion has to be considered mainly from written sources. A few people might disagree and insist that the remains have a lot to tell us. This immediately opens up the difference in religion between what people believe and what they do about it. As a broad generalisation the remains will help us to understand what people did about their religion, but the documents are needed to try to understand what they believed. A font, suitable for baptising people of any age, does not tell us directly who was baptised, at what age, for what reasons, and what eternal punishments were awaiting those who were not baptised. It is sad that the most interesting human characteristic, sin, is the least susceptible to material study in the past. It is seldom the physical action, which might leave a material trace, which is sinful, but the motive, which is unrecoverable. It might be that the decorative scheme inside the church will tell us something about the hopes, fears, and beliefs of the congregation. An excellent example would be the depictions of the last judgement, the division between heavenly bliss and writhing torment, which is the last thing the penitents see as they leave the west doorway of the church to continue their pilgrimage to a chosen shrine, such as Compostela, in quest of grace. But we have very few late Roman churches whose decorative schemes are complete, and of those which are complete, almost all have been suitably amended in later ages to fit in with changing ideology. The example of San Apollinare Nuovo in Ravenna will provide an example later. If the material remains say little about sin, the writers make up for it.

Images

Art, in the shape of paintings, mosaics, sculptures, carving and craftworks as well as architecture, forms a rather odd section of the study of the past. Few people have tried to plumb the deepest thoughts of the Roman potter by studying his undecorated output, yet there is a constant attempt to look at spatial and pictorial products in order to find out what was the spirit of the age that produced them. A second oddity is the fact that the most interpretative subject, art, bases itself almost completely on a body of material. Written sources play little part because they say little about decorative art or architecture in the later Roman period. The justification here must be twofold: that what is expressed goes straight from the mind of the artist to the finished product, so that intermediate words are pointless or impossible, and interpretative words are at best tangential, and that decorative arts are the product of a spiritual effort, while the production of a cooking pot is the product of a purely practical effort. If you want to know of aspirations look at art. If you want to know about cooking look at cooking pots.

Few art historians will be happy with this analysis, and I completely agree with virtually any criticisms that might be made. Most obviously, this concept of the tortured artistic soul expressing its struggles through the medium of paint or marble is only known from the eighteenth century onwards, the Romantic movement. Up to then the painter may have had his tantrums, but they were those of a superior craftsman rather than an 'artist'. The reason for beating the apprentice who put on the coat of wet plaster too early so that it had dried out before the maestro had got out of bed is simply that the colours of the resulting painting would lack the glow of the true fresco and the customer would be critical. Inability to express deepest feelings about life would probably not surface till later in the day, and further down the wine-jar.

Yet, given all the ifs and buts, a substantial amount of interpretation is hung on the surviving art and architecture of the ancient world. This is mainly because there are great changes to what is portrayed or built, and how it is done, and people inevitably want explanations for these changes.

Two dimensional art consists mainly of painting and mosaic. The great mosaics of the third century are on floors while the great mosaics of the sixth century are on the superstructure. The set piece of the Great Hunt or mythological scene has its finest hour in the fourth century and then seems to die away. There are large expanses of coloured mosaics in the fifth and sixth centuries but most of these are fairly conventional patterns and geometric motifs (4). There is evidence of wall and ceiling mosaics from at least the second century onward but since so few superstructures survive intact from before the fourth century complete examples are unknown. A wall mosaic was freed from utilitarian needs to stand up to hard wear; all it had to do was stand up. It could therefore be made of more brittle, colourful, and even precious materials such as coloured and gold glass.

Painting is less durable, in situ, but more restorable when decayed. Thus stains of damp on plaster can destroy painting even before the plaster falls off the walls, whereas so long as the mosaic clings in position its materials are far less affected by decay. Once the decoration has come away from its seating matters reverse. If the plaster holding mosaic decays the mosaic crumbles down fairly quickly to separate tesserae and there is virtually no way of getting back from separate coloured cubes to the original pattern. Painting, however, usually decays in chunks and there is a chance of piecing the chunks back together. As a very general rule mosaics are therefore a matter of survival more or less intact, while paintings can sometimes, but rarely, be intact, but more often rescued by archaeology.

The number of secular buildings surviving in secular use with intact mosaics is small. Religious mosaics are more common. Surviving paintings are more common underground as in catacombs, while painting restored from excavation is more often secular than religious. In summary, mosaics up to the fifth century will tend to be secular, excavated floors; from the fifth century they are more likely to be surviving, religious superstructures. Paintings up to the fifth century will be excavated and secular, or

4 *Rome, Palatine Hill. A late pavement in the area of the Imperial palaces with green and red porphyry inlay (opus sectile). As mosaics became more common on walls and ceilings, floor pavements tended to become simpler. Copyright Richard Reece*

surviving and religious, while after the fifth century they are less common.

Three-dimensional art will be sculpted or cast, stone or bronze, and up to the fifth century a series of large state monuments, such as arches and columns, gives a dated sequence. Smaller carving or casting such as ivory work, bronze, silver, wood or bone presents very different sets of problems from the larger material. A mosaic in situ belongs without doubt to a place, and often to a time. It may have been pre-fabricated and transported, it might even have been re-used, but the limits of our knowledge are reasonably well set. The small ivory carving is not tied to any place or any time, even the source of the ivory is irrelevant to a discussion of where the carving took place. With an engraved silver plate you would not even have the radio-carbon date possible, in theory, on the ivory, to give a rough idea of when the object was created. Smaller works of art and decoration, if not inscribed and taken utterly by themselves, are only datable by the style and technique of decoration, and these are clearly open to substantial questioning. One group of later Roman art that has virtually no forerunners is the illuminated manuscript or picture book. These luxury products are in a sense an invention of the period, and some do give help on both dating and place of origin. They survive mostly out of context, though one example, the St Augustine's Gospels, is still in use in Britain.

This has developed into a listing of types of art. But the Later Empire has been defined as a period of change, and art styles are part of this change. What do the changes consist of and how can they be explained? This cannot be examined without getting down to detail and looking at examples, so perhaps the first thing we ought to do is to consider some examples of later Roman art.

1. Official sculpture and representation

There is one major qualification for a work to be included in the corpus of late Roman art: it must have a date. A minor, supporting, qualification would be that the work looks like other dated pieces of late Roman art. This suggests a two-stream approach in which the running is made by the dated pieces and the catalogue is filled out by the look-alikes. If this approach is not followed, if atmosphere rules, then every different commentator can construct different catalogues and go on to outline totally different schemes of change and development. Argument between schemes becomes impossible because there is no agreed body or sequence of information about which to argue and the subject spirals out of control. On the other hand, if a body of information on which to argue is agreed, then there is total freedom within that framework to construct any schemes that fit within the framework. So late Roman art can rise to a peak unknown to earlier art, or it can plumb vulgar and incompetent depths to which early art never descended. The two schemes can be constructed using the same series of works, but putting different interpretations on them.

It will annoy some people, but comfort others, if I start by saying that I totally reject the theory that late Roman art looks as it does because technical standards declined and the poor artists could do nothing better. I shall not give the theory any further publicity other than wondering why anyone suggested it in the first place. I assume it is because they were raised on 'classical' art that late Roman art looks different, and the only way the classical concept can retain supremacy is to assume that everything else wanted to look the same, but failed. If later art has not 'failed' to look like earlier art then, horror of horrors, it actually wanted to look as it does. And if workers started out trying to make something different from earlier art then other concepts of what is perfect, or what art is for, are possible. Which, of course, cannot be the case.

With these two points in mind, first a dated sequence, then a commentary on what people were trying to do, we need to start on structures with similar purposes, put up by highest authority and therefore presumably carved by good sculptors. Public arches and columns are perfect for our purposes from about AD 80–400.

A good point to start is under the arch of Titus (5-6) which, was completed shortly after his death in AD 81. One of the panels lining the roadway through the arch shows the triumphal procession after the sack of Jerusalem with the emperor in a chariot moving from right to left (5). Yet that is not quite true, for the path of the emperor and the plane of the panel are not the same. If the procession continued its way out of the stone, and you

5   Rome, Arch of Titus. Triumphal procession of the Emperor. Copyright Peter Clayton

6   Rome, Arch of Titus. Spoils from the sack of Jerusalem in the triumphal procession.
Copyright Musea della Civiltà Romana

7 *Rome, Trajan's Column. The Emperor addressing the legions. Copyright Peter Clayton*

walked forward in the same direction, the chariot would cross your path a few yards down the way. The whole procession is there, except that the crowds on our side have been carved away to give us a unique view of what is going on. People continue into the stone, several layers deep, and if their heads are shown, then their feet will be there somewhere, unless blocked from view by other items. Everyone relates to the same ground level, and everyone has similar anatomical proportions and dimensions. If you had been one of the guards lining the route then you might just possibly have seen what is now set in stone.

If we move forward to Trajan's column **(7)** these rules still apply. The column was clearly built by Trajan because it appears on his coins, but it has been suggested that the carving was done after his death. Dating between 110–120 cannot be very far out. Trajan also had constructed an arch at Benevento in Italy which is dated around 117. On both the column and the arch the scenes keep to human proportions and likely arrangements. That is, the emperor, when present, is no larger than anyone else, and has to be interpreted out of the crowd by the arrangement of people around him or the focus of the group. The people who do form the group are reasonably set out, more like an action shot than a wedding group, except that the sculptor has put us in the front line of viewers, and we are unaware of anyone else on our side of the event.

The column of Antoninus Pius does not survive, except for the panels which decorated the base, but the column of Marcus Aurelius does. The base of Antoninus' column shows two main scenes, the apotheosis of the emperor and his wife, Faustina **(8)**, and a scene from the funeral ceremonies and games **(9)**. Two things have happened. The scene

21

8 Rome, Column of Antoninus Pius. The emperor and empress ascend to heaven.
Copyright Peter Clayton

9 Rome, Column of Antoninus Pius. Parade of mounted soldiers in the Decursio, part of the
Emperor's funeral rites. Copyright Peter Clayton

in which the couple are borne aloft by a winged Genius differs from the scenes on the arch of Titus or the monuments of Trajan in that no one ever actually saw what is represented in the sculpture. True, the army of Trajan leaves the gates of Rome with the blessing of Roma herself in human form, but this is to add a personification to an actual scene. For Antoninus something is being represented which is difficult to define. To say it did not happen is well beyond the evidence. To say that no one saw it is not very helpful. To say that it was a matter of belief rather than record at first sounds safer, but it suggests quite wrongly that only visible facts are suitable matter for the record. If a chronicler can write that 'on this day the emperor ascended to join his wife, who had gone before him to the company of the gods' there is no reason why a sculptor cannot depict it. If this were a single episode due to an individual sculptor it would probably not be worth detailed comment. But since it is the first of a line of depictions of ideas and ideal events rather than photographic representations of flesh and blood events, it deserves the comment.

The decursio scene has broken other conventions. There are military standards in the centre of a parade of mounted soldiers riding in a circle. If a complete circle is depicted, and the viewer is on the outside, then the standards will be invisible. If the circle is halved to allow the viewer in, as happened at Titus's triumph, then in this case the nature of the event is destroyed. The answer has been to sculpt from a high vantage point, in fact a bird's-eye view. Yet this is not true, for each person is seen side-on without the expected perspective and foreshortening. Distance has temporarily been wiped out so that the near and far sides of the circle are similar. The elimination of distance by perspective means that the central group, who are the same size as both sides of the circle, are unplaced. They need some ground to stand on, and this is arbitrarily created beneath them. A further result of this drastic re-arrangement is the virtual elimination of the real ground surface and the background.

One interpretation would be that the scene is being edited for us before being depicted. The central group of standards is important and so cannot be obscured; the circle is essential to the ritual and half cannot be disposed of to let us in, so we must look over them. The setting and the grass say nothing which adds to the information, so they can be left out. This interpretation works for a formal or official monument whose purpose is to make a point and communicate it to the viewer. It is almost the opposite of the artistic television commercial where high marks are given for introducing the point, or product, almost as an extra half way through. I assume that the idea here is to make people puzzle over the motive for the commercial, and to influence them subliminally by the 'background'. The state sculptor in the second century and later took a very different view. If you are communicating, then pare the message down to the absolute essentials and hit hard. A victorious general should not be human and handsome and mingle with the troops, but big and ugly and alone.

This has set up the reliefs of the column base of Antoninus as a signpost and mission statement for later Roman art. Quite clearly, at the time this was not the case. But when the monuments are seen in sequence of date, then the middle of the second century does seem to be a turning point, or a quickening point of change. The column of Marcus Aurelius, which does exist complete, though it gets far fewer photographs taken of it than

10 Lepcis Magna, Libya, Arch of Septimius Severus. Imperial procession. Copyright Peter Clayton

the column of Trajan, illustrates some of the points just made in a rather gentle form. If scenes from the two columns are compared, battle scene with battle scene and official event with the like, then tendencies are fairly clear. Scenes are more posed and less untidy, groups of people are usually reduced to one or two deep, backgrounds are minimal and sometimes dispensed with altogether.

By the end of the second century there are two further arches to consider, both of the reign of Septimius Severus (193–211). One is in the forum at Rome and the remains of one are in the emperor's home region of Lepcis Magna in modern Libya. The Rome arch has large-scale scenes which are helpfully divided by ground surfaces to help our understanding. The figures are rather regimented, and far less free-range than the crowds of Trajan's Column, but they still have the freedom to form a crowd, huddle in one place, move in any direction, and be obscured if necessary. The Lepcis reliefs are much more organised. There is a triumphal procession **(10)**, yet it seems to be a set piece with everyone posed so that the viewer of the relief gets a perfect view. The emperor and those with him in the chariot, though moving from left to right, have suddenly all turned at right angles to their direction of movement to face us. In the scene of sacrifice only two rows of participants are allowed, set out neatly with the back row lifted up for good visibility. Yet these carefully posed figures still have considerable individuality, and they are allowed to look to right or left, up or down, at the sacrifice or perhaps the emperor, who is out of the picture. Clothes, as always up to now, have their form determined by the human body within them. This may seem an odd point to make, but its importance will be obvious later on. A further point on the same lines is that if one of the participants dropped dead and was to be dissected the result would be perfectly normal. The bone structure determines the body, and the body determines the clothes.

There is one further point that we need to take in at this point. The earlier monuments were all from Italy, mostly from Rome. The arch of Severus at Lepcis is the first foreigner. It would be good to be able to say that this arch represents the African tradition making itself felt against the Roman norm, but the African emperor, Severus, seems to have gathered craftsmen from different parts of the Mediterranean world to reconstruct his birthplace. Africa, with its lack of native marble, is unlikely to have been the home of a vibrant marble-carving school, and there is some evidence that the marble carvers were imported from Asia Minor. Mosaics tell a rather different story, but that has to come later.

The question which this raises is whether we are looking at a Roman tradition in art which has suddenly hit a bumpy patch, and accelerated fast in its own development, or whether different forces are at work. Besides accelerated home-grown development there are at least two other possibilities, one native, one foreign. Frontality is a buzz-word in late Roman art, and it could well be applied to the emperor and his court who, in their triumphal procession at Lepcis turn smartly to the front to face the viewer. The tendency grows stronger in later art. But it is also seen in art from the East of the empire. Palmyra is often quoted, and sometimes much earlier than in Rome. Thus the Lepcis arch could be more influenced by eastern art than art deep in the city of Rome. The other possible influence does not come from outside, but within. The great Italian art historian Bianchi Bandinelli, the Red Count, maintained that art in the City of Rome had always had an aristocratic, Greek-tending, form as well as a less ethereal, dumpy, popular form. I mention his friendly nickname applied to him in the 1950s and 1960s to say that the interpretation of art is rarely a disembodied mental exercise, but usually incorporates individual interests and feelings. In the case of il Conto Rosso this was explicit and you can take it or leave it. The dangerous ones are those who pretend to be unworldly scholars divorced from the life of their times. If the dumpy popular Italic style of art is taken as an influence then what is happening from the middle of the second century onwards is that the Greek-tending and the home-grown styles in Rome are fusing to form a single late art of Rome.

We must move on, but this means jumping nearly a century because the third century is a desert for dated monuments. A lot was happening in forms of depiction and techniques of sculpture. This can be seen clearly almost year by year on the coins, but the dated monument next after the arches of Severus is the arch of Galerius sculpted around 296. This is a vital but rather sad monument, the remains of a four way arch. The main road from the West to the East, say from Rome to the future Constantinople, ran through the arch, and the main road into Thessalonica still brings juggernauts thundering past it.

Since we have used scenes of sacrifice earlier we can home in on the sacrifice scene on this arch. In this scene, more than the others, frontality rules. All extras, in the film sense, have been swept aside to show the emperor and the main figures lined up in an over-tidy way. All face the front, almost to the detriment of what may be happening on the altar, and the depth of the scene is restricted to one person . Other reliefs are more complicated and untidy, in particular the battle scenes, but when the court is depicted a very formal style of arrangement is used.

The fourth century brings the Arch of Constantine at Rome **(11)**, put up by a 'grateful' citizenry after their 'liberation' from Constantine's rivals in 314. The arch has fuelled

11   Rome, Arch of Constantine. General view showing the sculptural panels of different dates brought together by Constantine. Copyright Richard Reece

many debates because it is a pick and mix of earlier sculptures together with reliefs newly made. Current orthodoxy includes, in the re-use, some Trajanic (98–117) panels, eight Hadrianic (117–138) roundels with two new ones to make up the number, and reliefs of the time of Marcus Aurelius on which the heads are smaller than expected and show features like those of Constantine. The decoration is completed by long thin reliefs in a totally different style, with dumpy figures arranged in regimented rows with a strong frontal lay-out (12). Poor things, they could not equal the grace and anatomical detail of their predecessors. Even though they could remodel the elderly, bearded Marcus Aurelius to look the spitting image of the youthful, clean-shaven Constantine. Switch to the 'new' reliefs, and the emperor whose features have been removed, whoever he may be, is surrounded only by identikit courtiers.

The 'new' roundels are quite obvious, and in a different style from their earlier prototypes (13). In the sun roundel the flying cupid is unpleasingly posed in mid-air but otherwise the sun god in a four-horse chariot is a fair approximation to the other roundels. New figures decorating the roadway through the arch stand out as very different from the Trajanic reliefs beside which they are fixed. The figures are not balanced as they would be in real life, and some of the anatomy is inexact. But it is the long thin friezes above the

12   Rome, Arch of Constantine. Panel of the time of Constantine (c.315 AD) showing a speech to the people. Copyright Musea della Civiltà Romana

side (footpath) arches which worry many commentators. The great central inscription says in words all that needs to be said about the reasons for putting up the arch. The collection of sculpture from earlier buildings marks it out as a major monument. The reliefs of Marcus Aurelius have been re-cut in good portrait style to show the emperor Constantine in formal events. Why spoil the thing by getting a ham-fisted local gravestone carver to carve four thin panels showing two scenes from Constantine's wars of 'liberation', and two court events, the emperor's speech to the people and the distribution of largesse?

I start from three main points: the panels must be important or they would not be there; they say something that the rest of the monument does not say; they were not seen as out of place at the time. What they say, and why they say it in that way, must be left for the present. Here we can only use the panels to show how far the extreme codification of official scenes had moved since the Roman arch of Severus. Virtually everyone faces the front. Except in the heat of battle, individual features and even positions have been drastically reduced. All figures at formal events are reduced to two rows with the back row invisible except for their heads. But there is a formal background of architecture whose purpose seems partly to organise the scene into exact symmetry with the emperor dead centre.

All these characteristics have run to completion on the last well-dated and surviving monument, the base of the obelisk set up by Theodosius the Great (378–395) in the hippodrome at Constantinople **(14-15)**. The court scenes there are totally rigid and an extra characteristic is the grading of important people by size to emphasise their status. A

teenage prince who could be taller than his father must be shorter, but a babe in arms who has imperial rank must clearly be a properly sized person only little smaller than the senior emperor. Symmetry is exact, with the emperor in the centre. All face the front, but, even if the monument survived in perfect condition I suspect that the faces would be very little use for identifying the individuals depicted.

So we have sorted out a sequence of dated official monuments, all decorated with sculpture, and when the monuments are put in order of date the sculptures show a progression in style from the Arch of Titus to the Column of Theodosius. I think it is true to say that there are no fragments of clearly-dated monuments that disagree with the progression, and all major monuments have been included. The maximalist view would be that we have seen the change from early to late Roman art. The minimalist would say that we have demonstrated a progression of style in sculpture on official monuments dated between AD 80–400. The minimalist is clearly right, though the maximalist is not

14-15 Constantinople, Obelisk of Theodosius. Scenes of the imperial family and court on the base of the obelisk which was set up by Theodosius I in the circus near to the serpent column. Copyright Peter Clayton

necessarily wrong. What is needed is a lot of hard work to see whether the ideas derived from official sculpture hold good in other works of other materials and different status. Thus official amber carving, if there were such a thing, might hold to the rules, while tradesmen's carved tombstones follow a different course. The problem in almost every possible category is the question of date. Amber beads, official or not, are never explicitly dated. Tradesmen have never been heard of, and in the later empire they never refer to dated personages on their tombstones.

There is one further point that must be taken into account even if it suggests diversity and confusion rather than a single-line development and simplicity. The very fact that it is mainly the state monuments which are dated means that a dated sequence has to be constructed out of official art. Virtually all the items discussed have been sculptures in stone or marble intended for display to as wide a public as possible. All the items had a clear purpose, which was at the very least to be seen, but probably, in being seen, to communicate to the viewer. The monuments are not decoration of public spaces but elements in a programme. Mention of a programme ought to lead on to say what the programme seeks to do, but this is a very difficult thing to do. We could read the inscription, if any, and take it as evidence of the programme and intention. This is not always wise because the words may well have a purpose as well as the pictures. We might take a purpose from contemporary texts, but this has the difficulty that there is no need, or even likelihood, that the text and the monument are part of the same programme. We might disregard the text and try to derive the programme from the pictures, but here we need some method, probably comparative, by which certain purposes can be drawn out of either the subject matter of the pictures or the way or presenting it. Some of these points will be developed later on different material, but for the moment all that is needed is a warning that official monuments probably always have their own agendas which might well dictate or influence the style in which they are embellished.

Before looking at a selection of different types of art and decoration in the later Empire we need to consider which of the developments in official art between 80–400 might be influenced by officialdom? The most obvious feature must be that official productions probably have a didactic purpose, while domestic products may be simply pleasing or decorative. At its most polarised the official product may be a teaching aid, the domestic product may be wallpaper. The teaching aid, the didactic sculpture, needs to follow certain rules. It must be uncluttered so that the main point gets through easily, it must be comprehensible to those who have to learn from it, and it must know what it is saying, and say it as clearly and firmly as possible.

If some elements in this analysis are correct then most of the developments of later Roman official art can be explained away as developments in communicative techniques. The scene has to be stripped down to its bare essentials, extra sightseers have to be shaved away for they detract from the main point of the scene. If the scene itself is complex then it can often be simplified by taking a bird's-eye view. But since all parts of the scene are likely to be equally important to the communication, the effects of distance must be disregarded. Viewers concentrate more on big figures in a picture than on small figures, so the most important people must be the biggest. On an empire-wide view the emperor can be known to very few people so when monuments spread out from Rome, where the populace are used to seeing the emperor, facial characteristics are useless to identify him among a group. Diadems and brooches are widely known, the message can be reinforced quite easily, so these signs are far better imperial characteristics than a short nose or a large chin. As the need to get messages across becomes stronger so the technique used must be pared down until only the essentials remain.

There is therefore the strong possibility that any pictures on official products will follow the development outlined, while private and domestic material may remain in a more decorative, perhaps classical, mode. But it is not only the state that wants to teach or inform. The estate owner who builds a new villa and hires a mosaic firm to set the floors may well have just as strong feelings about what he wants the floors to do for him as the builders of a triumphal arch. On the other hand, not everyone is out to impress the neighbours all the time, and there must be room for personal choice and, more difficult to judge, personal indifference. It does seem likely that sculptors, and designers of pavements, would find it easier to work in one vein, the didactic, or the other, the decorative, and would make a speciality of one rather than trying to maintain a split artistic personality. Even that can be countered with the idea of work-art and relaxation-art from the same craftsman.

2. Portraits

A hard-line sceptic could say that the study of portraiture in the Roman Empire is impossible without coins. The reasoning here is that there is no such thing as an identified portrait of a dated individual such as an emperor outside the coinage. This may provoke outrage: 'What about this, that and the other well-known portraits of emperors?' But none of these well-known portraits is actually identified, named, titled or has an associated inscription. A few have regalia such as diadems which only emperors wore, but this gives us only the class, not the individual. Every such sculpture has been associated with the name of a particular emperor either through tradition or by comparison with the named coin portraits. True, there are Roman portraits named Socrates and Alexander, but these are of little use for discussing how portraits were sculpted at different times because, being of clearly Roman technique, they can say nothing direct about the times of their subjects. Not only are coin portraits named, but they are often dated to relatively short spans of time, and as such form an unrivalled gallery of portrait art.

The dating varies from period to period. Clearly an emperor like Otho who reigned only from January to April AD 69 has very well-dated portraits. Since he only became Pontifex Maximus, (chief priest) in March, and put that on his coins, it is possible to separate out coins struck in January to March and others struck in March to April. In fact no new portrait would have been needed, and so far as I know the subject has not been examined in depth. Hadrian reigned for 21 years and his coins are not so well dated. There is an element of intuition in ordering his different portraits, for he appears to have changed his image as he got older. This is always happening on coinage, and a new portrait of Elizabeth II has just (1998) been produced which clearly shows the march of time.

These simple and rather obvious points have already introduced important possibilities. Portraits within the frame of letters HADRIANVS are visibly similar to one another, so that Hadrian can be said to be recognisable in a series of slightly different forms. We can never know whether the coins reflect the actual features of the man because we have not got him here to compare with the coins, but at least he has an individual image, and that image changes appropriately as the man gets older. The simplest assumption we can make is that the images corresponded to the man. All this may seem irritatingly obvious, but it is not. Emperors of roughly the same time varied quite strongly in their approach to ageing; Augustus (27 BC–AD 14) became more youthful on his coins as he became bent and wrinkled in life. Nero (AD 54–68) seems to have admitted to becoming gross, fat, scowling and ugly. So in the first century AD there are different approaches to sequences of image. I am dealing all the time with coins here because they are dated in themselves by imperial years and consulships. Sculpture, especially of Augustus, has a very detailed sequence from the changing styles, but ultimately all this depends on the coin portraits.

In the fifth century AD such change has lost all connection with the individual features of the imperial subject depicted. This is the major change which we have to look at more closely.

Some of the most detailed and exuberant coin portraits are seen in the second century. My own favourite is one of the young prince Marcus Aurelius (AD 150–160) before he became full emperor **(colour plate 1)**. By the time of Commodus (181–192) change is visible, partly due to the fact that Commodus was convinced that he was the reincarnation of Hercules and had his portrait adapted accordingly. There is a fall in detail from the middle of the century, and perhaps the beginning of stylisation. With Septimius Severus (193–211) the portrait seems to become more formal. From the middle of the reign his beard is always shown divided into four 'ringlets', just as the god Serapis is shown, and this association seems to take precedence over either ageing or exact physical detail.

There are portraits of people other than emperors, but the problem here is that in virtually no cases do we know who they are. Even if we have a name attached we are none the wiser because we know nothing about the people named. The most remarkable series of portraits from the second and third centuries, dated by similarities to emperors and by general changes of style, are those from the Fayyum in Egypt. There the practice of embalming the body after death and wrapping it in linen continued from the Pharaonic period into the Roman period, but the modelled cases which were set over the head were replaced in the early empire by portraits painted directly onto the shrouds. In other cases portraits were painted on wooden boards, set over the face, and bound with the rest of the body. The effect is strikingly life-like and, seen in a gently-lit museum gallery on a winter afternoon, can give an unexpected shock.

The portraits must presumably have been painted from living models; they are certainly nothing like painted death masks. A few are painted on both sides, and these could have been used in the funeral procession before being bound into the shroud. The people look out with pleasant concentration, sparkling eyes and perfectly portrayed hair. If you saw them after the museum visit in the street you would immediately recognise them even in modern clothes. While it is impossible to say that these are remarkably realistic portraits of the person embalmed, the combination of excellent technique and very strong appearance of life make it very likely. One glance at the portraits used by modern publishers on book-jackets, or by newspapers in obituaries, makes it quite clear that, apart from gender, there need be little correlation between the recent appearance of the deceased and the representation. The portraits are dated by association with people whose dates we do know. Thus a lady from the Fayyum with a bun on the top of her head rather than on the back 'must' be of a similar date to the empress Faustina I, wife of Antoninus Pius, who died in 141. Faustina is the only empress whose coin portraits show such a bun. One portrait of a man brings strongly to mind the emperor Trajan (98–117) and he is usually dated to the early second century. More schematic people are relegated to the third and fourth centuries as their portrayal demands. It is important to remember that none of these portraits is of any help in constructing a sequence of changes in portraiture through time because none of them has any independent date. But once such a sequence has been constructed these portraits can be used as quite remarkably detailed examples within the type series.

What we know existed, but are now completely missing, are the highest levels of the painted portrait, the imperial imago or icon. The introduction of the word icon is useful here because it introduces some of the power which the Roman state believed to live in the portrait. This power is still a part of the belief of the Eastern Orthodox church. But just as it is an incorrect and insulting thing to say that the Orthodox church worships icons it would be wrong to say that the portrait was the emperor. In any Orthodox church there will be many icons of saints and visitors to the church will kiss the icons and will pray in front of them. The portrayal of the saint has in some way a part of the power of the saint and it is this which is being reverenced and respected. The images or icons of the emperor were painted soon after his accession and copies were sent out round the provinces. Each provincial governor needed the icons to validate his power and his acts. The governor was, in a sense, an extension of the emperor, and the presence of the emperor, as an icon, increased his power. The best direct illustration of this comes from an illuminated manuscript, in the Rossano Gospels, where two full-page pictures show episodes in the trial of Jesus **(36)**. These are set very much in a late antique setting, perhaps the fifth century from the clothes worn, and the brooches, and behind the magistrate (Herod) are two icons, each on a stand and each portraying two emperors. In a sense the judgement is being made by the emperors who are present in some degree through their icons, and delivered by the governor. The Fayyum portraits of quite ordinary individuals show us something of what we have lost from the ranks of official portraiture.

The third century, which has already been called a desert of dated monuments, shows a quite remarkable free-for-all in coin portraits. These certainly were troubling times in the empire with problems in the economy and on the frontiers, so some worried-looking marble portraits are firmly dated to the time of trouble. They are usually compared with the coin portraits of Philip I (244–249) and Trebonianus Gallus (251–253). But the most worried emperor must surely have been Gallienus (253–268), whose father Valerian was captured by the Persians after a military defeat. While Gallienus was away trying to set things right in Persia and liberate his father a rebel empire was set up in Germany and Gaul based in Cologne. Gallienus therefore had more trouble than any other emperor. Unfortunately for general dating methods, which assume a simple uniform progression from one form to another, Gallienus is shown on his coins in perhaps the most tranquil and ethereal of portraits of the third century **(colour plate 1)**. His coins are, in general, not well struck, and the flans used are badly prepared, the gold is of variable fineness and inconsistent weight, and large bronze coins had almost disappeared. In these senses the coinage of Gallienus is very poor. Yet the standard of die engraving is good, apart from atrocious lettering, and the portraits are sometimes of excellent technical quality.

The rebel emperor in Gaul, Postumus, brings in a contrast with Rome which ought to have appeared earlier. It has been tacitly assumed so far that all the coins of the Roman empire were roughly the same. In the western empire this is true, because until the middle of the third century virtually everything was struck in Rome. In the Greek-speaking east there was a great variety of mints and they produced some very unusual portraits. Unfortunately these rarely equal the Rome coins in either detail or consistency, and when a particularly 'good' portrait is seen, as in Cyprus under Trajan, there are often signs that Rome workmanship was involved. But the Gallic Empire seems to have had its share of highly-skilled die cutters from the beginning so that portraiture through the Gallic Empire is of the highest quality. In a sense the limits of stylisation which can be seen slowly increasing at Rome are pushed back, so that the best portraits of Postumus (260–268) compare well with the middle of the second century at Rome **(colour plate 1)**.

The Gallic empire ended in 274, so that Rome once more controlled the production of coin in the West with branches in places like Milan and Trier/Cologne. Between 274–294 there is nothing like the dreamy Gallienus as a series of heavily armed, closely shaved, determined looking emperors fill the coinage. Diocletian (294–305) continues this trend, still allowing some individuality **(colour plate 1)**, and his co-emperor Maximian is at this time a distinguishably different person. When the two emperors chose an assistant each and formed a college of four, the tetrarchy (293), portraiture on coins suddenly changed. Spears, shields and breastplates which had earlier been a warlike feature were eliminated, all hair and beards were closely trimmed, the portrait ended at the neck rather than showing the shoulders, and individual features were drastically reduced. The head on the coins became that of The Emperor instead of the emperor A, B, C or D. The sudden change involving four people seems most likely to have been a matter of Imperial policy for obvious reasons of communication or propaganda. The cult of the individual was highly undesirable at a time of collegiality, and the position of emperor over-rode personal preferences. Even in the matter of wives. When the new assistants were chosen they had to leave their former wives — for instance, Constantius I divorced Helena the mother of Constantine — and marry into the senior partner's family.

Seen in this light the suppression of facial features in the Imperial interest is rather less surprising. We must add to this the tendency to stylise throughout the third century. The Emperor from 270–294 was a military leader and was shown accordingly. Personal features were visible, but they made less impact when beards and hair styles seem to have been minimal and identical, and when the main feature of the depiction was not the face but the military panoply.

The time of the tetrarchy, 293–*c*.308, produces such distinctive portraiture that the lessons of the coin can be applied fairly easily, and perhaps fairly safely, to sculpture. This does not mean that it is safe to declare a tetrarchic sculpture a portrait of Diocletian or Constantius, but it probably is safe to declare it a portrait of the time of the four emperors. The most obvious candidates here are two groups of the four emperors themselves. Both are in porphyry, and both come in two pairs. The smaller set are in the Vatican museums, the larger set are still public sculpture in the fullest sense of the word in that they are built in to the outside of the south-west corner of St Mark's basilica in Venice **(16)**. More simply, they are on the right hand corner as you look at the façade from St Mark's square.

Since they clearly are not in their original position, for Venice was little more than a mud-bank at the time the sculptures were made, any discussion of what they were for has difficulties. The fact that they are cut from a block of purple porphyry, kept in the later empire as an imperial monopoly, agrees with everything else about them — that they are imperial portraits. At present the two groups, each of two emperors, are set at right angles to one another, actually forming the corner. One pair look west, the others look south. Yet

16 Venice, St.Mark's basilica. Porphyry sculpture of four emperors, the Tetrarchs, set into the south west corner of the church.
Copyright Richard Reece

their background is not that of the flat slab once set side by side; their backgrounds are curved. If the curves of the two slabs were intended to be continuous then they need to be reset. One part of the sculpture is missing, the bottom right-hand corner of the south facing, right-hand, group. This turned up in the filling of a thirteenth-century rubbish pit in Istanbul. It seems fairly clear that the rubbish came from tidying up after the Venetian sack of Constantinople in 1204. It is therefore not surprising that the Tetrarchs appear together at St Marks, with a very large number of looted capitals, columns, sculptures and pieces of church furniture made for Constantinople and removed by perverted crusaders.

It is perhaps odd to spend considerable space on a group which cannot tell us anything about features of an individual person from the past, and thus portraiture in its narrow sense. One glance at the four people will show that their individual facial features have been submerged in a common form of portrayal. Even if the accidents of time were repaired perfectly to their original form the people shown would still probably not be recognisable among the crowds of visitors who pass by them each day. Or perhaps that is wrong, perhaps they would stand out, but they would be very worrying people to see. They would suggest a total impersonality, perhaps as important figures in disguise, perhaps victims of brain-washing, perhaps potential robbers masked in latex, making for St Mark's rich treasury.

Safely in stone, they extend the idea of portraiture into the format of the later empire. The individual is little, the position held is much. The length of a nose says nothing much of interest to anyone outside the family circle. The fact that the four emperors stand in two groups is an important statement, very useful for any observer at the time. There were two spheres of influence, East and West, and each sphere had its chief and its assistant to rule it. The chief and the assistant are immediately apparent from the grouping with one figure in each group putting a conferring or caring hand on the shoulder of the other. Perhaps this is even a sculpture of the inception of the rule by four emperors, the creation of the tetrarchy? It appears again in the Vatican group, who are backed by another column. If this is so then the detective work leading to Constantinople is rather pointless because Byzantium, as it then was, is one of the least likely places for such a monument to be set up. A possible place for its original siting would be Nicaea, on the Asian shore, but not far away from Byzantium, where Diocletian had his palace. Whatever the details, this was a monument to imperial collegiality.

The boat of Collegiality hit a rock with Constantine I. From his accession in 306 until 324 his main purpose in life seems to have been working out from his first power base in Britain and Gaul to eliminate all colleagues outside his own family. From 324 to his death in 337 he ruled supreme with his sons and some other relations as helpers. He came to the throne in a time that I have just described as one of decreasing individuality in portraiture. Just as he destroyed the Tetrarchy he tried to destroy the idea of uniform portraiture. His portrait types seen on coins through his reign are probably the most varied of any emperor, yet there is nothing which compares with the finely chiselled detail of the young Marcus Aurelius. This is not a matter of technique because some of the reverses required highly competent and detailed engraving. It must be a matter of style. The quest ranged from a young prince **(colour plate 2)** to a mature, but foxy, man, a three-quarters facing portrait with full military regalia to a wistful upward-looking portrait trying to leave earthly cares behind, with many other less well characterised intermediate stages. The end result is fully identifiable as a person in its own right, but fine detail is eschewed.

His sculptural portraits are few but distinctive. On his arch there is little remaining of individual features on the long thin Constantinian panels. It seems unlikely that there was ever much there to start with. Yet studies of the panels taken from monuments of Marcus Aurelius show first that the emperor looks nothing like Marcus and second that the head is too small for the body. The heads do look very like some of Constantine's styles of portraiture and the assumption is that the heads were re-cut at the time that the panels were incorporated into the arch. There is one other portrait which is usually taken to be that of Constantine but it is more a study in power than a personal representation. The shade of Constantine might, with typical modesty, ask what the difference was. This head, which is much larger than life size, was found in the basilica first built by Maxentius and then re-modelled by Constantine. It was accompanied by a very large arm-and-hand, and a foot. My favourite example of scale comes from a postcard which shows a kitten extended on the foot taking up about one joint of a toe. These parts could very well be put together with a solid rubble body, and the rubble could be covered by magnificent cloth. The parts sculpted would then be the only parts of a brilliantly attired monarch sitting in majesty with one hand outstretched and one foot forward that anyone would expect to see. The head does not convey a detailed likeness and this was probably not intended. An onlooker would be standing on the floor of the basilica looking up some metres to the face of the statue. That, in turn, totally disregards the onlooker for the eyes look out not on the level but slightly upwards. People may observe the monarch, but the monarch has much greater things to do than observe the people. If the head were now alive it would seem more individual than those of the tetrarchs, but it would still appear very much refined, almost purged of idiosyncrasy, the curse of common people.

When Constantine's three (337–340) sons ruled after him, then two (340–350), then one (350–361), the spirit of rebellion against the trends of the age waned. When Constans and Constantius II ruled together and struck coins for each other in their respective areas of influence the portraits are fresh and interesting, but not individual **(colour plate 2)**. Even on gold coins, which had always been the most carefully prepared, it would be unsafe to identify a coin which had lost its imperial legends by reference to the face. By the time the sons of Theodosius the Great were ruling together (395–408) the portraits of Arcadius and Honorius are neither fresh nor interesting, and they show no individuality at all except in very rare and highly erratic cases.

The great bronze statue formerly in Barletta is of an emperor **(17)**. No-one else could be publicly represented with the diadem and jewelled round brooch. The diadem was first shown commonly on coins after about 330. The statue is therefore of an emperor after about 330, and before the Gothic take-over of Italy in the late fifth century. Guesses have ranged from Valens (364–378) to Marcian (450–457). One portrait with a diadem which does stand out is that found in Constantinople and usually called Arcadius (383–408). It stands out because although it has an imperial diadem, and is therefore later than about 330, it has individuality. It is usually called Arcadius because of the 'Theodosian Renaissance', a renewal of art styles, and a harking back to earlier models which has been attributed to the court of Theodosius and his family. I am sceptical because I have never

17 Barletta (now moved), S. Italy. Large bronze statue of a late Roman emperor. Copyright Deutsches Archäologisch Institut, Rome

18 Madrid. Large silver plate (missorium) with an inscription of Theodosius I.
  Copyright Ellen Swift

found out how this burst of new-old style is dated, and how it can all be attributed to one particular time and place without a circular argument. Once a Theodosian Renaissance has been decreed, then any unusual or unusually good works can be attributed to it, and so the corpus of work can grow. But if few, or any, of the works can be firmly dated in their own right, grouping them together has to be seen as purely subjective. There is nothing wrong with such subjectivity so long as it is remembered as a hypothesis rather than a firmly based fact. It could well be called a model, a way of making sense of the evidence we have, which is not necessarily more than that.

It may be that coin portraits are disappointing because they are of single figures who are not allowed to have any individuality. When four rulers are seen in a group, as with the Venice tetrarchs, the relationships within the group, and the original meaning of the scene, become interesting. One ruler alone can only be portrayed as a single emperor, and the only way that that message can be emphasised is to load the one human shape with more

19 Ravenna, church of San Vitale. Portrait of the emperor Justinian from the apse mosiacs. copyright Peter Clayton

and more imperial signs. This results in the human body, devoid of personality, being hidden under a heap of insignia.

An example of group portraiture which can take us further into relationships and meaning is the plate in Madrid known as the Missorium of Theodosius **(18)**. Its inscription tells us that the main emperor is Theodosius the first in his tenth year. This means the plate dates from 388 and the subsidiary emperors must be Valentinian II and Arcadius, so the scene is fairly well set in words before we look at the image. The most obvious feature of the composition is the seated figure of an emperor set in the centre of the plate within an architectural surround. The architecture also encompasses two other diademed figures, therefore other emperors, but they seem to be less well defined, almost in the background. Theodosius stares straight out of the plate at us, so his face gives us no idea of what he is actually doing. Closer inspection shows that, crouched at his knee, is another figure with a prominent crossbow brooch who is being handed a rolled document. Each of the subsidiary emperors is flanked by two identikit soldiers, the gable of the architectural surround encloses two flying cherubs, but there is still about a third of the surface of the plate below the platform on which Theodosius is sitting. This is filled with wheat ears and a reclining figure, perhaps a personification of the earth, who is gazing up towards Theodosius. From her, three more winged cherubs (one is obscured by damage to the plate) carry fruit and flowers upwards towards Theodosius.

The soldiers have been described as identikit soldiers in that they could be replaced by any other late antique soldiers without altering the scene in any way. The facial features of the emperors and the recipient are extremely regular and virtually interchangeable. The female figure below the platform has more individuality, but the side view of a reclining figure has strained the anatomical abilities of the engraver. Features like these are not the important points.

The focus in every sense of the word is Theodosius. The recipient half-kneels before him, the other emperors and the soldiers flank him, even the earth looks up to him and flying cherubs bring all the good things towards him. In return he takes no notice whatsoever; but this is the correct imperial attitude. The historian Ammianus Marcellinus describing the formal entry of Constantius II to Rome in 356 cannot give higher praise than to say he never moved a muscle, he might have been a statue. True imperial behaviour. The interest therefore is the relationship of each of the figures to the centre. The recipient is presumably someone important. His brooch makes the point that he is not a member of the imperial family, for they all wear round jewelled brooches, but he is important enough to receive a document, perhaps the title to a job, or the instructions for project, on this formal tenth anniversary. He presumably also gets the plate as a commemoration of the event, and if other examples are followed, the plate when presented might have been heaped with gold and silver coin.

Theodosius sits so that his footstool is on the edge of the platform. Not so Valentinian II (aged 13), who is properly smaller than Theodosius and has his footstool set further back from the edge. Nor Arcadius, whose footstool is even further behind as befits the youngest of the emperors. He is in fact a child of five years old, but that is not what is being shown. He is an emperor, and has been for five years, and he must therefore be greater than any common soldier or recipient of the emperor's favours. Valentinian II and Arcadius are literally in the wings, emperors in waiting, and they can move into the central slot when necessary. When they are there they will rule over everything in earth, and the goods of the earth will be offered up to them. With this sort of detail and implication clear in the decoration, details of an emperor's facial features clearly pale into insignificance.

Dated people in painting, mosaic or other materials are rare. On ivory panels known as diptychs there is a series of representations of consuls, and other high dignitaries, but they are seldom represented and named in any other contexts. In general they belong to the late fourth and fifth centuries and follow a rather stylised sequence. The great exception which tests the rule is that of the emperor Justinian, his wife Theodora, and their attendants in the apse mosaics on the wall behind the altar in the church of San Vitale in Ravenna **(19)**. The people in the mosaics, except for the bishop Maximianus, are not named, but the history of the building of the church, the brick stamps in it, and the links in materials to Constantinople all agree with the identification of the emperor. Justinian's coins have no individual features at all and this is exactly as it should be in a single line stream of development. Yet the person on the mosaic is not only different from those around him but gives a strong impression of individuality. High-ranking people beside him, all wearing the crossbow brooch of office, and the bishop Maximian, all have individual features but the soldiers to the side come from an identikit bureau. The Empress Theodora is so bedecked with jewels that only her face can be seen, not even her hairstyle, so it is difficult to assess her individuality though she comes across as a firm and powerful personality. Her ladies-in-waiting have their own distinct personalities, as do the men of the court, but the background court women are relegated to a row of almost identical faces.

None of the rules created for the interpretation of the Missorium of Theodosius really apply here. There are identifiable individuals about their usual functions. In this case it seems as if the emperor and empress are on their way to the new church and the processions have been halted for us to see. The emperor and empress are in the centres of their scenes, but not aggressively so. Stature is rigorously equal so that even a soldier is the same height as the emperor. There are no great distinctions such as footstools one or two inches from the edge of a platform to interpret. We are almost spectators at a real scene. And this might solve the apparent contradictions.

The mosaics are in the apse, behind the altar, in a main church of the Imperial capital in Italy. Photographs of this church taken with wide angle lenses make it look large. It is in fact small and in floor space intimate. The larger dimension is height. One hundred people standing in the central space in front of the altar would be fairly crowded. Others, in the ambulatory, would have a poor view of things happening and could see nothing of the upper story gallery round the central space. The emperor, when in residence in the palace, would sit in the balcony opposite the altar and take part in the service from there. The few people who could see him could also see the mosaic from a distance. Since the mosaic is in a place where the few important people who would see it could also see the original, and would probably be a part of the court ritual, this is a matter of commemoration and representation rather than communication and instruction.

The mosaic of San Vitale would stay at the intended centre of things as a reminder of a court event. The Missorium was sent out with the recipient to his possible new post and would be something like his pictorial contract. The fine print of what he had to do was written in the document the emperor handed to him in the ceremony, but that was for his instruction and reference. The Missorium would be on display in his official residence, or while he was performing his duties. It told whoever saw it that what was being done came directly from the emperor and was by the will of the emperor. The official had been sent out with a representation not just of the emperor but of the whole system centred on the emperor. The spectator would never see this central character himself, so the plate helped to convey to him the great organisation which ran the world and some of its elements.

The final example is also in Ravenna where some of the mosaics of San Vitale (about 540) were copied over a hundred years later at the church of San Apollinare at Classe, the port of Ravenna. The Imperial group of Justinian was copied to show Constantine IV and his associate emperors (668–685) but although the faces differ to some extent there is little evidence in them that they really represent the people named. This panel forms the first of many in later Byzantine contexts in which the emperor appears in religious setting. Secular imperial representation, apart from the coinage, seems to die out. By this time the whole subject of portrayal and depiction was being called into question and interpretations are probably better left aside.

3. Painting and mosaics

Official monuments were to be found mainly in the homelands of the emperors, Italy, Lepcis for Severus, and then Constantinople. Portraits, through coins, formed an almost complete sequence which was well dated and from a known mint city. Paintings and mosaics form a much less well-organised group of material. Wall paintings can be known either because they survive in situ or they have collapsed and been excavated. The two classes are almost completely mutually exclusive in both time and space. Floor mosaics follow the same rules. Ceiling and wall mosaics can only be known if they survive in situ, and they form a group which is almost completely late and religious. By putting together floor mosaics and wall mosaics a continuous sequence can be formed, but in many ways it remains two sequences joined together rather than forming one uniform group.

It is probably easier to start with the mosaics, as they are numerous and widespread, and some are dated. The reliability of dates for mosaics varies considerably. The scenes including Justinian and Theodora, and Constantine IV and his fellow princes, at Ravenna have been briefly discussed as portraits. The Justinian mosaic must be dated after the reconquest of Italy from the Ostrogoths in 540, but fairly soon after, since the written sources say that the church was begun before the re-conquest and brick stamps confirm this. A date for the mosaic of 534–565 (death of Justinian) must be likely. The Constantine IV mosaic actually names the chief emperor and his associates and the mosaic should therefore belong to the time of his reign, 668–685. So far as I know no other mosaic is dated in this sense apart from the floor of the basilica at Aquileia.

Clearly, if the date at which a building was put up, or re-built, is firmly known then any mosaics within it are likely to be after that date. How far after is unknowable unless, like Justinian's cathedral of Hagia Sophia in Constantinople, it changed its purpose and became, for instance, a mosque after 1453. The unique collection of mosaics in the churches of Ravenna have no closing date, for they have been continuously cared for, which is good, and restored, which is bad, to this day. In a few cases the restorations are insensitive and can be clearly seen and even fairly firmly dated. The most obvious, and liturgically the most annoying, is the blatant ?seventeenth-century (Van Dykeish) repair in the Orthodox baptistery. I say that it is liturgically annoying because the fact that it depicts John the Baptist pouring water over the head of Christ from a dish cannot be taken to represent early Christian practice. It may, but we cannot be sure. Restorations referred to as 'good' usually mean that they are undetectable. To the archaeologist, as opposed to the aesthete, they are both unfortunate and dangerously misleading.

These problems do not apply to material which is newly excavated. Mosaics were certainly repaired in antiquity, but this is usually quite clear in the bedding mortar if nowhere else. Wall paintings could be restored, but this is unusual in domestic circumstances. When the decorations of a room became worn or dirty the whole room was redecorated. Only when the paintings are held to represent something worth keeping, a sacred likeness perhaps, are they preserved and re-touched. The idea of connecting the words beautiful and old is relatively recent. Judging from the material which does, and does not, survive, and the circumstances, the Roman attitude was that decoration had to have a very high status if it was not to be swept away in restoration and re-decoration.

Excavated material can be dated in two ways. If the excavation is careful, stratigraphic and thorough then a date range for the material on top of the mosaic can be found, the mosaic can be lifted, and a date range for the material below the mosaic can be found. The date of the mosaic ought to be between the two. The problem is that until recently a mosaic was an evident good in itself, so that it justified clearing the debris away from on top without record and should be left undisturbed if at all possible. Thus we know for most mosaics nothing about what covered them and nothing about what is underneath them. In that sense we do not know their dates. In cases such as these, the great majority, the art historians have moved in and given the mosaics a stylistic date. Since such dates are dependent on a sequence of changes in style, just like those changes that can be deduced from sculpture on official monuments, the validity depends on the pegging of the sequence to some fixed and well known dates. It also depends on the assumption of a single line of stylistic development always progressing in the same direction. Stylistic dates are also influenced by historical events which may, in fact, have had nothing to do with the sequence at all. Thus, as an almost imaginary example, the barbarian raids into France in the third century were a major catastrophe for towns, which never recovered. Good mosaics in towns are therefore likely to be before the catastrophe and poor examples may well be later. The 'likely' can easily get forgotten, so that good mosaics should be dated before the third century and poor mosaics after. This is a crude caricature which (I hope) has not been used for many years. Yet, if it was used at any date, and that use has not been detected and deleted, reasoning as crude as this could still be infecting modern, more careful, analysis. Unfortunately there is a general rule which states that the better the mosaics the worse the excavation; perhaps it is better to leave such a broad generalisation without going into detail.

There are two possible starting points for paintings and mosaics which ought to be as tightly dated as official monuments. Anything at Pompeii and Herculaneum ought to be before the eruption of AD 79, and there have been no challenges to this so far. One other remarkable survival is the villas built by Hadrian (117–138) at Tivoli. This was not destroyed or otherwise brought to a clear end, so there is the possibility of later addition and remodelling, but many aspects can safely be dated to the reign of Hadrian. Mosaics at the Vesuvian cities are not vivid, colourful depictions of events and landscapes. They are far more often in black and white, usually patterns, and where scenes do occur these are usually smaller set pieces such as mythical scenes within wide decorative borders. The wall paintings in their four styles are more ambitious with scenes of seascapes and landscapes receding into the distance, and ornate architectural frameworks with windows through to the outside world.

We could start at Hadrian's villa with the colourful mosaic showing centaurs and wild beasts. There is a clear foreground scene, with plenty of action, and from this the ground surface recedes into the distance, ending up as a misty blur. The position of each animal can be firmly fixed from the receding perspective, there are several layers of depth in the picture, anatomy is well observed, and colour is reasonably lifelike. But the landscape is partly schematic. Stunted trees stand for vegetation in general and rock forms provide suitable platforms and gullies for the composition rather like a carefully made stage set.

After this we have to launch out into a stylistic sequence. Here there are too many stylistic variables to control before we can make a safe theoretical path through the material. Mosaics of the second, third and fourth centuries are empire-wide and divide themselves up into regional schools. The mosaics at Antioch are visibly different from the mosaics of the North African tradition and these differ from North Italy, Britain and Germany. In most cases dates are unknown, so that even if each tradition can be put into a sequence it is almost impossible in our present state of ignorance to compare possible dating between traditions. As a final blow each area has a number of firms at work with different techniques, different clients and different costs. Contrasts between two mosaics drawn at random may therefore be due to date, place, workers, or status.

As a start we could compare two mosaics associated with North Africa: those at Cherchel in Tunisia **(colour plate 3)** and those at the great villa at Piazza Armerina in Sicily **(colour plate 4)**. The mosaic at Cherchel comes with a warning; the panels illustrated are by far the best mosaics at Cherchel . I say this because for many years I had admired photographs and longed to see 'the rest'. Then the chance came to visit, and, magnificent as the Roman monuments of Algeria are, there is nothing up to the standard of these rather small panels. When I saw them they were displayed on a wall, all four panels together perhaps three metres high by two metres across, rather dusty and with colours partly obscured by algae, but they made the whole journey worthwhile.

The mosaic is undated but ought to be later than Tivoli. Why? Four scenes show agricultural pursuits: ploughing, sowing corn, weeding and pruning vines. The scenes have their own ground levels and are shown one above the other. The ground levels are not just lines produced by a straight edge but undulations in the ground surface, and although they have a finite width this allows for grass and trees to grow out of it, shadows to be cast on it and an element of depth to be portrayed. Anatomy is well observed, the men have muscles, and the oxen would have provided juicy steaks in their youth. Colour is rich and highlights have been used on quite large areas. These reflections of light in white or near-white tesserae were very sparingly used at Tivoli and are often used by commentators as an indication of date. One area of highlight quite reasonably shows the glossy hide of the oxen glinting with sweat, but the edges of the highlight sometimes finish on straight lines rather than being gently smoothed away in curves. Off the narrow ground surface that is behind the scene, there is nothing. The tesserae are arranged round the figures, rather than just blocked in in straight lines, and this, if observed, gives an impression of a background, but there is nothing there. The scenes have been filleted out of existence for us to observe rather as scenes of imperial sacrifice are pared away to reveal the centre of the group free from incidental sightseers. We could take this to be the mosaic equivalent of the funeral rites scene on the base of the column of Antoninus Pius, or the layered scenes on the arch of Severus at Rome. The mosaic is usually described as Severan.

There is no information on the status of the customer who ordered and paid for the Cherchel mosaic, nor on the house in which it was found, but the find-spot is fairly safely Cherchel, and the date cannot be more than 100 years from AD 200. If we move to the sprawling villa at Piazza Armerina in the middle of Sicily we are changing the place by a few hundred miles, but it is generally agreed that the mosaic workers who laid the floors came from North Africa. The date is now thought to be somewhere in the years around 330, on the basis of pottery found in modern excavation. Since we do not know the status of the Cherchel mosaics the fact that Piazza Armerina has often been called a palace neither helps nor hinders. If we home in on the capture of a bison then the subject matter is similar to the oxen at Cherchel.

At Piazza Armerina the great hunt of which the capture of the bison **(colour plate 4)** is a part unfolds on a single surface which has been sliced in the same way as the base of the column of Antoninus Pius. The scene is carefully set out so that the capture of a remarkably tame tigress is seen behind the capture of the bison, yet the top of the bison scene is finished off before the bottom of the capture of the tigress starts. The two scenes which are shown to be happening in the foreground, the bison, and the background, the tigress, are of exactly the same scale and distinctness. To give the illusion of distance there are shadows and fragmentary bushes on an otherwise featureless ground. All this makes perfect sense in the delivering of a scene which happened in three dimensions, through a two-dimensional floor covering, to a customer who wants a full representation of what was there. If he is going to pay for a tigress then he does not want her either indistinct in the distance or half obscured by the men necessary for the capture of the bison. The use of spacing and perspective has therefore developed from the Cherchel mosaic, but the change is gradual and could be accounted for by different workers, different ideas, or different patrons, rather than different date.

A larger difference comes in the depiction of the men in the scenes. One clear difference is in the way that action is shown. The Cherchel men are working hard. If they stopped for a snack they would be hot and sweaty and would unpack varied things to eat carefully packed for them the night before. The Piazza Armerina men can hardly stop since they do not give the impression of actually exerting effort. If they moved from their poses they look as if they might have difficulty in adapting to real life, and they no more look as if they eat than do models in a shop window. They all have postural problems, but the main offender is the man giving orders and not doing much else who has posed for the scene so awkwardly that he is almost certainly going to be tripped up by the tiger when the frame moves. The men occupied with dragging the reluctant bison along have again posed for the picture, but they give the impression more of a corps de ballet than a work force.

The bison looks in some ways much more real than the men. There is strong movement and it would certainly be interesting to see what happened if one of the men tripped, for the bison has clear intentions. But again, the bison's body is not fully involved in its action. The right pose is there but there is no sense that the animal is being propelled by its muscles. The Cherchel oxen, firmly ploughing on over rough ground, give a greater impression of harnessed energy. The colouring at Piazza Armerina has moved in the same schematic direction as the overall composition. Highlights are used, but they are less obviously necessary. Shadows around the joints of the haunches are so strong as to be almost black. The muscled shoulder has been turned from an anatomical detail into a nicely regular ovoid with colouring shading neatly from black to buff. This impression is strengthened by the regular contours with which the colours change.

Piazza Armerina provides parallels for almost every possible occasion, so examples have to be chosen economically. One mosaic, which shows in detail the method of slicing a complex scene to make it clearly visible, comes from the vestibule of the small circus and shows a chariot race in progress. This is almost a caricature of the common decoration in North African villas in which important races and favourite horses are commemorated for posterity. In this case the charioteers are boys, or appropriately clothed cherubs, and the animals in harness are different types of fowl from pigeons to geese. The importance of the scene is the way in which it takes the Antoninus column base scene of the funeral ride and splits it so drastically as to make almost two scenes of it. It is clearly meant to be a circus race because all the details of the circus are there: the chariots, the central spine, the obelisks and the turning points. But neither the contestants nor their shadow ground surfaces show any signs of turning, and what is so important in the actual race, the scramble at the turning point, has been totally lost. A circular race has been turned into two straight sprints.

Another type of scene at Piazza Armerina involves the sea. The sea is obvious in association with the hunt scenes because the animals are being captured and loaded onto boats to be taken for sale abroad. The simplest explanation is hunting in Africa for sale in Rome. True to the mosaic tradition in bathhouses which was well developed in the second century, the sea is heavily populated with many different varieties of fish. There are conventions here, and similar peculiar fish can be seen in quite widely spaced sea scenes. Another sea scene is brought down in scale to show cupids fishing. This is a variation on the general sea scene in which the same sorts of fish are being caught by cherubs with rods and lines, sometimes from boats, sometimes in the water themselves.

This type of scene was of great help to the workmen who were called in to make a floor for the new cathedral of Aquileia, at the northern tip of the Adriatic between Venice and Trieste, in the time of Bishop Theodore (died 318). It seems fair to suppose that they needed help because their previous commissions would have been almost exclusively secular, mosaics for all sorts of rooms, patrons, houses, and shops. These rooms would have been of sizes up to those suitable for receiving numbers of guests, but they would usually have been of a single roof-span rather than long aisled halls. Now the firm had to provide the floor covering for a whole basilica, a long rectangle divided up only by two rows of columns, and the basilica was a church. What designs were in stock to cover such a large area, and what designs were right for a church?

The problems were solved by using up a number of different designs and putting them to some extent as if in rooms with the nave columns at each corner of the 'room'. This involved considerable use of decorative bands and borders, and it does mean that the whole floor never looks like a single space. However the amount of design which any member of the congregation could see at any one time was limited, and our modern wish to see an eagle view of the whole design is rather unnatural. An alternative view of this method of flooring would be to see each part of the floor as signifying some different activity within the basilica. This makes it sound rather like an open-plan office and it does pose major problems for any possibilities of a living liturgy which needs to change over decades.

If the problem of covering an unusually large space was fairly easily if not particularly aesthetically solved, there remained the uncertainty what designs might, or might not, be appropriate for this new thing called a church or cathedral. Simple patterns are non-committal and fill the spaces well. A few portraits, or representations that could be taken for portraits, do not come amiss since it is impossible to decide whether a human being is a great saint or pagan sinner simply from the face. Some old designs could easily be given new life. Some of these were so obvious that they must have been invented or discovered in many different places at the same time. Other conflations of old and new, pagan and Christian, were worked out separately, and sometimes in different ways in different places. This means that in the early fourth century some forms of representation were becoming standardised and agreed. Some of those have come down to us as the correct way to represent a Christian truth or event, and others were still being worked out. If a scene does not follow our modern conventions it may be because it was one of the unsuccessful attempts at depiction rather than that the modern commentator has got the interpretation of the scene wrong.

The most obvious borrowing can be illustrated at Aquileia by the panel showing the Good Shepherd **(20)**. A shepherd has a sheep across his shoulder, and that is more or less the whole story. To the spectator of the first century AD this was a well-known scene of the slave bringing the sacrificial animal to the sacrifice. The person is clearly a slave since he is a rustic of the lower classes, and the animal is unmistakably a lamb that is meant for sacrifice. Why else would a person be carrying a lamb? Because the fourth century convert has read or heard the parable of the good shepherd who, when he has lost one sheep, leaves the ninety and nine who are safe to go and look for it. He finds it and brings it back on his shoulder. And of course this good shepherd is The Good Shepherd, a way of depicting Christ without getting into wrangles about the Commandments. So while a statue in the mithraeum beneath the church of San Clemente in Rome is clearly a slave bringing the lamb to the slaughter, the panel on the floor of the basilica at Aquileia is clearly of the Good Shepherd. Nothing in the form of depiction has changed, since shepherds are often slaves, and it is impossible to tell from the expression of the lamb whether it is due for slaughter or redemption.

Our move from Piazza Armerina to Aquileia was caused by sea scenes. These were of great use to the mosaicists since by nature they do not have edges and so can be extended indefinitely. But after a time the variety of fish has to be repeated, and seascapes without detail are uninformative. Someone therefore imported into the sea scenes at Aquileia details which were instructive, or could be interpreted in an instructive way. One of the most obvious, and often used, stories of the old Testament is that of Jonah, who was swallowed by a great fish (our modern whale has no textual foundation). The sea is obviously the setting for this story and panels of Jonah being thrown out of the ship and swallowed by the sea monster, being vomited up by the sea monster, and later reclining under the shadow of the gourd plant, are set in a background of waves and fish which

20 *Aquileia, Basilica. Floor mosaic showing the Good Shepherd. Copyright Ellen Swift*

21 *Aquileia, Basilica. Floor mosaic with events from the life of Jonah. Copyright Ellen Swift*

would be totally at home at Piazza Armerina or anywhere else **(21)**. This is direct use of, and representation of, the biblical text.

Interpretation is important for other scenes. Near to the memorial inscription to Bishop Theodore, set in the sea, is a boat from which two naked winged cupids and one probably clothed are fishing. They are trying to pull up a net full of fish. If they are successful there is little hope for the boat since the draught of fishes is positively miraculous. Put in these tendentious terms it is very difficult for anyone reared on Bible stories to avoid an interpretation with the apostles as fishers of men and the conflation of that with the one particular parable. Though the fact that many of the apostles were fishermen of course strengthens the case. True, the apostles did not go round naked, looking like chubby small boys and with wings on their shoulders, but then no direct statement is made. This is all a matter of interpretation.

This is a major point, which needs to be emphasised. The decoration of all the new churches built in the early fourth century could not be completely Christian because no one had yet worked out exactly what Christian decoration was to be. Anyone who doubts the ability of the preachers and writers of the time to interpret almost anything in a Christian sense must go back to the sources and read. There is no great gulf between pagan imagery and Christian imagery at least partly because Christian imagery was in the process of becoming.

There are some pagan themes that are not used. Other virgin births such as that of Mithras would be counterproductive, as would his slaughter of the bull and the creation resulting from its blood. Some themes are taken over, and the suckling of Horus by the goddess Isis has quite remarkable similarities to depictions of Mary and the infant Christ. Some Christian themes are not used at this time, the most obvious one being the crucifixion itself. The usual explanation is that in the fourth century this is still a recognisable form of capital punishment for the worst type of criminals, so that to an unconverted Roman the depiction of Christ in this form would signal a disgusting religion.

The theme of pagan and Christian, and the development of some aspects of Christian imagery, can be followed by moving to paintings, and specifically the catacombs at Rome. To some people the catacombs are Christian refuges during the times of persecution. This does not square with what evidence we have. The earliest catacombs rarely have evidence of Christianity in them. The clearest evidence of Christianity in the catacombs comes in the fourth century when there is no need for underground activities. Except for burial, which has become both crowded and expensive up above. Most catacombs are long narrow tunnels, just about the worst possible places for holding services where people need to hear, and see, and move about.

One of the best-published catacombs is one which was discovered by building work in 1955 near the Via Latina south of Rome **(22)**. The site engineer found a cavity during drilling operations and had himself lowered into what is now known as Hall I. This was a painted chamber which was part of a series of passages and rooms almost covered with painted decoration. A new shaft was sunk in a nearby roadway, the catacomb was cleared rather than excavated, but the pictures were well photographed and published so that we now have the complete documentation of the decoration of one underground burial

22 Rome,
Catacomb
on Via
Latina. Plan
of the
catacomb.
Copyright
Ellen Swift
after
A.Ferrua, in
Ferrua 1991

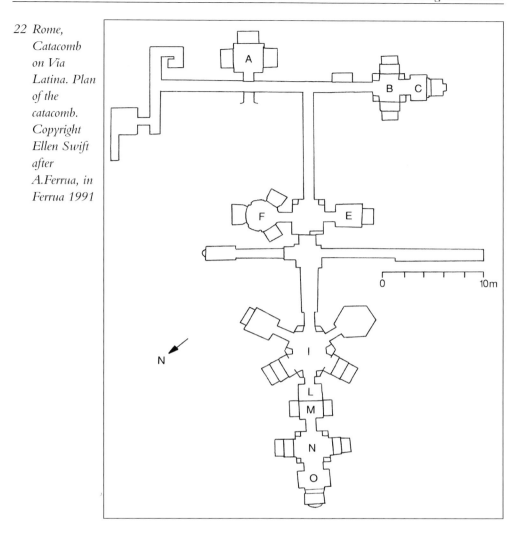

complex in Rome. The decorations of other catacombs have been published, most notably that of Saints Peter and Marcellinus, but most of what is illustrated from the catacombs involves single pictures or scenes rather than complete catalogues of whole areas.

The dating of the catacomb is reasonably safely based on the form of the epitaph inscriptions and symbols which survived associated with some of the individual burials. They suggest that most activity happened in the early to middle fourth century and that burial was tailing off towards the end of the century. As the original visitors entered the catacomb they walked down a tunnel from which branched separate rooms or cubicula. A right-hand turn at a T junction led to the main series of burial chambers, which were arranged along the main axis. Each chamber contains several burials which were inserted in the walls of the small rooms with the grave then plastered over and usually painted. Many paintings have been partially destroyed by looters, ancient and, unfortunately, modern, looking for treasure buried with the burials. Some modern looters, between the discovery of the catacomb and its clearance, were after modern treasure and tried to take some of the paintings themselves for the illicit art market.

The different rooms have their own characters and often contrasting styles of painting. Subject matter varies, presumably according to the wishes and preferences of the families of the dead, and perhaps sometimes their own wishes. Clearly a complete description has no place here, so it will be necessary to select from the series of paintings available.

Room A has a series of paintings that are fairly easy to interpret. A naked man and a naked woman stand either side of a tree round which coils a snake. A man stands with arms upraised with a crouching lion on either side. A figure is ejected from a boat towards a sea monster, which looks likely to swallow him. So far, so good. While many interpretations are possible, Adam and Eve, Daniel in the lions' den, and Jonah and the sea monster all spring fairly quickly to the mind of anyone with a reasonable knowledge of the Old Testament. This suggests that the room belongs to the Jewish or Christian tradition. After this interpretation becomes more subjective. A young woman between two men has been interpreted as Susanna and the elders. Susanna was being spied on, but there is no sign of this, and the somewhat indistinct men do not look particularly aged. A group of people in the centre of a painting are being addressed by another, probably male, figure on a hillock to the right. While it might be quite proper to call this an address from a hillock, to move on to the Sermon on the Mount is a major step. If this interpretation is accepted it moves us on from the Old Testament to the New and makes this a Christian burial chamber. It would however make sense of another scene which shows three men, with the curly hats typical of the East, who line up before a woman with a child on her lap. The painting is badly damaged, but is a good candidate for Mary, Christ and the Three Magi.

Room B, which leads on to the dead end of room C, has a substantial series of paintings which are set on an architectural background chipped out of the solid rock. Thus there is a vault which is 'held' on columns and even a cornice 'held' on corbels. Among the paintings a man reclining as if asleep with a ladder above him with men ascending and descending suggests Jacob's dream of a ladder. Another person reclining on a couch with seven sheaves of corn above him suggests Jacob's dream. Someone ascends in a fiery chariot leaving someone else on the ground amid a pastoral scene, and Elisha is a clear favourite here. A couple clothed in skins are pushed through a door by a figure with a sword: Adam and Eve expelled from Eden. Women in very fine dress stand above a baby floating in a basket near rushes, watched over by a simply-clothed woman: Moses in the bulrushes **(23)**. This gives a very firm base in the Old Testament without anything specifically Christian.

Room C has Old Testament scenes such as the intended sacrifice of Isaac by Abraham, a man thrown up by a sea monster opposite a man reclining under the shade of a gourd: Jonah. But it also has two major panels opposite one another which occur again in the same conjunction at the end of the catacomb in room O. On one wall is a gap in the centre with on one side an army rushing towards the gap, probably eastern judging by the curly caps, and on the other side a general collection of ordinary people. One particular figure on the people's side points back at the gap with a rod. The suggestion must be the crossing of the Red Sea with the Egyptian army pursuing the Israelites led by Moses **(24)**. Opposite

23 (above, top) Rome, Catacomb on Via Latina. The discovery of Moses in the Bullrushes.
Copyright Nardini Editore
24 (above)Rome, Catacomb on Via Latina. Moses supervising the crossing of the Red Sea.
Copyright Nardini Editore

25 *(above, top) Rome, Catacomb on Via Latina. The raising of Lazarus.*
   Copyright Nardini Editore
26 *(above) Rome, Catacomb on Via Latina. Perhaps the death of Cleopatra.*
   Copyright Nardini Editore

is a crowd of people behind a man with a wand which is pointing at a small isolated building set up a flight of steps to the right. We have to compare this with the similar picture in Room O before the very strong suspicion sets in that this is the Raising of Lazarus **(25)**. If this is correct then room C shows clear Christian influence.

Room E is rather different. The vault has a large head of Medusa in the centre. Around her are animals and plants. On the wall below are two peacocks, and in a niche below them reclines an almost naked woman with a nimbus round her head, poppies or other flowers growing around her, and a basket on which she reclines and out of which comes a snake **(26)**. The publisher of the catacomb favoured a figure of Tellus, the earth. Others have seen in the snake a reference to the death of Cleopatra. The walls are decorated with a series of winged Victories. While there is room for several interpretations here they must probably all have a pagan flavour. Room F with Balaam and the ass, Samson and the jaw bone of an ass would take us to the Old Testament. If a commanding figure facing a woman drawing up a jug of water from a well is Christ and the Samaritan woman, then we move back here into a Christian setting. Rooms E and F are set back from the main corridor so their different allegiances need cause no trouble.

After that I, M, N and O are part of the main corridor, so that you have to go through I to get to M, and so on. Room I has many standing figures but few that can be firmly identified. In the niche above a sarcophagus is a scene with a seated figure, with a hand raised, and a standing figure, each with a scroll, on either side. This has been interpreted as Christ with St Peter and St Paul. The main painting is the most difficult to interpret in the whole catacomb. A man naked to the waist, sits in the centre of a seated group, perhaps 16 in all, while before them lies a naked figure with a hole in its abdomen. One of the seated figures points to the chest of the victim, but most of the group look towards the central figure rather than what is being pointed out. The possibilities are almost endless as different commentators try to win the scene for their particular viewpoint. Probably the best that can be done is to say the scene seems to be a unique representation of an anatomy class with the central figure a respected doctor who is buried in the catacomb. After a series of metaphysical insights this comes as rather an anticlimax, but it economically interprets all the evidence.

Room L has Adam and Eve again, Abraham and Isaac, and Samson slaying the lion, with an earlier victim beside him already the home of bees and honey. M has Adam and Eve and Jonah, both being swallowed and resting under the gourd. But N has pictures of Hercules, with Minerva, with an enemy (dead), with the Hydra, and the Apples of the Hesperides. Someone determined to prove that everything in the catacomb is Christian, who has not been deterred by the Gorgon's head in E, might cite Hercules as a good hero who wins through a series of struggles and is redeemed in the process. But this has about it the ring of desperation. Room N, the way through to room O, is basically pagan.

The end of the long main passage widens out to form room O and here we have another set of varied scenes. Daniel in the lions' den accompanies three men who appear to be dancing in the middle of flames. A figure with a rod or wand addresses seven baskets, which could contain loaves. A man stands in the centre of a wooden box, which only reaches up to his knees, but this could well be Noah and the Ark. All these are overshadowed by another crossing of the Red Sea opposite a crowd behind a figure who points out towards a possible tomb on a hill. But this time, at the door of the tomb is a figure swathed in white. This is difficult to interpret as anything other than a resuscitation at the least. With a figure in the background receiving stone tablets from a hand in the sky it is probably perverse to delay the identification as the Raising of Lazarus. If this information is applied back to room C we have two examples of these scenes used together. Room O seems to be firmly Christian.

The painting, by many different hands, ranges from the accomplished to the competent, from a very spare mix of colours such as red, white and yellow to richly painted scenes with the more exotic and expensive blues, greens and purples. Backgrounds are rarely fully shown, but backgrounds are rarely needed to tell the relevant story. Figures are generally well drawn, naked figures such as Adam and Eve have well-painted musculature, and clothes usually cover credible bodies rather than oblong dummies. Crowd scenes are crowded as in the witnesses to Lazarus being raised and the crossing of the Red Sea, but this is necessary for putting over the story. These points apply just as well to the labours of Hercules, which provide well drawn and painted people. They lapse a little in the Gorgon tomb, room E, where the effect is more decorative than didactic. This does not mean that the standard of painting is any lower, simply that most of the frames contain single decorative elements rather than carefully posed statements.

Perhaps the most informative feature in the whole catacomb is the apparent harmony in which different persuasions died, and therefore presumably lived. Room E, pagan, opens off the main corridor opposite room F, possibly Christian, and this arrangement only means that two groups have to share the access through the same corridor. But Room N with the labours of Hercules is the only way of getting at room O, Christian. Burials in room O and visits to graves have therefore to come and go continually through the Hercules cycle.

There are two points at issue here. One is that of date, the other concerns the relationship between written sources and real life. The date of the main use of the catacomb is early in the fourth century, roughly the same time as the laying of the pavement at Aquileia which showed the miraculous draught of fishes being hauled up by naked winged cherubs instead of fishermen apostles. Some sources, mostly later, do suggest total distaste of Christians for pagans, and to some extent vice versa, but others remind us that in the fourth century many families contained at least two ideas and practices on religion with women favouring Christianity and men sticking to the old ways. There is a telling possible parallel from a novel of Chinua Achebe, looking back to the nineteenth century in Africa, in which a chief with an eye to continuing the family power sends one son to the mission school and brings the other up at home in the traditional religion. In the fourth century the emperor was favouring this novel mystery religion, and it had many adherents, but no one could predict how things would be at the end of the century.

The tremendous amount of tomb painting of the fourth century in the Roman catacombs, much of it still awaiting full study and publication, has parallels in other parts of the Roman world. The main feature has to be underground burial because the remains of above-ground painted mausolea are usually scattered beyond recognition. One exception that has been partly reconstructed comes from the cemetery at Poundbury outside Dorchester in Dorset. There are good examples below ground at Pécs in southern Hungary. When scenes from Pécs such as Daniel in the lions' den and Adam and Eve and the serpent are put side by side with similar scenes from Rome there is very strong resemblance. The lions come up to Daniel's thighs, but no farther. The grouping of Adam, Eve, the tree and the serpent are almost identical. This strongly suggests that some scenes, whether from the Old Testament or the New, have reached a firm form by the middle of the fourth century, which was to remain for a long time.

It might be suggested that Old Testament scenes, such as Daniel, would be the favourites since they might have had four hundred years or more in which to develop among Jewish communities. That is usually opposed on the grounds that it was specifically the Jewish communities who were forbidden to represent either the divine or human form. Dura Europos, a city of the East near the river Euphrates and the site of the possible Christian house church, also provided for excavation the Synagogue, and that, in turn, provided a whole series of mural paintings of scenes from the Old Testament. Such things are virtually unknown back in the areas around the Mediterranean, so perhaps distance from the centre of things had a strong effect on how laws were interpreted. It seems fair to say that, in general, it was the Christian painter and decorator who developed the fixed forms of most of the biblical scenes. Since this was rare before the fourth century, unless underground or under cover of analogy, it is during the fourth century that the scenes take on an accepted form.

To jump straight from the choicest catacomb to the most brilliant collection of mosaics in the late Roman world may seem to be picking out the plums and ignoring the standard, well-distributed monuments. The reason is that there is no such thing as a standard monument, and when the monuments that do exist are well distributed the amount of information that can be gleaned from each one is severely limited. The lack of standardisation is perhaps an overstatement. What it means is that very few of the fifth and sixth century paintings and mosaics that do exist in many parts of the empire are individual productions, not often well dated, and with no comparative material close at hand. Thus particular features, details and quirks of style may be due to any of the influences that have cropped up with earlier works. The style may be a local variation, but there are no comparable works within a hundred miles. The style may be a chronological feature, but the work is not well dated. The style may owe something to a high-ranking patron, but no information on the circumstances of the work's production are available.

The obvious antidotes, or comparisons, with Ravenna should be Constantinople and Rome. Constantinople for the fifth and sixth centuries has very little to offer. The great churches that do survive are either ruinous, St John Studion, or built or rebuilt in the age of Justinian (527–565). Even Hagia Sophia, which does exist almost intact and whose mosaics presumably survive fairly well under coats of whitewash, provides mainly conventional pattern and acres of gold tesserae. The other great cities of the East in the fourth, fifth and sixth centuries are not in good shape. Alexandria has no building surviving intact from pre-Islamic days unless the theatre of Pompey and the pillar of Diocletian are included. Antioch has very little to show above ground at all, and most of the excavated remains pre-date the disastrous earthquake of 365. An 'early' church in Jerusalem means 'Crusader'.

One exception is Thessalonika, but even that has been severely shaken by modern earthquakes. The rotunda of St George has a superb set of mosaics on a gleaming gold ground but a date other than 'fifth century' eludes us. Some panels of mosaic survived the 1912 earthquake and fire at St Demetrius, but it is difficult to tie these in to any sequence. The little oratory of Hosios David, up on the hillside outside the ancient town, has a superb apse mosaic but, again, any close or reasoned date is missing. Many individual mosaics can be added to this list. Naples and Milan both have substantial fragments surviving, the monastery of St Catherine on Mount Sinai has a Justinianic mosaic as does the church of Pula in Slovenia. The monastery of Bawit in Egypt preserved some of its paintings intact into this century. The Levant has many floor mosaics of both churches and synagogues. Some church mosaics and paintings in Cyprus go back to the sixth century. But even if a mosaic in Naples and another in Cyprus can be dated firmly to the years around 480 they belong to different traditions within a rapidly diversifying empire, and they may look totally different. The final argument against assembling and comparing a large number of individual examples here is that almost all of them would have to be analysed by comparing them back to the appropriate mosaic in Ravenna. Since it is the whole purpose of this book to provide a starting point for the study of the Later Empire, an introduction to Ravenna will allow any reader to work outwards from that fixed point.

Ravenna today is a bustling capital of one of the provinces of Italy. It is a substantial port and a major railway focus. With government, administration and commerce there is more than enough to cope with without spending effort on showing off the heritage. As a result you can wander round its unique set of buildings with no bombardment and very little restriction. The town seems to say to you 'nice to see you, congratulations on having the knowledge and good sense to come and see our mosaics, it's up to you, but ask for help if you want it'. All the mosaics, except for those in the archbishop's chapel, are in churches so the entry, up to the last time I saw them, is free. You may get trampled underfoot by coach-loads of tourists, but they sweep through the monuments and then leave them pleasantly empty until the next wave. This may seem a snobbish point, but it is important because of lighting. The guides want their parties to see the mosaics as clearly and as quickly as possible, so they almost always use the powerful lights provided on a time switch. Every illustration you will ever see published is taken, usually on the horizontal from a scaffolding platform, with full lighting. The slides which I have used for lectures for thirty years come from a full set which was made in the mid 1960's, and they are perfect for showing style, colour, and detail. But the mosaics were created for fairly shadowy churches, illuminated, if at all, by lamps and candles, and some of the mosaics are totally incomprehensible from the ground. In the ancient world the only people who ever saw them were their creators, and workmen on ladders making repairs.

The word unique has been used about Ravenna. I hope I have been very sparing in its use in general, but in this case the word is justified. In the modern city, and just outside it, are seven buildings whose mosaics dating from between 425 and 680, are completely, or largely, intact. They are products of imperial patronage while this was the imperial capital, and of the patronage of the Ostrogothic king when he was in charge. Nowhere else is there such a concentration of well dated mosaics of such high quality.

27 Ravenna, Mausoleum of Galla Placidia. The exterior. Copyright Richard Reece

Light is vital in the first church, the Mausoleum of Galla Placidia **(27)**. This redoubtable woman built the nearby church of Santa Croce, now completely destroyed, and this small building was an adjunct to that church. It may have been intended for her own burial, but in fact she died in Rome and was buried in a mausoleum added to Old St Peter's. If she was involved in the building this dates it to between 425 and about 450. It is very small in Roman terms. It has the form of an equal armed cross, and its outside walls are about two people high, so twelve feet or four metres. There are three great marble sarcophagi, additions after the ninth century, in three of the arms, and the fourth arm is the entrance. The sarcophagi almost block the arms, but you can squeeze behind them, and that is a very useful retreat in the face of other visitors. The walls are faced with marble veneer up to shoulder height, and above that every inch is covered in mosaic. The ground is a deep blue, out of which the patterns, designs, and pictures sparkle **(colour plate 5)**. All the mosaic stones, the tesserae, are coloured glass, and all have a rough surface which catches even small amounts of light. It seems best on a sunny day, with the door open, the lights firmly off, but enough time for your eyes to get used to the very gentle light which comes in through the small alabaster windows. Fifty people will fill the space uncomfortably and give little room to move.

This is a complete reversal from public or imperial monuments of the early empire, where size and space were the major factors. Even something of restricted access like Hadrian's villa at Tivoli is spacious and open. The imperial baths and palaces were on an imperial scale, and if money was given to a community it was intended to produce a major monument such as a great theatre, library or fountain. In this small oratory, seen by very few people at the time it was built, we can get an idea of what people of the later empire judged to be important. This is a building for the privileged individual, built for quiet, private thought, with decoration that encloses the persons in it so that they can almost reach out to touch any part of the design.

The colours are difficult to describe in purely factual terms. Words that suggest themselves are fresh, clean and intense. The scenes are simple, and backgrounds are minimal. Christ appears as a young, beardless, good shepherd clothed in gold and purple and seated on a rock in a simple landscape. In the arch opposite the door St Lawrence on one side hastens towards a well fired gridiron in the centre while the other side of the picture gives us one of the two representations of a book-cupboard from the late Roman world. The gospels, each in a separate leather cover with thongs to close them with, sit on apparently sloping shelves. The doors of the cupboard can clearly be closed and locked. St Lawrence has his copy of the gospels in one hand, leather ties flying as he moves, and he carries a gold cross over his shoulder. The drapery of his clothes is in turmoil, suggesting violent motion towards his martyrdom. The drawing of human figures is good, but not anatomically perfect. Clothes suggest the form beneath them rather than being tubes fitted over dummies. Colours are fairly realistic, and shading follows form rather than creating a pattern of its own.

The cathedral of Ravenna ought to be the high point of any visit, but in fact it is best avoided. It was totally rebuilt in the eighteenth century and is not even good for its time. Fortunately the baptistery beside it is a completely separate building, and that is virtually intact. The decoration is attributed to bishop Neon and given a date around 460. The font takes up the centre of the building, and around it is an ambulatory. The lower parts of the walls hold mosaic, marble and porphyry panels. Higher up much of the original stucco work survives. This is important because stucco is much more delicate than mosaic, and it suggests that in many schemes of decoration elsewhere we have probably lost the stucco element. The dome has a series of panels in architectural surrounds, pillars and arches, rather like the decoration in the rotunda of St George at Thessalonica. But while the background at Thessalonika is gold, the Ravenna background is mainly deep blue. In the curvature of the dome twelve apostles move towards the axis of the scene in the top of the dome. That roundel shows the baptism of Jesus in the river Jordan by St John the Baptist **(colour plate 6)**. The twelve apostles are well drawn figures in white and gold clothes shown as individuals of different ages and characters. The background of the central roundel changes to gold, and a large part of it is clear restoration. This means that the head, shoulders and arm of the Baptist, the head of Christ and the descending dove are not original. The lower parts, with the wavy water of the river Jordan, duly labelled and presided over by the river god himself, and the stylised rocky background can be relied on.

The archbishop's chapel is in the palace on the other side of the cathedral from the baptistery. This is on an upper floor, which ought to mean that a substantial part of the fifth century palace still remains in place to hold things up. The chapel has a series of panels on the walls, some of which have been very heavily restored, and a mosaic in the vault in which four angels hold up the central roundel filled by the chi-ro, while between the angels the symbols of the four evangelists emerge from clouds. The mosaics in the chapel are usually dated to around 490.

28 Ravenna, Arian Baptistry. The exterior. Copyright Richard Reece

This takes us beyond the last emperor of the West, Julius Nepos, who was killed in 480, and on to the time of the kingdom of the Ostrogoths. The most famous name here is Theoderic, and he is linked with the two next monuments. Since the Cathedral baptistery has just been described it is good to move on to the Arian Baptistery **(28)**. A second baptistery was needed because of the religious divisions between the Romans and the Goths. The Romans, as good imperial citizens under the control of the Bishop of Rome, were orthodox (straight) in their Christian beliefs. The Goths had been converted while outside the empire at a time when the balance between central orthodoxy and different interpretations such as those of Bishop Arius was less firm. The missionary to the Goths was Bishop Wulfila, who was a follower of Bishop Arius and therefore an Arian. Arianism was condemned as a heresy in the fourth century, which to some extent settled things inside the empire but had no effect on the Goths. When they arrived in Italy in the 470s they were Christian, but 'separated brothers'. When the chief person in Ravenna was the Ostrogothic king the firm Roman balance was shifted again, and there were two cathedrals, each needing a baptistery, one for the Orthodox and the other for the Arians.

The Arian baptistery retains only the decoration of its dome, but this is complete **(colour plate 7)**. It ought to date from the years around 490, the early years of the Gothic kingdom. It is similar to the dome of the Orthodox cathedral baptistery, but the background has changed to gold and there are only two elements in the decoration. The architectural frieze is omitted, and the whole of the curve is taken up with the twelve apostles. The flatter central part shows the baptism. The apostles are very well drawn and are given individual features again. They have only white clothes, but like the other

63

apostles they carry their crowns of martyrdom. Those in the cathedral procession are all labelled, those in the Arian procession are not. The cathedral Peter and Paul carry crowns like the other saints, the Arian Peter carries his keys and Paul his scrolls. The cathedral apostles are separated by fairly stylised acanthus plants, while very stylised palm trees are used to separate the Arian saints.

The central roundel of the Arian baptistery **(colour plate 8)** has a design which is reversed from the cathedral plan. John the Baptist is on the right, the river god of the Jordan is on the left. John's hand touches the head of Christ and the Holy Spirit as a dove sends a cone of influence and blessing from above. The dish with which John pours river water over the head of Christ, which has been restored in the cathedral roundel, has no place here. The human figures are very well drawn with fully-muscled bodies in good proportion. The scenery on the other hand is even more schematic with simply a river and a fractured green platform for John to stand on. The colours are perfectly pleasant, tones and shades are excellently deployed on the bodies to give a near-natural account of the musculature, but the greens are verging on the khaki and the reds tend to browns. What I described as the cleanness of the Galla Placidia colours seems to be failing. One other difference comes in the relationship between the procession of apostles and the central scene of baptism. In the cathedral baptistery if you position yourself to look at the baptism, the procession meets in front of you. In the Arian baptistery, if you look at the baptism the right way up, the procession is going away from you to meet, upside down, either side of a throne, above the head of Christ.

The orthodox baptistery is by the orthodox cathedral, and in just the same way the Arian baptistery was beside the Arian cathedral. This is now the church of Spirito Santo, but only the structure of the church remains, and all decoration has gone. If we want an Arian church then we have to go to the next monument on the list, the new church of San Apollinaris, or San Apollinare Nuovo. The name is complicated because the church is not 'newer' than the other church of San Apollinare in (at) Classe (the port of Ravenna), but the detailed story has no effect on a discussion of the mosaic decoration. The church survives almost completely covered in mosaic except for the apse, which was rebuilt in 1950 inside the war-damaged baroque apse. I wish more restoration like this had taken place. Top of my list would be an agreement between Christianity and Islam that if the heavy late gothic cathedral could be removed from the superb Great Mosque at Cordoba, the Islamic decorations could be removed from the superb Great Church of Hagia Sophia in Istanbul. Not only would this result in great improvement of looks and atmosphere, but it would be a very practical exercise in reconciliation and a retraction of ugly triumphalism.

Even though the mosaics of the church of San Apollinare are the result of just such anger there is not enough evidence available to make restitution a practical proposition. I described the church as almost covered in mosaic, rather than almost intact, because there are at least two major campaigns of decoration. The first belongs to the building of the church, and the Ravenna sources quote an inscription on the former apse mosaic as saying that 'King Theoderic built this church from its foundations in the name of our Lord Jesus Christ'. The materials are mainly re-used from earlier Roman buildings and are quite unlike the columns, capitals, and veneer imported from near Constantinople for the later

29 *Ravenna, Church of San Apollinaire Nuovo. The south arcade, saints in procession.*
Copyright Peter Clayton

church of San Vitale. The early mosaics of around 500 include a series of small panels just below the roof line and above the windows, a series of figures between the windows, and parts of the long frieze just above the columns of the arcade.

The top panels show 26 scenes from the life of Christ. They are in brilliant, clear colour, the drawing of figures is good, the scenes are not too formally posed, and they are virtually impossible to see. Even with binoculars there is the problem of glare from the large windows directly below the panels, and in the absence of outside light only electric light can illuminate them. When they were put up there was no possibility of good illumination by lamp or candle. They share some characteristics, of colour, drawing and composition, with a series, of the earlier fifth century, in the church of Santa Maria Maggiore at Rome which is equally difficult to see. The Rome series provides a series of panels by which the Old Testament leads from the entrance up to the triumphal arch which shows New Testament scenes.

Directly above the columns of the nave there are two processions, one of virgin saints and one of male martyrs **(29)**. These are visibly inserted into the decoration, with straight line junctions with earlier work, and the Ravenna texts tell us that they were put in after the church had been 'reconciled' to the Orthodox tradition and all trace of heresy removed. They therefore date to around 550. The virgins start out from the port of Classe and merge into a panel showing the three wise men who, after a straight-line join, present their gifts to Christ on the knee of Mary. The male martyrs start out from a building labelled Palatium and arrive at a scene of Christ, young and beardless, enthroned in purple and flanked by angels **(colour plate 9)**.

The main points of interest centre in Classe and the palace. The port shows a city surrounded by walls with a harbour entrance and ships at anchor inside. The town has the usual town appurtenances, the dome, the colonnade, the open space and perhaps the theatre. There is a strong tradition of showing just these characteristic buildings right through the Roman period, from the newly discovered fresco on the Oppian Hill of the first century AD right through to manuscripts of the seventh century, so it would be very unwise to plan an excavation at Classe using the mosaic as a guide to the likely position of the main buildings. The Palatium shows an ornate frontage to an apparently rambling complex of buildings of different forms which may, again, be conventional, and its main feature is a colonnade partly closed by curtains **(colour plate 10)**. Closer inspection shows signs of interference with the original mosaic, for parts of hands appear on columns and shadows of bodies and heads appear in the curtained openings. This strongly suggests that when first set up the palace was inhabited by its royal family duly posed in the appropriate openings. As they were both barbarian and heretic they have been purged and replaced with conventional decoration, but the purge has been rather carelessly done. It is likely that we have here Classe at the time of Theoderic and Theoderic's palace. What connected these two scenes with the east end of the church, now replaced with the two processions, we do not know. It seems unlikely that such an expanse of mosaic could have contained much undesirable Arian detail, and the replacement may have been practical rather than triumphal.

Triumph is at once more and less obvious in the church of San Vitale which forms a uniform interior decoration. It is less obvious because there is no argument visible between different parts of the decoration; it is more obvious because to anyone knowing of the reign of the Gothic kings and queens the great panels showing the court of the Byzantine emperor Justinian and his wife Theodora **(colour plate 12)** are a massive statement of re-conquest. Ravenna sources say that the building was begun in 525 under Gothic rule, but it was not consecrated until about 548. The Byzantine army occupied the town from 540 onwards, and it seems likely that much of the decoration is post-conquest. Unlike the furnishings at San Apollinare Nuovo, everything at San Vitale is newly cut in the most up-to-date Constantinopolitan style and materials. The panels of the court figures have already been discussed as portraits. Here it remains to point out the vivid colour, the figures, which are anatomically accurate, and the extreme luxury of the dresses of the women of the court. The materials are presumably woven of silk, the culture of which had been 'liberated' from China at this period. But the repeating designs are intricate and highly effective and allow the women courtiers almost to challenge the heavy imperial purple of Theodora. The men of higher rank are locked in formal, presumably official, dress, mostly of white, but the soldiers of the bodyguard wear colourful tunics.

Two of the most interesting scenes are set on the wall either side of the altar, which is set forward from the apse and the court mosaics. They are simple references to what goes on on the altar between them, the communion service. Abel, on one side of a draped table, offers up a lamb, and on the other side of the table Melchisidek the priest offers up bread and wine in an Old Testament prefiguring of the Eucharist **(colour plate 13)**. On the facing panel Abraham first entertains three seated angels to refreshment, and then is about to kill his son Isaac as a sacrifice, but is stopped by the hand of God appearing from the clouds. The three angels as persons of the Trinity, the sacrifice of a son, the providing of a meal, the making of an offering and the offering of bread and wine have connections to the communion service which most spectators would have grasped without difficulty. The figures in the scenes are fairly rigidly posed, and their bodies are not perfect anatomically. The colours form for me a watershed between the freshness of earlier mosaics and the muddiness of some later examples, but this is a personal judgement which it is almost impossible to put into words. Readers need to see the mosaics for themselves because all colour reproductions have a colour bias in one way or another.

The representation of Christ is another way in which San Vitale seems the end of the Roman line and the beginning of Byzantine representation. Christ in the apse mosaic is a young, gentle, clean-shaven figure seated on a globe. Christ above the arch which separates off the choir from the rest of the church is a heavily bearded, older figure of authority whose facial features are already beginning to be used as parts of a regular pattern. This conjunction of the young human Jesus with the formal second member of the Trinity of God the Father, Son, and Holy Spirit balances the mosaics of San Vitale in the 550s narrowly between two different worlds of the past and the future.

The final set of mosaics in Ravenna has settled firmly on the Byzantine side of the divide, in the church of San Apollinare in Classe. The site is about four miles to the south of Ravenna itself, but of the port city virtually nothing but the church remains above ground. The decoration is the direct opposite of that in San Apollinare Nuovo, which was almost complete except for the apse. In Classe the only mosaic surviving is in the apse and the arch which separates it off from the rest of the church. The arch has on it another bearded Christ, together with the symbols of the four gospel writers: Matthew, a man, Mark, a lion, Luke, a winged bull, and John, an eagle. The date is disputed, but is certainly later than the sixth century. In the semi-dome of the apse is a jewelled cross, and beneath that the figure of Saint Apollinaris. Between the windows are figures of priests and saints, and either side of the altar, on each end of the apse, are panels which recall, or copy, panels at San Vitale. The semi-dome mosaics are assumed to be of the later sixth century, while the end panels are firmly dated, by mention of Constantine IV, to the 670s.

One panel copies the Justinian panel but the drawing is much more stylised with figures who can hardly be detected within their cloaks, and faces without any individuality. The other panel conflates the two panels which at San Vitale flank the altar; Melchisidek is in the centre at the table, Abel is to one side with his lamb, and Abraham is at the other with Isaac. The colours in the semidome are not very strong, and they merge into different shades of green and yellow without much purpose. In the lower panels the colours are abrasive rather than strong, glaring rather than bright. This description of Classe might tempt the visitor to cut short the tour with San Vitale, but this would lose most of the benefit of having this series of seven sets of mosaics within a comfortable and gentle day's study.

The points which emerge from this remarkable collection of ancient material are many but three can be emphasised. First comes the richness of the collection, for what survives is only a part of what once filled the city in the sixth century. We know of several churches which were built and fully decorated but of which no trace remains above ground. There are as many churches, built in the sixth century, still surviving without decoration as with. We therefore have to multiply the examples by at least three to get an idea of what the sixth-century resident would have seen. Second comes the standard of the works, for this was the Imperial capital and produced the best work of its day. I have made value judgements setting the different mosaics at different levels within my own scheme of preference, but each one is at the height of fashion when it was made. A study of variation of 'attractiveness' is no less than a study of the changes of the best that fashion could offer. Third comes the chance to see the development of a particular type of art, mosaic, in a particular setting, religious, at a particular level, imperial, and most important of all, over a well-defined time period, from 425–680. This is why the monuments have to be seen one after another, within a fairly short time, to get the maximum out of them. The tendencies which, at San Vitale, might only be temporary blips, can be seen at Classe to be part of a decided change in the art of late antiquity.

The last two examples of late mosaic and painting close in, first to a series of almost disembodied scenes, and then to a single painted wooden panel. The disembodied scenes come from a definite location, in fact many of them were uncovered in excavation of the great palace of the emperors in Constantinople, so their place of manufacture and use is not in doubt. By contrast their date is almost unknowable. The single panel is in the Vatican museum and so has certainly moved well away from its point of origin, yet it is of a firm time and place.

The mosaics from the Constantinople palace were uncovered in the 1950s and have had a varied life since then. They were lifted and for a long time were to be seen stacked in wooden frames, on their sides, in odd corners of the church of Hagia Sophia. Now they are displayed in a new mosaic museum and can be properly appreciated. But they are totally out of context, and it is no fault of the museum that we have no detailed archaeological information about them. This leaves us at the mercy of dating by style, and they are probably the most difficult examples on which this could be tried.

Wide, general, date brackets can be settled but they are not very helpful. The mosaics clearly post-date the imperial move to Constantinople and so belong after about 340. Written sources tell us that the palace, like much of the centre of the city, suffered from the Nika Revolt of 532 but unfortunately the excavations do not place the mosaics either before or after any destruction. It might be correct to say that the mosaics look nothing like the styles used during or after the banning of icons (iconoclasm), so an end date before about 750 seems safe. This gives a time bracket of 400 years, which in Britain would be the equivalent of saying 'Roman' but not being able to get any closer.

One panel stands out and may well be earlier than the others. It is part of a border that has a human face within a scroll of plants. The face has so much detail of flesh and bone structure that it ought to belong to the middle of the second century. The lips are well drawn and coloured, the eyes look rather anxiously to the left, and the worries are accentuated by the wrinkles on the brow. But the face is framed in leaves and outside that frame there is no context whatever. Neither the white background nor the dog which runs to the right, help any discussion. Even if this face belongs to the time of Constantine it is very unusual, and it might make better sense for it to be a Justinianic throwback or copy

30 *Rome, Vatican Museums. Lid of wooden reliquary box painted with scenes from the life of Christ.*
Copyright Ellen Swift

than a remarkable piece of Constantinian excellence. The other scenes are very well drawn, gently-coloured pictures of animal fights, rural labours and everyday events.

The best known may be the guide leading two boys who are perched on a camel **(colour plate 14)**. There is a tree behind the camel but otherwise the background consists only of white tesserae. My knowledge of camels is not good enough to discuss this one critically, but it looks as if it is a young animal, and if this is the case then it seems to me a perfectly able representation. The children are certainly not idealised cherubs but fair-skinned boys, one of whom carries a black bird which might be a jackdaw. The guide, a tanned youth with clear, well-developed muscles moves forward and the camel follows him on a slack rope. There is very little, if any, use of highlights and the shading on the boys, the camel and the guide are very naturalistic. In these areas of colour and form this panel is less stylised than that of the oxen ploughing at Cherchel with which we began. The workmen hoeing in another panel are very well drawn though they have posed for the picture, and when the frame unfreezes it is uncertain what their next movement will be. The man milking the goats is crouching down on the ground behind the goat and, again, the scene is very well observed and portrayed. In all these scenes there is very little evidence of communicating a point by stylisation of colour or shape or texture, or even by organising the scene, which has been taken as a main characteristic of the development of Roman art from the second century onwards.

Since these scenes have few points of comparison with all those which are reasonably well dated the only obvious point to follow is the equally sudden return to individual features in portraits which is seen in the Justinian and Theodora mosaics in San Vitale at Ravenna. These upset the general tendency seen up to that point in the development of late Roman portraiture, and it may be that at the court of Justinian conventions of style were suspended. This suggestion of stylistic anarchy obviously upsets the attractive idea of Justinian using real likenesses in an imperial church where few ever went, and those few knew the people behind the portraits. The same argument could be extended to cover the palace mosaics, but it would stretch it almost beyond belief. Since there is no obvious message in the mosaics, and since they seem to have no imperial elements in them, then the suggestion would have to be that decoration in the imperial palace could be more purely decorative in its form and function than decoration anywhere else. The emperor at home is the one person who does not need to make points to his guests about his powers and his possessions. This goes so strongly against what we know of the hierarchy and the power struggles of the later empire that I think it can be safely forgotten.

It is almost a relief to turn to the lid of a small wooden box painted with five scenes of the life of Christ **(30)**. Starting at the bottom left we have the birth, with the swaddled baby being examined closely by a curious ox and ass. We move quickly on to the baptism, and then the middle panel takes up a double space for the crucifixion. After that at top left is the discovery of the empty tomb and top right the ascension. The box can be thought of as a reliquary, filled with earth and stones from the vital sites any pilgrim to the Holy Land ought to visit. The painted scenes form a visual record. The ascension is very similar to that in the Rabbula gospels (chapter 4), with Mary in the centre of the group, and the crucifixion shares with Rabbula Christ in a long dark robe. The visit to the tomb in Rabbula has only a small ornate mausoleum with columns and a curly pediment, but the box-lid shows the tomb as perhaps the pilgrim would see it in the sixth century under the dome of Constantine's rotunda of the Resurrection (Anastasis). The baptism is similar to those in Ravenna, but the river god has gone and two angels waiting with cloths, or clothes, for the emergence of a wet Christ from the Jordan take his place.

The way in which this small object has a place and a time, and even a purpose, of its own is very satisfying. If it had been discussed earlier, the suggestions would have seemed strained. With a proper sequence built up, they seem pleasantly sensible. This might of course simply mean that divergence of opinion on the Constantinople palace mosaics leads to discomfort and anxiety whereas consensus on the Vatican box-lid leads to false security.

4. Illuminated manuscripts

One area of art which developed dramatically in the later Roman empire is the luxury manuscript with many illustrations. Such a simple statement causes many people considerable discomfort. What about all those Egyptian Books of the Dead? Are there not reams of papyrus covered with both writing and pictures?

The strange thing here is the total absence of any link between the Egyptian papyrus and the Roman painted book. Many people want to put one of the great production centres of painted books in Alexandria, and if that were true the non-communication between the two cultures is even more obvious. But this example of non-communication in Egypt is only one of several — Greek imposed coinage being the most obvious. The simplest way to look at it is to assume that Books of the Dead were bound up in the Egyptian cultural package, that vellum books with pictures were part of the Classical package, and not only did the two packages stay separate but transfer of elements from one to the other was not proper and did not happen.

We therefore have to make sense of what we have, while remembering that our ideas can easily be overthrown by any new discoveries. Classical papyri may at first sight offer more hope. There is one papyrus with a coloured picture, the five charioteers, and this is quoted on every occasion and often reproduced. If more were known they would certainly be mentioned. But, runs the argument, only a proportion of papyri are published, there is a considerable backlog awaiting detailed scrutiny, more coloured pictures may turn up. One specialist to whom I applied for help on this made the very simple point. Yes, there are thousands if not millions of fragments waiting to be worked over. But virtually everything has been looked at at least once and there is a general rule of thumb. A drawing, whether coloured or not, is usually recognisable for something and will probably get mentioned. A line of verse can probably be tracked down without too much trouble, and that will receive immediate publication. The friendless fragments which await study are not the obvious but the obscure. This leaves the illustrated manuscript of the late fourth century without any surviving ancestors, but clearly they cannot have been created out of nothing.

The manuscripts surviving can be put in a general chronological sequence by the letter forms of their texts. Hundreds of plain unpainted manuscripts survive from the later Empire, some of them actually dated in Roman terms, and the scripts of these have been put in time brackets, and often in geographical groups. Dating here may be by a century or more, so there will never be certainty on dating a manuscript to a shorter time period by script alone. The small numbers, tens rather than hundreds, of painted manuscripts can be fitted in to the sequence of scripts, and art historians are then free to imagine closer dates as they will. The very general sequence shows the first parchment books, perhaps of the first century AD, as descendants of papyrus rolls with occasional drawings where they are relevant to the text. There may be a portrait of the author at the beginning, and a diagram where words fail. In the roll there is almost no constraint on where diagrams can be put. A roll copied directly onto sheets of vellum and then bound will show illustrations scattered erratically over the pages. By the fourth century a book had to be thought out with words and pictures to be placed to best advantage and constraint began to creep in. A square picture will not fit in the narrow rectangle which is all that is left at the bottom of the page after the relevant text. The text must be continued and the picture put in the middle of the next piece of text on the next page, to which it is irrelevant, or the text must break off in time to get the picture in, and the story may be finished after the picture on the next page. If you are going to prepare a sheet for painting rather than writing, and different people will paint and write, then it might be better either to have a full-page picture opposite the text, or save up a series of episodes and set them one below the other in narrative order, on one page. This development seems to be fairly generally agreed, it fits with the other aspects of dating the manuscripts, and it makes good sense as a progression.

The two manuscripts which are always put first are copies of the works of Virgil. Both are in the Vatican library. The *Vatican Virgil* is usually dated earlier, around the year 400, and the *Roman Virgil* is dated up to 100 years later. Their paintings are very different and this is usually made the basis of the dating. But there is the other aspect of place as well as time which needs to be considered. We may be looking not at a single line of development by which *Vatican* gives rise to *Roman* in the same place, but more or less simultaneous painting in two different styles in two different places. *Vatican* is cool and well drawn with colours well-blended and matched. Scenes are usually seen from a distance so that details of bodies are less obvious. Where people are seen more closely, as in the death of Dido **(colour plate 15)**, there is little to complain of. *Roman* is clearly outlined, has bright colours and rather naive figures which somehow match the colours. The people are far more immediate, in closer focus, and anatomy, especially the shoulders, is not perfectly observed. In one case I get the impression of formality and reticence; in the other I see the freshness of a painter working things out as he goes along. My favourite picture is of Dido and Aeneas during the Royal Hunt sheltering in the cave during the storm **(colour plate 16)**. Aeneas looks almost apprehensive at Dido's advances. The cave in which they shelter is only just big enough for them and the soldiers have to stay outside. One horse looks up at the storm, one soldier very sensibly puts his round shield over his head and shelters under that.

If *Vatican* is properly dated to around 400 somewhere round Rome I think I would prefer to place *Roman* at roughly the same time, but in a 'provincial' setting. Slaves in the banquet scene have long hair and are blond, and Trier has been suggested. Weitzmann says of the artist that he has 'limited experience in the design of the human body' but 'is more concerned with patternisation'. This might fit well with what little we know of artists in the NW of the Empire. One of our main problems here is in fitting something so intimate as a manuscript written and painted for an individual into the political history of tribes, wars and disasters of the fifth century. The two do not fit for they belong to totally different parts of the fifth-century world.

*31 Berlin,
Staatsbiblithek.
Quedlinburg
Itala
manuscript,
Saul and
Samuel.
Copyright
Berlin,
Staatsbibliothek
zu Berlin,
Preußischer
kulturbesitz,
Handschriften
abteilung.*

If looking back to classical traditions in blending, not to say merging, colours is a feature of Roman painting around 400 then the six leaves of an Old Testament manuscript including the Books of *Samuel* and *Kings* is perfection **(31)**. The pages show us, with four scenes to a page, episodes from the Books with text above and around the pictures. These pages survive because they were used in a binding done in Quedlinburg in 1618. The loss of the rest of the pages of what must have been a manuscript of considerable size and great luxury adds fuel to the argument from non-survival. The drawing is close to the *Vatican Virgil* and the colours hover around pinks, purples and blues.

With the copy of the *Iliad* kept in the Ambrosian library in Milan strong changes appear **(32)**. Put in modern terms, what we have left are the pictures which have been cut out of a book and, even worse, someone has scribbled all over them. Put in more scholarly terms, we have only the pictures from this manuscript, hacked rather unevenly out of the pages of text. These have been annotated so that the viewer who reads Greek knows who is who in each scene, and what is happening. This in a way fits with the drawing of the pictures which have been opened up in the late antique way to make the scenes clearer. Faces are an almost brutal opposite to the clear, open faces of the *Roman Virgil*, colours are strong, but blend, and sometimes it is necessary to tell several parts of a continuing narrative in the same frame, separated by blank background. Since this is the first illustrated manuscript with a Greek text its possible point of origin is likely to be eastern, and dates usually range in the fifth century.

With the copy of a book on herbs and medicines, the *Materia Medica* composed originally in the first century AD by Dioscorides, we reach much firmer ground. The book was

32 Milan, Ambrosian Library. Ambrosian Iliad, Nestor and Patroclus. Property of the Ambrosian Library. All rights reserved. Reproduction is forbidden

copied by order of Juliana Anicia in the early years of the sixth century and probably around 510. She was one of the old order of Constantinopolitan aristocracy with imperial ancestors, considerable property and a healthy disregard for the new, jumped up, type of emperor represented by Justinian. Her great church of St Polyeuktos was partially excavated in the 1970s. Her manuscript was in Constantinople at the Turkish conquest and was sold by the Sultan's physician to the Holy Roman Emperor in 1569. Hence the shorthand title of the *Vienna Dioscorides*. The picture that accompanies the dedication is of Juliana herself. The manuscript follows the usual tradition of having a portrait of the author (33), but in this case there is a unique representation of the writer and the artist at work. Detail is such that the artist works at a drawing board on which his sheet of vellum is held by thumb tacks. His pots of pigment are on the table beside him, and the muse holds up for him the mandrake root that he is painting (34).

It is impossible to compare this manuscript with others because most of its drawings are of plants and natural curiosities. To some extent all that useful information in the first few paintings is wasted because there are no other early herbals with which to draw parallels. But it is worth pointing out that in the portrait of Juliana the artist has no problems with one person sitting clearly in front of two others who go into the background. They have no setting, but their physical appearance is unexceptionable. On another early page seven physicians are shown. Here all setting is avoided and the seven bodies are placed against a gold background. The scene of writing and painting is much busier with a full architectural background and several layers of events. The perspective of chairs, tables and benches is not perfect, but a sense of space is firmly there. These three pictures therefore show many of the characteristics of late Roman art, but on the other hand show that depth and perspective are still available as techniques, if wanted.

33 Vienna, National Library. Vienna Dioscorides, portrait of painter at work. Österreichische Nationalbibliothek, Wien

English readers deserve a mention of the few charred fragments which are all that is left of a luxury manuscript of the Book of *Genesis* that survived intact up to a fire in London in 1731. The outline of the complete manuscript has now been reconstructed from the fragments, both the Greek text and the setting of the illustrations, but this gives little idea of what the pictures looked like. It does seem generally agreed that the manuscript was in Venice when the mosaics in the porch of St Mark's were being set, so we probably have to use those mosaics to fill in the overwhelming blanks. A date in the 500s is usually given. We could, if were being nationalistic, call this the *London Genesis* to compare with the *Vienna Genesis,* which conveniently comes next.

34 Vienna, National Library. Vienna Dioscorides, the painter at work. Österreichische Nationalbibliothek Wien

This manuscript turned up in Vienna in 1664 and has no earlier known history other than a brief appearance in Venice, so that the name of *Vienna Genesis* is a simple statement of fact. It is a luxury document with the Greek text written in metallic ink on parchment stained with Imperial purple dye. The illustrations at the bottom of each page are directly related to the selected text above and sometimes have two ground surfaces, with one scene directly above another. One of the most striking pictures shows what was left, apart from the Ark and its cargo, after the flood. Mount Ararat stands out, surrounded by flood water in which swirl numbers of dead bodies and a few still in the process of drowning. There is very little material with which to compare this scene because the *Cotton (London) Genesis* picture has been lost, and the relevant panel of mosaic at St Mark's shows a flat sea with mainly dead faces showing above. The only Latin Genesis, the *Tours pentateuch* to be

35 *Vienna, National Library. Vienna Genesis, Rebecca at the well. Österreichische Nationalbibliothek, Wien*

considered later, has a full-page picture of the Ark, in ancient, chest-like form, not the medieval and modern toy form, with men and animals floating freely on the water **(colour plate 18)**. The Vienna picture is much more communicative because the living, but drowning figures are still a healthy pink, while the dead are a pale grey. The presence of drowning as well as drowned adds to the horror and all sorts and sizes are there from a child to an adult couple clasped to one another. Formality, and firmly decided rules for the depiction of each scene have perhaps not yet settled in, so the painter was to some extent free to invent. On the other hand, he might have been copying from a much earlier painting in which freedom of expression was greater.

This brings in the question of date, place of writing and what we know about the artists. The luxury of the manuscript, silver ink and purple dye suggest an imperial setting. The clothes and ornaments worn are close to those on mosaics of the sixth century, and a date during the reign of Justinian (527–565) or a little later is often quoted. Different detailed studies have separated out the pictures into the work of several painters who range in number from about four to about eight. The strong variation in style would certainly be very unusual for a single painter. If the date in the middle of the sixth century is right then the manuscript was probably made in the eastern part of the Mediterranean, but there is no way at present of deciding between Constantinople, Antioch, Alexandria or some smaller centre of excellence.

In general, colours are bright and clear, the figures are well drawn, and many of the scenes show a strong sense of movement. Many of them can be linked in to the general sequence of late antique pictures by details either of what is shown, or how it is shown. The meeting of Abraham's servant Eliezer (and ten thirsty camels) with Rebekah at the well outside the city of Nahor **(35)** has several elements which have cropped up already elsewhere. The most obvious is the city, with its ring of walls and towers, a simple gateway and then a sample of suitable buildings inside the walls. The roofs are tiled in red and grey, and there is a colonnade and possibly a small tower. Outside the walls there is nothing except for a way, bordered with columns, down to the well. The well is conflated with a river, or perhaps a spring, because a stream of water comes out of the jug held by the lightly draped river nymph. The camels are an unusual feature with no obvious points of comparison. Here we have the city, as in the mosaic at San Apollinare in Classe, and the river nymph in a specifically Judaeo-Christian setting, just as in the baptisteries in Ravenna.

The New Testament equivalent of the *Vienna Genesis* is the manuscript of the Gospels which was for many years in the Cathedral at Rossano in southern Italy. The illustrations are gathered together at the front of the volume. There are some full page pictures, notably two scenes with Christ before Pontius Pilate, but on other pages there is a combination of a New Testament story, such as the raising of Lazarus, and below it four Old Testament figures with quotations from their writings which lead forward to the New Testament. The raising of Lazarus which we saw firmly posed in the Via Latina catacomb in Rome in the fourth century is here much more of an action picture. Via Latina has a mass of spectators and Christ is posed to draw Lazarus from the tomb by his authority. Here Jesus hurries towards Martha and Mary, sisters of Lazarus, who are kneeling before him to ask for his help. Other men bend towards the approaching figure of Jesus, and one more figure brings the corpse from the tomb, with his nose buried in his tunic. Something is happening in front of us, but there is no background at all, and the only impression of depth for the scene comes from the superimposition of the spectators. Colours are bright, and figures are well drawn.

The two great scenes are those showing Pontius Pilate in judgement **(36)**. He sits in a gold robe, with two pictures, each showing two imperial figures on stands behind him. These are the Imperial Images or Icons which share with him, the person on the spot, some of their power. The table in front of him is draped, again with two portraits on the white cloth, and on the table are writing implements. In the first scene Jesus and his accusers stand on one side, on the other are five officials of some sort, each with a prominent brooch holding his cloak. Below this scene is another part of the story in which Judas takes the thirty pieces of silver back to the chief priest, who rejects them. Judas then hangs himself. The chief priest sits under a dome-like shell on four columns, a baldachino, in a chair which gives the impression of being woven like basketwork. It is the typical official chair, next down from the throne. In the second scene Jesus has been brought back to Pilate and stands in front of him with the other prisoner Barabbas. Pilate, with his short-hand writer taking notes in front of him on a wax tablet, asks the Jews all around him which prisoner is to be released.

36 Rossano, S. Italy. Rossano Gospels, Christ before Pilate.
   Copyright Hirmer

One further full-page picture deserves description even though it has been claimed as a later, Byzantine, replacement. It is the portrait of the writer of the gospel, the evangelist, at work. He sits in one of the wicker chairs and bends forward to write on a scroll. In front of him, almost dictating to him, stands a female figure in blue. They are set against a light blue background and within an impractical architectural framework of columns, an arch and two pyramids. This could perfectly well be the classical author at work with his muse dictating to him, as Dioscorides was shown at work on his *Materia Medica*. A pre-existing idea has been taken over for the authors of the gospels, and these are to be major elements of book decoration from this time onwards. It is interesting that the figure, bound in a book of separate sheets, is shown writing on a continuous scroll. There are two possibilities here. Either the painter is copying an earlier model, made when the typical form of the gospel was a scroll, or, much less likely, there is an awareness that scrolls were the early form, so that is what would have been used at the time of the first writing of the gospel. The author is always said to be St Mark, I assume because of the position of the picture within the text, but it could remind us that tradition brought the Virgin Mary to help St Luke add particular details to his gospel.

A final note, which always intrigues me is the portrayal of the parable of the wise and foolish virgins who went to greet the bridegroom at a wedding. He was late, the lamps were still burning, and some of the virgins had thought to bring a good supply of oil, while others had not. They go to get some more oil, the bridegroom arrives, the doors are locked, and the foolish virgins are left outside. This is where we join them with the wise virgins in white with the bridegroom, who is shown as Christ, on the right. Then there is a closed door, and to the left are the foolish virgins in coloured robes, duly excluded. All carry torches, rather than lamps, which goes against the text. The point which always worries me about the scene, which I know is the intrusion of a modern and literal mind on an ancient symbolic representation, is how the virgins knew when they came, to dress whether they were to be wise or foolish?

Apart from several other fifth- and sixth-century painted manuscripts such as the *Syriac Bible* in Paris and the *Codex Sinopensis* (the Book from Sinope, on the Black Sea), there are four more manuscripts which each makes a separate point. The *Rabbula Gospels* are not only my favourite illustrations, but they are placed and dated. The *gospels of St Augustine* are vital to a knowledge of what was going on in Italy in the sixth century. The *Tours (Ashburnham) Pentateuch* seems to me to lead on to one particular area of later book illumination. And the *Codex Amiatinus* is a British product that stands at the head of a remarkable line of British and Irish book production.

The *Rabbula Gospels* have a note in Syriac, like the whole of the manuscript, to say that they were written in 586 by the scribe Rabbula in Mesopotamia. Their pictures are brightly coloured, well drawn, attractive representations of ideas and scenes which are down to earth and full of life and motion. They come as a splendid antidote after the rather fragile posing of the Greek manuscripts. The canon tables, passages in different gospels which correspond with one another are set out in sections. These are divided by columns and covered by a magnificently decorated arch. The smaller arch over each column is in fact a horseshoe arch which will make most people think of the Moorish architecture of Spain. Islam, however, has still to arrive.

37 *Cambridge, Corpus Christi College. St. Augustine Gospels, portrait of St. Luke.*
    Copyright The Master and Fellows of Corpus Christi College, Cambridge

38 Paris, Bibliothèque Nationale. Tours Pentateuch, Moses receiving the Ten Commandments. Cliché Bibliothèque Nationale de France, Paris

The most vivid scene is that of the Ascension **(colour plate 17)**. A long-haired and heavily bearded Christ is carried up in an oval frame by angels, and beneath him is the chariot of Ezekiel powered by the wings of Cherubim and Seraphim, set with eyes, and joined with the four evangelists' symbols. Below, the apostles look up and point, and two helpful angels tell them what is going on. Mary stands in the absolute centre apparently with no need of instruction. To put Mary in this position is unusual in Late Antiquity in general; it is a speciality of the area from Egypt round to Asia Minor. A more staid scene is that of Whitsun, after the Ascension, when the Holy Ghost in the form of a dove descended on the Apostles and a tongue of flame was seen on each head. They form a posed group of different individuals, but centre stage is Mary again, a demonstration, if one were needed, that the picture of the ascension is firmly in line with local thought.

St Augustine's Gospels are known to have belonged to Canterbury from about the year 800 and are still used every time a new Archbishop of Canterbury takes his oath of office. The Gospels were given into the safe keeping of Corpus Christi College Cambridge by Archbishop Parker. The illustrations come in two full pages of painting, one of which has twelve gospel scenes, the other an author portrait of St Luke **(37)**. The twelve scenes take us from the entry to Jerusalem on Palm Sunday to Simon of Cyrene carrying the cross for Jesus. The crucifixion is not shown. The scenes are quite easy to follow, but in some cases a title is given. Colours are mainly red, orange and blue; backgrounds to ten scenes are provided, and figures are reasonably drawn. The one full page divided up into sections could be taken as an economy model, but the provision of any illustrations puts this manuscript into the luxury class.

The author portrait of St Luke shows a white-haired figure seated on the sort of throne that Pontius Pilate occupies in the Rossano Gospels holding a book on his lap. Luke is framed by double columns supporting an arch in which is his symbol of the winged calf. Between the double columns is a further set of eight small scenes, this time all from St Luke's Gospel. All these scenes are labelled.

The script and the style of the painting fit well in Italy in the later 500s and are separate from the Byzantine court. This means that the manuscript would have been available for St Augustine to bring with him when he was sent to Britain by Pope Gregory the Great in 597, and this is the tradition. There is nothing which conflicts with the tradition, and if it is true this is not the only book from the Mediterranean area to reach Britain in the seventh and eighth centuries. Expeditions went out from Northumbria to collect manuscripts, and we have some of the copies of these that were made.

The best known is a manuscript called the *Codex Amiatinus* which was copied from an Italian manuscript, written in the monastery of Monkwearmouth-Jarrow about 700 and sent off as a present to the Pope. The messenger died, and the manuscript was becalmed near Siena. It is now in the Laurentian library in Florence. The frontispiece is a portrait of the prophet Ezra who re-copied the Scriptures at the end of the Babylonian captivity of the Jews. As an author portrait it combines several features we have seen before. This author, unlike the St Augustine Luke, is a workman-artist at his job. He is therefore seated on a padded bench with his feet on a footstool busily writing in a book. His utensils are around him, pens, inks and colours, and this has links to the writing scene in the *Vienna Dioscorides*. Behind him there is no great architectural confection but a basic book cupboard with leather-bound volumes on shelves. The one other example of this is in the mausoleum of Galla Placidia in Ravenna in the scene of the martyrdom of St Lawrence. The only faults are in the perspective of the bench, footstool and small table for pigments. Otherwise the copy is close to the Mediterranean style but there is still argument as to whether this is the work of an Italian in Northumbria, or a Northumbrian copying almost perfectly a foreign manuscript.

The main reason for including this codex is to demonstrate the movement of manuscripts even out to the edge of the world, and to indicate the later tradition of the illuminated manuscript. While very little survives from Italy and Gaul from the years between about 580 and 750 in the way of fully-painted manuscripts, this is a time when the idea was taking very firm root in Britain and Ireland. The *Lindisfarne Gospels* in the British Museum are often wrongly thought of as something quite different from the late Roman tradition of luxury gospel books. This was made at Monkwearmouth-Jarrow shortly after the *Codex Amiatinus*. A comparison of the *Amiatinus* Ezra and the *Lindisfarne* St Matthew suggest a workshop in the process of making the late Roman style all its own. In St Matthew this has not gone very far, for the furniture and the figure are very close to their model. The padded bench is almost identical, but the footstool has come apart. The colours of the author's robes, though changed round, are still red and green. But at the corners of the frame around St Matthew are the beginnings of an interlacing pattern which on other pages forms a main element in intricate decoration.

But British book illumination is not the only western direct descendant of late Roman pictures. While the British link is as secure as any art historical argument can possibly be, with historical references and surviving links, the Spanish connection is much less well documented. The manuscript which might provide a link is a copy of the Pentateuch (the first five books of the Old Testament) which was at Tours in France till 1843. It was sold to the Ashburnham family in England and is sometimes known as the *Ashburnham Pentateuch*. Since it returned to France, the Bibliothèque Nationale in Paris in 1888, I think the name of Tours should stay with it. In colour, movement, down-to-earthness, and sheer vitality it is close to the *Rabbula Gospels*. In the form of decoration it is totally different. The Flood, now a whole page of death and destruction, has already been mentioned **(colour plate 18)**. It is not so gruesome as the Vienna Genesis flood because the dead bodies are splayed out in rather schematic form and retain a healthy flesh-like colour. The large chest on legs with barred doors and windows is the ark, and this is the traditional late Roman form. Other full pages are stories rather than single scenes. Moses at the top of a picture receives the tablets of stone from the hand of God and then, below, brings them down to the people **(38)**. Below that the Ark of the Covenant is set up in all its glory with an altar very like that on which Melchisidek in San Vitale, Ravenna, makes his offering. Colours are brilliant and the people look perfectly human in shape and proportion. The women would be at home in the Byzantine court with rich clothes, necklaces, and elaborate head-dresses, but the men would not for they are virtually all in knee breeches. A study of the Latin of the text suggests that the mistakes of copying are far from random and begin to make sense if thought of as Latin in transition to early Spanish. The majority of commentators allow the suggestion that the manuscript was written and illuminated in Spain after the conquest by the Visigoths. It might belong to the sixth or seventh century.

The idea of setting the manuscript in Spain grows in attraction if it is compared with some of the earliest Spanish manuscripts. They contain full-page colour illustrations which give an impression similar to those of Tours. The main problem is that the earliest of these manuscripts belongs to the 900s and there is therefore a gap of at least 200 years to cross. A second problem is that most of the Spanish manuscripts are copies of a commentary on the Book of Revelation, and their apocalyptic subject matter is very different from the standard Old Testament narratives.

5. Churches

The scene is the court of Constantine the Great about AD 315. Christianity is tolerated everywhere and Constantine seems positively to encourage it. Three anxious imperial architects, who have so far avoided blotting their copybooks with this most impatient of patrons, enter nervously. After some general chat which seems to go well the atmosphere is good and the architects begin to relax. Constantine clears his throat to say:

> The reason we have called you here today is to order you to begin work on three churches that will be the wonder of the world. We intend to mark the tomb of Paul, of Peter, and when we have recovered the Holy Land itself from . . . , well, we shall mark the tomb of Christ himself.

There is silence. They are prodded with an imperious, 'Well?' The bravest suggests that the emperor seems to want a tomb. That was badly phrased but the slip passes as the emperor, true to form, explodes and points out that the bodies involved, or not as the case may be, already have tombs. He intends to build churches over the tombs.

Irritation breeds irritation as the bravest architect, who up to now has dealt with arches, gates, walls and theatres asks 'And what exactly is a church?' This stops the emperor in his tracks and they settle down for an amicable discussion. Well, it is partly to mark the site of the tomb, a memoria, so that could look a bit like a tomb if you like, circular, or square, or oblong, not too big in case lots of sightseers make the place smell. But then the sightseers have to be catered for, so add on an assembly hall. That is a basilica, you mean? Well yes, but a basilica for Christian purposes, none of your old superstitions. And you might as well add an atrium, a courtyard with a colonnade round in front of the basilica, for the sightseers to shelter in.

And with a bit of good-will and good designing this totally apocryphal and imaginary encounter produces the plans of the churches of Old St Peter's on the Vatican hill, St Paul's, always known as San Paolo fuori le mura, outside the walls, and the original church of the Holy Sepulchre in Jerusalem. It may seem affected to mix names like St Peter's, in good English, with San Paolo flm, but this is the usual way, and certainly helps if you are asking your way in Rome. Great St Mary's might get you directed by a well-travelled Roman to Cambridge, whereas Santa Maria Maggiore in Rome, is unmistakable.

But you can see the architects' point. What, when Christianity was only just becoming acceptable in the highest quarters, was a church? Archaeology cannot help because, so far as I know, no purpose-built church dating before Constantine has ever been excavated. If one of the very small number known from documentary sources does appear it would add to its credibility if it was built, destroyed about 303 and then rebuilt for its future life. On the other hand, there are places where Christians worshipped, but these are known as house churches, or in one case a flat or apartment church.

Perhaps the best evidence comes with an end-date soon after 257. This was the date at which the Persians captured Dura Europos, an outpost near the Euphrates. The city had been threatened many times. Under Severus (193–211) soldiers had been billeted in a quarter of the town. In 257 the existing wall was strengthened by an earth bank piled up against it on the inside. The wall had previously been of typical Hellenistic type and so was free standing. A road ran inside it, so no buildings actually touched it, but when the bank was piled up more than the width of the road was covered. A strip of the buildings nearest the wall was engulfed, and their walls helped to stabilise the earth bank as rooms were filled up with rubble and soil. One of these buildings had a row of three rooms, each opening off the corridor. Two of these had been knocked into one long room with one entrance, a dais and benches round the side. A local date, scratched in the wet plaster, equates with AD 231. In another room there were paintings on the wall which seemed to involve women and a tomb, and something which looked just like a small individual plunge bath, with a plastered and painted canopy over it and no source of water either in or out. General opinion seems to accept this as a Christian house church and baptistery of the third century. The room is the meeting room, the plunge bath is the baptismal font and the painting represents the women coming to Christ's tomb on Easter morning. We shall see again the idea of baptism being death to the old life and a rising to a new life, so that baptisteries and tombs are closely linked.

Apart from Rome, where house churches are much better known, the other main example at present is in a villa in Kent at Lullingstone. This was an upper room, above a half-basement or half cellar. The building began to decay, and when the roof came off and the rain rotted the plaster from the walls the painted plaster fell into the half cellar and so ended up sealed well away from later disturbance. When the villa was excavated in the 1950s the plaster was recovered and slowly pieced together and provided much excitement when two examples of the chi-ro, Constantine's sign of victory, the XP conjoined, were discovered. They were among a row of figures with their hands outstretched in the position typical of Christian prayer — the orans position. This upper room in the villa was converted to an oratory or a house church in the second half of the fourth century, and access from inside the villa was blocked off in favour of one entrance from outside.

In Constantine's Rome there was already a good organisation of Christians into areas, each with a meeting place. These meeting places were known as Tituli and distinguished by the traditional name of the founder or donor of the site. Thus the church now called San Clemente is above the remains of the house which, by tradition, one Clemens gave for church use. The house given by Equitius has been gutted to form the church of San Martino ai Monti. The best-preserved gift is that of the apartment block, built around 200, in which the church of SS Giovanni e Paolo has evolved (39). The best-organised example to visit is that of San Clemente, but only the basement floors of the Roman house survive intact. SS Giovanni e Paolo has an intact shell, obvious on the outside, and substantially intact basements since the block is built on a hillside, and you enter the present church from the hill top. But I have always found the unconverted Roman parts of the block difficult to get at.

*39 Rome, Church of SS
Giovanni e Paolo. View of
the outside of the S wall of
the Roman apartment
building in which the church
is constructed.
Copyright Richard Reece*

If Krautheimer, the great student of Roman churches, is correct in his analysis of the position of the altar in relation to the plan of the original apartment block then worship may have started off at a small shrine on a landing which later became encased in an early church. A modern parallel would be a plaque in a modern block of flats to commemorate the point at which someone was summarily executed in the 1939–45 war. House churches, except at Dura and Lullingstone, evolved slowly and fitfully into purpose-built structures in the fourth, fifth and sixth centuries. Since many have either lost their first forms in later rebuilding, or have them embedded in later masonry, there is little of the development which can easily be seen.

Outside Rome, where the organisation of Christian communities is less well known during the third century, we know virtually nothing of house churches. It is usually assumed that when the building of permanent churches was started a town community had several choices. In some cases they might well have developed properties in which house churches had survived, but in these cases we have only ideas to work with. At Aosta, if the earliest publication of the results of excavation are correct, the Christian community developed a site which opened off the main town forum in the fourth century. This suggests strong financial and political support from prominent townspeople. Outside the military settlement of Vetera, on the Rhein, just south of the Dutch border, the Christian

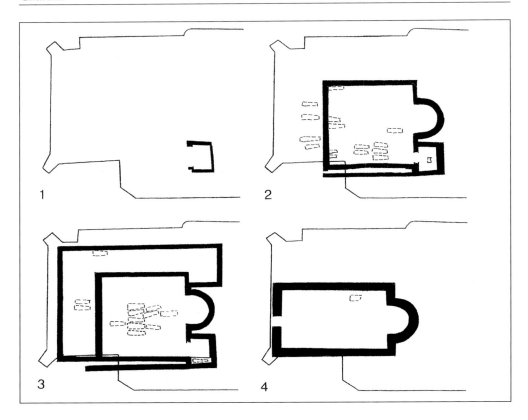

40 Geneva, Church of la Madeleine. Plan of the sequence of church buildings.
Copyright Ellen Swift after C.H. Bonnet/ Service cantonal d'archeologie, Bonnet 1986

community concentrated on the spot in a late Roman cemetery where certain people special to them had been buried. They constructed a church, people gathered to live round it, and the place 'at the Saints' or Ad Sanctos evolved. The name gradually shortened to Xanten. At Verulamium the Christian focus, at least by the seventh century, was on the other side of the valley where, by repute, St Alban was buried.

This gives us two main sequences by which town centre churches and suburban churches may have come into existence. At present the examples documented by the actual remains are few. We probably ought to take in the examples which 'failed', that is the sites important to the early church which somehow lapsed and never followed through to the medieval period. One example is the church of the Madeleine at Geneva **(40)**. This lies outside the small hilltop defended town of the fourth century. Inside the town about one third of the small area was taken up, as we now know from excavation, by the cathedral, another church, the baptistery and the bishop's palace. Outside there were cemeteries. One grave in the cemetery was given the covering of a small mausoleum or memorial chapel in the fifth century, and in the sixth century a small simple church was built beside the memoria with a passageway along the side of the church. This may have allowed access directly to the tomb without going through the church. In the years around 600 the church was enlarged and in the memoria the central grave was moved and a new special grave inserted in the north wall. There then seems to have been some sort of lapse, which is very common in churches of this area which have been excavated, because the new church of the ninth century was of a totally different plan. The memoria had been eliminated with the burial in it, and although the site continued as a church its original history had been lost or moved.

A final sequence leading to the establishment of a church which was to survive comes through conversion of a pagan site. This is obvious in Rome with buildings like the Pantheon, but most of those conversions happened well after the fourth century. However two examples of conversions of Romano-Celtic temples into churches can be claimed from excavation in France. The abbey church of St Martin de Boscherville in Normandy shows on one side of the nave what could be mistaken for the foundations of a demolished cloister, a square foundation with the church sitting on the fourth side. Excavation has shown it to be a typical temple with a square building within a square temenos or courtyard. It would probably be necessary to demolish the abbey to get any idea of the state of the temple when the building of the church began, and even then the building and re-building have almost certainly removed any useful traces. We are left with a statement that the wall of the church uses one wall of the temple. This might be direct continuity, or it might be the siting of the church on a convenient heap of stones, which not only provided good building material but also disposed of remembered pagan influence.

At Civaux, south of Poitiers, any visitor is aware that the church is at the centre of the village. The first strange point is the absence of a cemetery anywhere near, the second point is an open area of excavations to the south of the church. This shows a small square structure with a corridor around, with the south wall of the church built directly on the north wall of the corridor. Here there is more evidence of some sort of continuity because in the corridor of the temple building is what seems to be the earliest baptistery of the church. This suggests that at the very least the temple buildings were still in a good enough condition to re-roof for a baptistery. The cemetery is to be found on the outskirts of the modern village walled in by empty stone coffins or sarcophagi. Excavations alongside the cemetery have shown that it starts in the Roman period and seems to have a continuous use till the present. In the early Roman period the place of worship, the temple, was normally totally separate from the place of burial, and this can be seen at Civaux. Perhaps the continuity of the burial site strengthens the case for continuity between the community temple and the community church. We have to remember that we are talking on the one hand of ideas and human communities and on the other of stone structures, and the two can never be easily linked together.

If we have difficulties in finding remains of the simpler churches of the fourth century there are similar problems even for the major church monuments belonging to the reign of Constantine. Here continuity causes the problem rather than being the problem to be solved, for later 'improvements' mean that very few of these great churches retain their original form. St Peter's provides the visitor with two major attractions, the street of mausolea which spread up the Vatican hill, now under the crypt of the present church, and the sixteenth-century church. Of Constantine's St Peter's you can see virtually nothing.

Since it was not knocked down until the early 1500s there are engravings showing parts of the inside, but these hardly give a good impression of what it was like to be in a fourth-century church. The Church of the Holy Sepulchre in Jerusalem is almost a monument to vandalism. If Constantine's mother, Helena, was right, this was the site of the crucifixion of Christ, and near to that is the tomb in which He rested for three days. The present tomb stands as a block of rock hacked out from a slope and left standing naked on a level platform. Around this Constantine probably had built a rotunda, a dome on twelve great columns; the hall for the pilgrims and the major services was to the east. The church and the tomb were a focus for destruction and restoration from the sixth century to the twelfth, but the church the visitor sees today is what the Crusaders constructed out of the buildings and fragments that they found after they had contributed to the general destruction. Apart from some of Constantine's columns, now halved in height but still resistant to destruction, there is very little to give any impression of what the original churches looked like. The church of the Nativity at Bethlehem has had a similar but not so violent history. The general proportions are thought to go back to the church built by Constantine but the church as it now stands, remodelled by Justinian, belongs to the sixth century.

This leaves the church of San Paolo flm to the south of the Aurelianic walls of Rome **(colour plate 19)**. The first thing that some people say about it is that it was burned down in 1823. This, coupled with its position away from the tourist centre of the city, is enough to put many visitors off. This is a pity because a visit is probably the nearest anyone can come to experiencing a church of the fourth century. The problem is that it is clearly not a medieval church. It has none of the clutter of monuments and half finished alterations, subdivided chapels and odd changes of level which any church with a 'real' history should have. It looks as if it has only just been finished, and that is the wrong atmosphere for one of the oldest churches. On the other hand, the original church had a period when it had only just been finished, so any visitor has to decide between an old appearance, or an original impression.

There remain only two further problems. The church is not that built by Constantine, and most of what is actually there was constructed, furnished and decorated between about 1835 and 1900. Constantine's original church was of modest size and it was set with its altar at the west end. Valentinian II started to rebuild the church in 386, and he worked to a much greater plan and changed the axis so that the altar is at the east end. Yet it is one place you can go to see what a five-aisled nave looks like with the central nave, a row of columns in each side forming an aisle, and then another row of columns cutting off yet another aisle on the outside. In spite of a good set of windows the interior is dim because clear glass is not used. The five aisles run up to a north-south wall through which is pierced a great triumphal arch covered in mosaic, some of which is presumably of the original design. The high altar stands in the focus of the arch and so cuts the nave off from a transverse hall forming the top of a great T. Things go on either at the altar, seen from the nave, or in the cross hall, not seen from the nave. The decoration could perhaps be described as nineteenth-century Renaissance. For some people this is the final straw. For me it is much better than fake Early Christian because I can totally disregard it and concentrate on the building. It is difficult to think of another church with this open space

41 Rome, St. John Lateran. Exterior view of the baptistry. Copyright Nicholas Vella

of a cross hall behind the main focus, the high altar, and this marks out the distinction in the original plan between the smaller ceremonies attended by the privileged few and the large-scale events for the masses.

Yet in a sense these Constantinian churches on the great Christian sites are totally untypical of the church at the time. In most places there was no tomb of St Peter or St Paul, and in only one place could there be the Nativity and the Tomb of Christ. In the West there were not necessarily many martyrs to provide a focus, so the normal church was simply a hall. I can think of no surviving examples of the fourth century, so I have difficulty in raising the excavated plans to full building height. Such halls are known at Trier and Aquileia, to name two Constantinian cathedrals, and there are a number in North Africa. As excavations take place under cathedrals and churches in Europe, Geneva, Aosta, Lyon, Vienne, more of these simple plans first constructed in the fourth century come to light. But almost all of them are still churches, which means they have been rebuilt, altered, reconstructed and hacked about so that they all show the medieval and modern church plan of nave, crossing, transepts and choir.

Some years ago Krautheimer fulminated against those who, steeped in medieval plans, tried to force the late Roman churches into post-determined forms. He went to great lengths to show that Constantine's cathedral in Rome, St John Lateran (41), was of this rectangular plan even though it had small side projections at the West (altar) end. It may well be possible to find early signs of transepts, choirs and crossings in late Roman churches, but the important thing is to see them as accidental signs of future developments that probably had little meaning or importance at the time. I remain with

Krautheimer in saying that the best way to look at late Roman churches is to regard them as a different type of building from the plan which any well-informed school child would draw for a church. The exciting part of the story is the gradual transition from the one to the other.

Some years ago it would have been possible to say that late Roman churches ceased to be built, there was a Dark Age, and then, perhaps in the era of Charlemagne when new churches were needed, a plan had to be reinvented. Detailed study in Rome, and excavation elsewhere, shows that this is wishful thinking to magnify the big names of Constantine, Justinian and Charlemagne. The variety of plans of churches constructed and reconstructed between about 500–900 is possibly greater than at any other time. It is only when this diversity has been killed off by the medieval super-state church that the one true plan finally evolves.

That deals perhaps with the community church and the cathedral, although before the spread of Christianity from the fourth century onwards many community churches would have been the seat (cathedra) of bishops who were simply the heads of recognised communities. Some other types of church have greater surviving powers because, once built, they need little or no expansion. The baptistery is used only at certain times, for a very specific purpose, and the whole process is one of passing through, so that production lines to process larger numbers are quite proper. The mausoleum built for particular people or a special family group obviously reaches the end of its original purpose and can then survive without alteration.

The basic late Roman church, with no function other than to be the meeting place of the local Christian congregation, can be seen in many places, but examples easily reached and nearest their original form are in Rome and Ravenna. In Rome churches such as Santa Sabina **(42-43)** on the Aventine hill and Santa Maria Maggiore are simply long rectangular halls, basilicas, with the main axis being the longer one. This seems to be obvious, but to a Roman the word basilica would normally have meant a large public building forming one side of the forum or market place. The ends of such basilicas were usually completely closed, and access to the buildings was through monumental doorways from the forum, and thus halfway down the long side. This meant that on entering the hall people had to decide where they wanted to go, to the right, to the left or straight on. This was fully intentional because the hall sheltered several different activities. The main religious point was on the middle of the long side opposite the door, but this was usually a shrine to be observed and possibly paused at, but not in any sense a centre of cult worship. As an example of the change that came about, the Christian church off the forum at Aosta was reached through a short open space, and the hall that opened out stretched away from the forum rather than alongside it. Soon the church frontage was extended on to the colonnade of the forum, and the long axis became a progression from the forum to the baptistery and then onwards into the body of the church, and finally to the space set aside round the altar. The series of mosaic panels of the Old Testament at Santa Maria Maggiore and the New Testament at San Apollinare at Ravenna bring the spectator from the entrance up to the altar. The sequence is thought out as movement on the long axis of the building. It is a pity that the positions of these panels mean that few can ever have followed the sequence in practice.

1 Oxford, Ashmolean Museum. Coin portraits of the emperors Marcus Aurelius, Gallienus, Postumus and Diocletian. Copyright Richard Reece

2 *Oxford, Ashmolean Museum. Coin portraits of the emperors Constantine the Great, Constans, Valens and Theodosius II. Copyright Richard Reece*

3   Cherchell, Algeria. Mosaic of the agricultural work of the different seasons. copyright Cherchell
    Archaeological Museum. Every effort has been made to contact the owners of the copyright.
    Reproduction rights will be willingly paid for should they contact the publishers.

4   Piazza Armerina, Sicily. Mosaic of animal hunts, the capture of the bison.
    Copyright Mary Sullivan, Bluffton College

5   Ravenna, Mausoleum of Galla Placidia. Interior mosaics. Copyright Peter Clayton

6   Ravenna, Orthodox Baptistry. Baptism of Christ. Copyright Peter Clayton

7 *Ravenna, Arian Baptistry. The dome mosaic. Copyright Peter Clayton*

8 *Ravenna, Arian Baptistry. Baptism of Christ. Copyright Peter Clayton*

9   Ravenna, Church of San Apollinare Nuovo. Christ Enthroned. Copyright Peter Clayton

10   Ravenna, Church of San Apollinare Nuovo. The palace of Theoderic. Copyright Peter Clayton

11 *Ravenna, Church of San Apollinare Nuovo. Mosaic panel with an imperial portrait, perhaps of Justinian. Copyright Peter Clayton*

12 *Ravenna, Church of San Vitale. Apse mosaic with the empress Theodora and her court. Copyright Peter Clayton*

13 Ravenna, Church of San Vitale. The offerings of Abel and Melchisidec. Copyright Peter Clayton

14 Constantinople, Imperial Palace. Mosaic of boys riding on a camel. Copyright Artephot/A. Held

15 Rome, Vatican library. The Vatican Virgil, the death of Dido. Copyright Biblioteca Apostolica Vaticana

16 *Rome, Vatican library. The Roman virgil, Dido & Aeneas sheltering in a cave.*
   Copyright Biblioteca Apostolica Vaticana

17 *Florence, Laurentian Library. Rabbula Gospels, the Ascension.*
Copyright Firenze, Biblioteca Medicea Laurenziana, Ms. Laur. Plut. 1.56, c. 13v

18 Paris, Bibliothèque Nationale. Tours Pentateuch, The Flood. Cliché Bibliothèque nationale de France, Paris

19 Rome, San Paolo flm. Interior view of the nave. Copyright Nicholas Vella

20 London, British Museum. The Water Newton Hoard silver hoard, the Innocentia bowl. Copyright Peter Clayton

21 The Seuso Hoard. The Meleager plate. Copyright Peter Clayton

22 Oxford, Ashmolean Museum. Two gold coins, an aureus (60 to the pound of gold) of Maximian c.300, and a solidus — 72 to the pound — (obverse and reverse) of Constantius II c. 358. Copyright Richard Reece

23 Oxford, Ashmolean Museum. Gold coin, solidus, of Magnus Maximus c. 383. The mintmark AVGOB includes the name AVgusta by which London was known in the 4th century and assures the user that the metal is refined gold (OBryzium). Copyright Richard Reece

24 Wörms, Museum. Glass beads from a typical late Roman necklace, found in Wörms. Copyright Museum in Andreasstift, Stadtverwaltung Wörms

42 *Rome, Church of Santa Sabina. Interior view.*
   Copyright Nicholas Vella

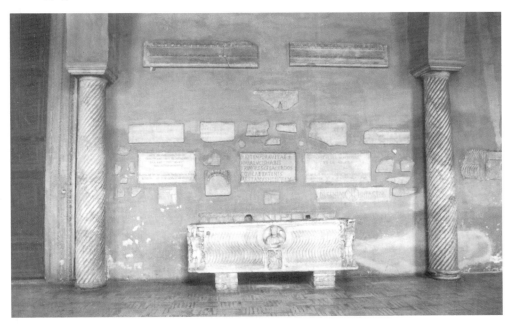

43 *Rome, Church of Santa Sabina. Interior view showing the nave arcade.*
   Copyright Nicholas Vella

The altar at St Peter's on the Vatican, and the original San Paolo flm, was at the west end of the building. This allowed the priest to face the congregation and face eastwards at the same time. By the time Valentinian II rebuilt San Paolo things had changed and the altar was at the east end. This became the norm. The whole subject of the positioning of altars, the direction in which the priest faced during the Communion, and much of the early liturgy is a hotly debated subject which cannot be dealt with here. It does seem safe to say that by the late fourth century a main altar not at the east end of the church suggests that some unusual forces are in operation.

The simple basilicas, such as Santa Sabina and Santa Maria Maggiore in Rome, and San Apollinare Nuovo and San Apollinare in Classe in Ravenna, usually have a main space, the nave, supported on a row of columns. The roof of the nave is high above a row of windows which light the nave, and its weight has therefore to be carried straight down to the ground on those columns. The arcade of columns ends to the east in a wall through which an apse is cut. This is not in any sense a choir, it may not even be for the altar, but it is a niche from which the president of the ceremonies may officiate. Where the original form of the apse survives there is often a series of benches round the apse with one seat marked out for the celebrant in the centre. This can be seen in Italy at Grado near Aquileia

45 *Vaison-la-Romaine, S. France. Fifth-century epitaph now in the cloisters of the cathedral.*
Copyright Richard Reece

(44), or in France at Vaison-la-Romaine **(45)**. In the eastern Mediterranean, where many churches did not survive the seventh century, this synthronon, or arrangement of seats, is more common. In a structural sense the apse formed a buttress which counteracted any lateral thrust from the nave arcade. If the balance of the roof, the windows, and the nave walls was perfect then that structure stood without pressing outwards in any way. If the building was not perfect then surrounding structures helped to correct faults. The west end was assisted by a porch which was usually a lean-to structure up against the west wall of the nave. The arcade opened either side into an aisle which was again a lean-to structure against each of the arcade walls.

I have stressed the structural points because one aspect of the development of the Christian basilica from the fourth century to the seventh is the way in which builders became more and more confident of this new form. The row of columns contains less and less material as the shape progresses, until it seems as if the whole church is supported on a very slender base. This of course would not matter if the load-bearing walls were the outside ones, the outer edges of the aisles, with the weight of the roof coming down on top of them. In that case the columns of the nave would be a pleasant decorative element which could help to support the roof. It is extremely tempting to reconstruct excavated floor plans in this way when nothing of the superstructure survives. The thick walls are all round the outside; that row of small column bases can only be decorative. One look at a standing building should convince you otherwise.

In front of the porch at the west end of the church, otherwise known as the narthex, there was often a colonnaded courtyard or atrium. This has been reconstructed at San Paolo flm and gives a good impression of what St Peter's might originally have looked like. It can also be seen at San Clemente, but here imagination is made more difficult because the west front of the church belongs to the sixteenth century.

The original plan of these churches belongs to a time when the congregation in each city was almost self-contained. The town or city had a bishop, and at first only the bishop could admit people to the church through baptism. So even if there were several churches in one city there was only one baptistery needed, and that was at the church of the bishop. This state of affairs changed from the fourth century so that even small churches had small baptisteries attached and then, later, fonts inside the churches. Here Geneva gives a good example. The first church which the excavators date 'third-fourth century' is a simple hall with an apse at its east end. A passage beside it runs down to the baptistery, which is a separate building level with the apse. The new members of the church could therefore go down the passage to the baptistery and then enter the church in both the spiritual and physical sense through baptism in the baptistery. It may be that they had been allowed in the aisles of the church, curtained off from the mysteries, before they were baptised, but the general scheme was to have another hall where the recruits, the catechumens, could be prepared for full church membership.

At Geneva in the later fourth century a second church was built parallel to the first and a larger baptistery was rebuilt symmetrically between them. In the fifth century the churches were enlarged, and then in the sixth century an even larger church was constructed over the earlier baptisteries. At Aosta it can be said that the baptistery was taken in by an extension of the church. The same can be seen at Aix-en-Provence, where the early baptistery is now surrounded by the later cathedral. At Geneva the baptistery expanded to become the main church, and the font retains the position it was given in the second baptistery. The next main building event came in the years around AD 1000 and so lies outside our period.

Within the lines of the walls of the church the main changes seem to have affected the placing of the altar and the organisation of the area around it. This is still a matter of difference between the Eastern and Russian Orthodox churches and the churches of the West. Orthodox feeling is that what goes on at the altar, the centre of the mysteries of the communion service, is not for general viewing. This leads to the altar being surrounded by a screen covered in icons, the iconostasis. The service takes place behind the screen and the priests act as a link between the altar and the people. The western feeling is that everything should be seen and accordingly there are now no visual barriers between the people and the altar. A fascinating half-way stage is to be found in the Greek catholic rite at Santa Maria in Cosmedin in Rome, where the officiating priest wears a long and voluminous cape (cope). At the vital moments of the Eucharist servers hold up the ends of the cope to form a complete barrier of cloth between the people and the mystery. I mention this to warn how the interpretation of archaeological remains can be led astray by the non-survival of wood and cloth.

Attitudes to the relation of the people in general to the priests and the altar changed throughout the later Empire and the excavated remains under the cathedral at Aosta give us a good example of this. At the end of the fourth century the altar had a space in front of it marked out by column bases so that it was presumably surrounded an arcade of some sort. In the fifth century the space was walled in with continuous blocks, though the wall probably stretched upwards only to about three or four feet. In the larger sixth-century church the space was once more delimited by separate blocks and by the ninth century the altar area was simply cut off from the rest of the church by a wall with an opening in. The sixth-century arrangement can be seen in full splendour in the church of San Clemente in Rome. It is not in its original position but has been reconstructed in the church rebuilt in the eleventh century above the older churches. It consists of a fully decorated marble screen which extends down into the nave of the church, marking out a major part of the space for the priests, servers and choir. The people in general are pushed towards the west of the nave, or outwards into the aisles. Adults can see quite easily over the screen, but there are two platforms, one on either side for communication, for preaching and reading.

This concentration on the basilica is a concentration on the ordinary and also a concentration on the west and the Mediterranean coastlands. The simple basilica is to be found around the Aegean and in North Africa, but it is not the main form of church building in Asia Minor away from the coasts and in much of the Levant. There the church is a rectangular box which sometimes encloses even the eastern apse. The load-bearing walls are the outer walls and if there are rows of columns inside they are more decorative than structural. There are often three apses side by side, with the larger in the centre, and these can be either in the thickness of the eastern wall of the rectangle or sometimes even boxed into an external rectangular framework. Many of these fifth- and sixth-century churches survive well above foundation level in Syria, so they give a good idea of how they functioned, but I do not know if any survive complete and in use.

Concentration on the basilica has meant a concentration on a building with a long axis, but there were of course many religious buildings with plans which concentrated on a centre. The two baptisteries at Ravenna, Orthodox and Arian, avoided integration with their respective cathedrals, and survive almost in their original forms. The font is in the centre, there is a passageway (ambulatory) around it, and then there might be niches in the external wall, which is usually an octagon. The earlier baptistery at the cathedral of Rome, St John Lateran **(41)**, had the form of an equal-armed cross which made excellent sense for its function. The ideal baptism took place in the river Jordan like that of Jesus. As Christianity spread beyond the Holy Land artificial forms had to be thought up. The candidates needed to leave their old selves, with their clothes, on one side, to go into the water and have the rite administered, and to leave the water on another side where new clothes and a new life awaited them. In an equal-armed cross the priests had arm one, the family had the opposite arm three, and the candidates gathered in arm two to pass through the water to arm four. At the conclusion of the ceremony the whole company proceeded into the church.

When the new life was finished the top people might expect burial in a mausoleum. This might be a simple square wooden 'hut' either put up over the grave, or constructed for the burial of a family inside. More permanent structures were in stone and could grow

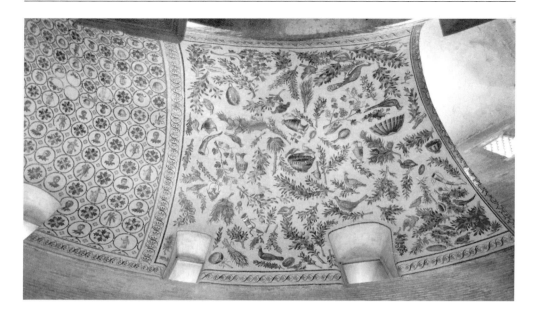

46 Rome, Church of Santa Costanza. View of the ambulatory. Copyright Nicholas Vella

in size to imperial proportions. It is difficult to find examples of such buildings in their original states because they either tended to get used for other purposes if they were attached to churches, or get demolished or turned into later churches if they were in cemeteries. The building in Ravenna called the mausoleum of Galla Placidia was probably not built with this function in mind, so it does not help us. The great imperial mausolea such as that of Augustus and Hadrian (Castel Sant Angelo) in Rome are again in a different tradition. Perhaps the best preserved are the mausoleum intended for Galerius (293–311) in Thessalonica, now the church of St George, and that of Diocletian in the centre of the palace at Split, now the cathedral. Neither of course was of Christian origin.

A better example is the mausoleum of Constantine's sister Constantia now known simply as Santa Costanza in the eastern suburbs of Rome **(46)**. Here it is assumed that the sarcophagus stood in the centre of the building with a cupola above supported on columns and an ambulatory outside the columns. The central space has been changed but the ambulatory is in its original form with its light and apparently unchristian mosaics on its ceiling. The sarcophagus may well have been a large porphyry coffin magnificently carved and decorated like the two in the Vatican museum, one of which is said to be that of Constantine's mother, Helena.

One mausoleum refuses to fit into any sequence either in plan or materials. This is the stone mausoleum built by Theoderic for himself outside Ravenna **(47)**. The stone had to be brought from the opposite side of the Adriatic, from modern Croatia, and it stands out very clearly against all the late Roman buildings which are made of brick. It is ten-sided and has two stories. In the upper chamber, which is covered by a circular capstone, is a late Roman porphyry sarcophagus. The upper chamber is smaller than the lower chamber and

47 *Ravenna, Mausoleum of Theoderic. View of the exterior. Copyright Peter Clayton*

there has been argument as to whether there was an external arcade around the upper chamber.

The most remarkable feature, apart from the choice of limestone as a building material, is the circular single stone which acts as a roof. Its weight has been calculated at over 200 tons and the problems of putting it in place are substantial. It has around and above it twelve protruding angles which have been hollowed out close to the curve of the dome. These could be used as handles when the dome was moved into place. The single stone is cracked, and local legend has it that Theoderic, warned that he would be killed by lightning, took refuge in the mausoleum in a thunder-storm. Destiny could not be thwarted, and a thunderbolt found him through the stone. A more prosaic explanation takes us into structural problems.

Moving the great stone around creates difficulties, but with enough resources these can be overcome. The stone can be hauled up to the right level by a ramp. It can be shifted from the ramp to its intended place with ropes, but the final moment of letting it settle gently on its seating is by far the most difficult. Blocks and wedges have in the end to be knocked away, and the impact of 230 tons dropping suddenly only two or three inches is enormous. One engineer suggested that if he were given the job he would fill the upper

48 Ravenna, Mausoleum of Theoderic. Detail of carving round the capstone showing possible 'tent hooks' as if Theoderic were to be buried in one of his ancestors nomadic tents, copied in stone. Copyright Richard Reece

chamber with wet sand, leave it a little above the seating level, and move the capstone exactly into position on the sand. The sand would dry out and the volume would decrease slightly, and then the dry sand could be allowed to trickle out of the doorway very slowly.

The outside of the mausoleum has little decoration remaining except round the rim of the capstone **(48)**. Here there is a constantly repeated motif of two pronged hooks suspended from discs. One theory has it that these are tenter-hooks, the hooks from which the cloth walls of a tent may be suspended. This takes us away from the Roman, rectangular, leather army tent and towards the open steppes of central Asia. There the tent has a basketwork dome, which is set up on poles. The dome is covered with felt, and felt drapes are hung from rows of tenter-hooks fixed in the dome to form the walls. This is the typical tent of the nomads of the Steppes, and the idea does account for the domed structure of the tomb and the decoration. If the idea is correct it suggests that the Gothic nomad who became Gothic King and Roman Viceroy of Italy wished to be buried with due acknowledgement to his ancestors.

The mausoleum of Theoderic takes us beyond the main types of religious building to the many types and structures which never became fashionable or which only survived in one or two examples. At Qal'at Sim'an in Syria there is a remarkable church which marks the site of the column on which St Simeon Stylites lived for many years before his death in 459. The site of the column has around it four separate basilicas which mark the four points of the compass. This is most emphatically not a single cruciform church but a

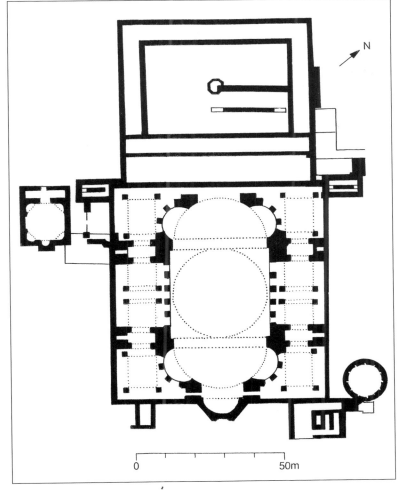

49 Constantinople, Church of Hagia Sophia. The ground plan. Copyright Ellen Swift after E.H. Swift/ P. Lampl, in Krautheimer 1965

N

0   50m

collection of four separate simple rectangular buildings which only communicate through the area of the column. At the other extreme is the church of St Laurent just outside Grenoble. This grew out of a series of mausolea in a suburban cemetery and in the sixth century several mausolea were linked together by a four-lobed structure to form a church. A three-lobed structure with simple apses had become fashionable in later Roman palatial dining rooms, and a similar structure had been used for small but important churches such as that of San Lorenzo at the imperial capital of Milan. But this four-lobed structure, which has hardly a straight line in it, is almost frenzied in its decorative effect. Both churches served a local purpose, of the needs of particular patrons, and had little, if any, general effect on architectural development.

This leaves us with the subject of the centrally-planned domed church, the structure and development of which has a whole series of problems and arguments. The obvious example is the great Church of the Holy Wisdom, Hagia Sophia in Greek, in Constantinople. There were some prototypes and there were copies in the centuries after

50 *Constantinople, Church of Hagia Sophia. Interior view from west to east. Copyright Peter Clayton*

it was built, but in a Christian sense it could be described as a glorious Dead End, for it never gave rise to a new line of church development. This should not offend those in Islam, but it might upset those of the Greek Orthodox persuasion. The plan of Hagia Sophia **(49)** is almost the starting point for the Turkish mosque, and the ideas contained within it have developed within Islam. After stagnation for several hundreds of years in the Christian East the plan, just like the actual building, was taken over by the Turkish conquerors and the architectural idea was given a totally new lease of life. Churches topped with domes continue to be built to the present day, though now of reinforced concrete, but the idea of building a dome and then working out a church plan underneath it, is almost confined to Hagia Sophia **(50)**.

The subject is to me one mainly of structure. This is because the building of Hagia Sophia today is dull, dusty and utterly unsparkling. The visitor who goes in having been told that it is the greatest church in the world will usually be sadly disappointed. Half an hour will suffice for a walk round and there are many more glittering and exciting things to be seen in the Sultan's palace a short distance away. But the secret of enjoying the church is to detach yourself from a group, to sit down, and to look up into the great dome. Very quickly you begin to wonder how it stays up, and has stayed up for 1400 years. The moment you wonder that and start looking for answers the church will grow on you.

The dome is remarkably flat. It is in fact the second dome, for the first, even flatter, fell after only twenty-five years. The builders of the church were mathematicians, Anthemios of Tralles and Isidorus of Miletus, so this emphasises the theoretical aspect of the work. The point which had to be solved is, given the form of the dome, how can it be supported. If a dome can be a half sphere it can be set on a cylinder of similar radius, and that cylinder can be converted into a rectangular base which will take all the weight downwards through four great piers. If the dome is a smaller slice of a sphere than a half then any support on which it is placed will have not only its downward thrust but a very large sideways thrust as the curve tries to flatten out sideways. The point of the dome, if you can get it to stay up, is that it provides a large open space on the floor of the building uncomplicated by pillars and other structural elements.

The choice of a dome for the church to replace that burned down in the Nika riots against Justinian in 532 meant that intricate structural planning was essential. An important element in the planning was the idea of containing the thrust on two sides of the rectangular base with half domes. All the weight of half a smaller dome leant against two sides of the central support, and this held in the terrific spreading forces from the flat dome above. On the other two sides major structures were needed to give the same effect as the semi-domes. The fact that the four sides were not treated equally in structural terms gives the church its plan. It is the great example of the central plan church yet a visitor could well emerge insisting that it had a long axis. Visually there is a clear progression from the western entrance to the east end, where the altar was once surrounded by great screens. The axis runs from the western end of the western semi-dome right up to the eastern tip of the eastern semi-dome. It starts outside the main structural rectangle to the west, runs through it, and ends way outside it to the east. It is hedged in on either side by the diaphragm arches which support the great buttresses which hold the sideways thrust where there are no semi-domes, to north and south. This is the structural creation of a very large open floor space with a longitudinal axis by covering the whole thing with an enormous dome. It is not an aesthetic operation, an exercise in beauty, unless the two at their best come out to be the same. It is for this reason that I maintain that it is essential to tangle with the question of why it stays up before you can ever appreciate its splendour. The best comment came from Ward Perkins 'It is a building to be appreciated rather than described'.

This type of plan was adopted quickly by Turkish architects for the mosques that they built after the fall of Constantinople. The idea is taken to its logical conclusion in the building only separated from Hagia Sophia by flower gardens, the Blue Mosque of Sultan Ahmet. There the thrust of the dome is taken by four semi-domes, one at each side.

Moving westwards, the most obvious example of the central plan is the church of San Vitale in Ravenna (51). Here the core is a central octagon in which a vault is supported on piers. This forms the central space with an ambulatory around it. Whereas in Hagia Sophia to be in the main body of the church is to be aware of the long axis, in San Vitale the height

51 Ravenna, Church of San Vitale. View of the exterior.
   Copyright Peter Clayton

of the central space somehow separates it from the choir and the altar. This is an extension from the octagon, but its width is not very much greater than the distance between all the other piers. The structure is in some ways like the structure of a coiled basilica. The central space is a round nave from which the choir and altar project. The weight of the nave is held on pillars or piers. Around the central nave is coiled a circular aisle which is a lean-to construction against the nave. This makes perfect sense if seen from outside at the right angle, the line of one of the sides of the octagon. Seen from any other point the building looks a quite remarkable jumble of jutting rooflines.

But the central plan in the west, apart from Romanesque copies of the church of the Holy Sepulchre in the years after 1100, produces few examples. The exception is Charlemagne's palace church at Aachen in Germany. But he is copying the outward form of the palace church of the Roman Empire rather than making any experiment with form or structure.

6. Silver

Weights are quoted as Roman pounds and ounces to try to avoid confusion. The Roman ounce is roughly the modern ounce of around 27 grammes; the Roman pound of twelve ounces is about 327 grammes

It would be wrong to say that silver was common in the later Empire, and it would be equally wrong to say that hoards of silver plate are constantly turning up today. Yet, from the amount which has been found, there was clearly a reasonable quantity about in the later empire, and every piece which is found now gets the maximum publicity, and then museum space.

A recent controversy about the social position of owners of sets of silver plate has reminded us that there was gold and that it was used for jewellery and ornaments, if not for plate. While gold is often referred to in the written sources, no hoards of gold plate have been found, and individual pieces are extremely rare. This suggests that gold was important; it cannot give us a guide to its distribution. The gossip columns of today's papers will almost certainly mention champagne, but they cannot be used to estimate what proportion of the British population drank it last night.

The earliest hoards of silver plate, one major find at Pompeii for example, were already decorated, and since this continues and even increases into the late empire, where the majority of pieces of any hoard are usually decorated, this does mark Roman silver out from much silver of later date. If visitors to a modern stately home see the dining table set with silver it will be of two sorts. Places will be set with fairly plain eating utensils and plain plates with perhaps a decorated border, and in the middle of the table will be some silver folly of a wine cooler or useless centrepiece. Silver to use is generally simple, silver to impress and flaunt is usually highly ornate. A second point about modern silver, which we might note for future reference is the progress of old plain plate to the centre of the table when its age is more impressive than its decoration. Finally, close inspection of the plates set out in stately homes shows roughened surfaces which demonstrate that they have actually been used for cutting up food and eating off. If a discerning burglar is looking over the stately home he is rather more likely to look at the cases of porcelain and fine china, for in the majority of examples these will pay much better dividends when liberated.

Many of these points are not relevant to the later Roman period. Hoards do not in general consist of plain eating and serving plates with exotic centrepieces. They consist of many decorated plates and bowls which depend for their effect on being empty rather than covered in salad, and only survive in good condition by not being continually used for actual eating. Some plain plates and bowls do exist, but the silver plate in a late Roman hoard is rarely of the right composition to cater for a family meal. Is this where the Roman equivalent of the china and porcelain come in? No, for we know of nothing ceramic in the later empire which is in any way highly valued or a status symbol. Glass forms include beakers, drinking cups and bowls, but rarely plates. The brilliant and breathtaking exception to this is the early plate from the first century found intact with the Dead Sea scrolls. Bronze may sometimes have been set alongside silver, but bronze vessels were more often the province of the common soldier. We do not know much of the Roman attitude to the value of decoration, but we suspect the worst. Plate is often marked with its weight in pounds and ounces; supplies of plate are quoted again in pounds and ounces. If it is decorated, so much the better, but it may not raise its value by more than 10 to 20% of its bullion value. This feeds through to the attitude to antique plate. Since it has the same bullion value as modern plate, and decoration does not seem to be highly prized, antiquity, unless related to major figures or events in the past, is probably to be seen as a liability rather than an asset.

The problem which dogs us is that we have to talk about late Roman silver through the medium of hoards. And by definition the vessels in a hoard were deposited in safety rather than used. Are we seeing the centrepieces from the stately home sent to the bank for safety, but the less valuable, and less heavy, ordinary plates carrying on in use, and hence not entering the archaeological record due to recycling? The question is obviously unanswerable unless a written source can be pressed into use, or a disastrous destruction deposit can be excavated — a late Pompeii.

Since we have to deal with hoards then it is worth summarising the latest work by Richard Hobbs on the epidemiology of hoards. In other words, where do hoards turn up today, and when were they buried? The answers are both unexpected and far from uniform. In general, Spain and North Africa are remarkably low on the finding of hoards. Italy does not have the pre-eminence that Imperial capitals might suggest, nor does the area round Constantinople. Gaul is fertile in hoards but of the third century and not the later periods, and, confounding all expectations, East Anglia in Britain easily tops the hoards per acre competition, but only after about 350. If you want hoards of the fifth, sixth and seventh centuries, Syria and southern Asia Minor will supply them, and hoards buried even later are found in northern Russia.

There is no simple correlation here to anything which is at all obvious. Gaul in the third century is under attack by barbarians; that causes those hoards. But equally famous are the attacks on the Danube frontier. That has coin hoards, but no hoards of silver plate. East Anglia was overrun by Anglo-Saxons in the fifth century, so legend wants us to believe, so that accounts for those hoards. But what about the even more terrible Goths and Vandals and Franks and Sueves and Alans who swept through France and Spain early in the fifth century? Where are the hoards that they should have caused to be buried? Hoards and hordes simply do not agree if any critical standard of consistency is applied.

Are the silver hoards visible signs of disposable wealth? Gaul in the third century buries hoards because it is a centre of wealth and excellence and has hoards to bury. The Danube provinces fail in these respects and bury no hoards of plate. Few people would agree that East Anglia is the Mecca of Social Success in the later fourth century, yet that is where many of the great hoards, even including gold coins and jewellery, are buried. One other obvious indicator of disposable wealth is to be seen in the mosaic pavement, which must have cost much more than almost any other form of flooring. The great late pavements are to be found in Antioch, in North Africa, Sicily and Spain, all noted for the absence of contemporary silver hoards. In Britain the best late pavements such as Woodchester and Chedworth, Frampton and Hinton St Mary are in the South and West, while the silver hoards are in the East. There is almost an inverse relationship between spending money on mosaic pavements and burying and not recovering hoards of silver plate.

From this it is clear that the possession of wealth is not the only factor which determines the burying of silver hoards. The people of the area must have had collections of silver plate or they could not have buried them. They must have buried them or we could not find them. If we assume that there is a general correlation between wealth and the possession of silver plate we would expect at least some collections of silver plate in each province. Threats, war, blood and mayhem do not correlate well with hoards of silver plate. This leaves the tendency to bury things as the deciding factor. What we are looking at in the epidemiology of silver hoards is the combination of possession of silver and tendency to bury things. To enunciate this clearly is quite a step forward yet, at the same time, it comes uncomfortably close to tautology.

So what sort of silver is in these hoards? As a very rough generalisation there are some church hoards, and the rest are domestic. One hoard from Water Newton (near Peterborough) may belong to the middle of the fourth century and could well be one of the earliest hoards of church plate. Apart from one older jug which is decorated all over, and some very delicate thin bowls, most of the pieces are plain, not to say simple. A large dish still has the circular marks where it must have been turned on the lathe, a cup with two handles is chunky and simple. A thinner cup of very simple shape **(colour plate 20)** has an inscription round the rim in excellent lettering saying that

> *Innocentia et Viventia ———runt*

The gap is caused by damage. The problem is that whatever *Innocentia* and *Viventia* did it is bound in Latin to end up — *ervnt*. They gave — *dederunt*, they promised — *promiserunt,* they dedicated — *dedicaverunt*. A more helpful inscription says that Anicilla paid the vow that she had promised, and hence this silver vessel was presumably added to the church treasury. Under the base of another vessel is the name Publianus, and the inscription on the vessel says

> *Alpha chi-ro Omega Sanctam altarem tuum D Alpha chi-ro Omega omine*
> *subnixus honoro.*

The spacing of the letters is not perfect as the splitting of the word Domine shows. The meaning of the words might come out in English as: 'I, Publianus, relying on you, O Lord, honour your holy sanctuary'. But, in a sense this gets us no further forward because the words themselves, altar in a Christian sense, subnixus?, are the least of the information that can be gleaned. There could well be a system of words behind this apparently awkward phrase which might have meant a lot to anyone reading the inscription. A modern parallel might be in phrases from the King James version of the Bible, to some people, not necessarily religious, almost proverbial, which would be totally lost on someone raised on a new translation of the Bible.

It is interesting that one other piece of plate, a rectangular dish, comes from Britain and has religious connections. This has a very strange history which involves being found hacked into pieces, and then the silver from the pieces being re-cast in a single piece in a mould taken from the fragments. An inscription mentions a person, Exsuperius, who is a bishop, and a place, Bogio. This is not a known place name from Britain, or anywhere else for that matter, so Exsuperius might have been the bishop of an area, an estate, or some other grouping of Christians.

Later church hoards, of the sixth and seventh centuries, seem mainly to be found at the eastern end of the Mediterranean in southern Turkey and northern Syria. Several of these, such as Kaper Koraon and Sion, have now been recognised. They contain collections which in variety of object and weight of silver completely overshadow Water Newton. Whereas the congregation represented by Water Newton had a decent set of vessels and a few decorations, the congregation represented by the Sion hoard had many vessels, lamps, candelabra and even silver coverings for some of the columns and capitals of their church. Even this luxury pales before some of the records of imperial benefactions, whether of Justinian in the East (40,000 pounds of silver to Hagia Sophia), or the continuous gifts by the Popes to the churches of Rome.

These hoards of objects of high intrinsic value and great historical interest are sometimes discovered in secure circumstances, and entire. At other times they trickle slowly onto the international market through clouds of obscurity. This means that some hoards such as Kaiseraugst in Switzerland and especially Hoxne, the latest hoard from East Anglia, can be studied as complete units. The other hoards retain an aura of uncertainty, which has no ill effects on the study of each individual object, but makes any study of the hoard as a totality very difficult.

The most recent hoard to emerge from the dealer's underworld is the Seuso hoard. This large collection of silver plate illustrates several aspects of study which are difficult to answer. Its great virtue is that the pieces accepted as part of a hoard in about 1988 have been fully published, in reasonably accessible form, in English. This means that discussion of individual pieces should be firmly based, but the collection as a whole may well be subject to further argument.

It appeared on the antiquities market with very little information to explain itself. The first country to be named as a find-spot was the Lebanon. People in Croatia have a very convincing story of the treasure's finding during the lifetime of Marshal Tito. Hungary too is a possible source. Any study of where hoards are most likely to turn up would implicate East Anglia but, in this case it is unlikely for chemical reasons. The silver vessels were packed away, fairly roughly, in a bronze cauldron which has survived intact with the pressure marks of various vessels inside it. The cauldron had on and in it evidence that it had been hidden in a limestone hole or cave, thus eliminating many possible areas of finding.

If it were known that the collection was a unit and was complete it might be thought that we ought to be able to suggest a find-spot from knowledge of where all the pieces were made. That would be a first step if we had any notions at all on the subject. At one time the finest decoration was always related back to Alexandria as one of the main artistic centres of the Empire. If not Alexandria, then certainly a great city in the Mediterranean area. Opinion now is far less definite, and it is admitted as possible that since a silversmith and his workshop can travel without too much difficulty the provinces might have been producing silver plate of high quality on the spot. It may not be so much the craftsmanship, which can indeed travel anywhere with relative ease, but the silver, which has limitations in time and space.

In over-simple terms the theory was that the earth, the physical world, belonged to the emperor. Everything that came out of it was his, but some things were clearly more worth claiming than others. Simple building stone or potting clay had little financial potential because they were so common. Special stone deposits, some marble, some granite and porphyry, were kept as an imperial monopoly. Metal ores and deposits were more valuable and the precious metals were obviously vital to the organisation of the state through coinage. Gold and silver were therefore claimed monopolies, though the actual production of the metal might be leased out to people or companies. Gold and silver in the late Empire ought to go to the Count of the Sacred Largess (Comes Sacrarum Largitionum), who would then send what was needed to the imperial mints, while the surplus was available for purchase. Some metal seems to have avoided the process of going into the centre and coming out again, and this may have been managed by a form of creative accounting.

It is uncertain to what extent raw silver could travel freely within the Empire because gold and silver coin were forbidden to cross provincial boundaries in private hands. This might mean that silver was only easily available in provinces which produced it, or provinces to which the state sent it. Important people who could persuade authority to send them silver for making into plate should be concentrated in the great cities and then fairly well scattered round the empire. Britain has not only a large number of late hoards of plate but has always been noted for the hoards of silver coins of 357–411. It is not noted for concentrations of well-known people, but it is throughout the Roman period a producer of silver from the lead mines of North Wales, the Peak District, and the Mendips. Lead was commonly used in late Roman Britain for making pewter vessels and lead coffins as well as all the usual plumbing and roofing, so silver production ought to have been quite high at this time. While this point cannot account for the strange British habit of burying hoards of silver coins in the fourth century, and the East Anglian habit of burying hoards of gold and silver objects and coins, it does demonstrate that the raw materials were probably available, so that only the importation of a silversmith was needed to produce the plate on the spot.

The collection of silver found in the late Roman fortifications at Kaiseraugst (52-53) is generally agreed to exist now in the form and numbers in which it was found with the possibility that two or three vessels have gone missing. The objects range from the great decorated plates (usually referred to as dishes) weighing more than 15 Roman pounds each to spoons of around an ounce. Together with eating implements and toilet utensils there are eleven cups and bowls, eleven dishes, a candelabrum, a statuette and three ingots.

As always, once a silver treasure has been described, people start asking whether it is complete. This is a dangerous question because it cannot be answered until the word complete is defined. If the hoard is the contents of a display case or sideboard taken down hastily from display and crammed into a chest to take away to be hidden, then it is of

52-53 Augst, Museum. The KaiserAugst silver hoard.
   Copyright Humbert & Vogt, Römermuseum Augst

course complete. If, as with some hoards, it is the decorative part of a large dinner service then it is very clearly not complete. Since we have no hoard which could possibly be used to furnish a complete dinner table for, say, six, we have no idea at present what 'complete' in this sense might mean.

Kaiseraugst does have cups and bowls which could be part of individual place settings. The joint could be brought in on one of the big plates, and the meat transferred to individual bowls so that each person may eat a share. There are the individual cups to drink from, but where are the jugs and flagons known from many other hoards? Some earlier treasures are made up of smaller plates, small dishes and cups, but they in turn rarely have the full decorative suite as well.

The problem here is with words and expectations. In the Seuso collection the main silver plate, the hunting plate, is 70cm (28in) across. In comparison my Victorian pottery charger or serving dish suitable for a large turkey is an oval only 20in long. A large roast joint, obviously not a turkey, would look lonely on the hunting plate unless it were the hindquarters of a lamb. A boar's head would look ridiculous. It is rather wide for one person to grip comfortably when loaded, and even unloaded it weighs nearly nine kilos or 19 pounds. The rim has a hunting design cut into the silver and filled with black silver sulphide or niello so that the silver figures are outlined in black and stand out very well. In the centre is a scene of a hunting party in the same technique, arranged round a picture of the stop for a picnic lunch under an awning. Round this is an inscription which includes the chi-ro, the first two letters of the name of Christ in Greek, and hopes in Latin verse, that these things will belong to SEVSO for some time and be of use to his offspring. The metre of the verse requires SEVSO to be three syllables and that is the reason for writing it Se-u-so rather than Seu-so. There are two other words on this plate. A horse is labelled Inocentius, and a stretch of water has the letters Pelso on it. This might refer to the water, which looks more like a stream than a lake, or the boar or the hunting dog beside it. Perhaps the main point about the plate, apart from its totally unpractical nature, is that all this luxurious central detail which Seuso must have intended to be seen, would be totally obscured by a haunch of venison with a redcurrant coulis. This, like the other Seuso pieces is for the sideboard or dresser rather than the table.

A second plate from the group is more practical and has only a central roundel with a geometrical decoration. A diameter of two feet and a weight of 15 pounds makes it a little more manageable but still in the bulk-catering class. Two other plates have raised decoration round the rim and in the centre and are known by the figures shown, the Meleager plate **(colour plate 21)** and the Achilles plate. Both of these sets of scenes are of interest from the point of view of what is shown and how it is depicted, but for the moment it is only necessary to point out that the plates are again totally unpractical for use, and no inscriptions of any sort are given to help the viewer interpret the scenes. On the reverse of the Meleager plate is a scratched inscription which might read 26 pounds, 7 ounces, 15 scruples. This would give a modern weight of 8722 gm while the actual modern weight of the plate is 8606 gm. The hundred gramme (four modern ounces) difference is small, and it may point out once again that the vital part of this plate is not the legend of Meleager but the weight of solid silver.

54 London, British Museum. The Esquiline silver hoard from Rome, the marriage casket.
  Copyright The British Museum

A quite different set of silver was found on the Esquiline Hill in Rome in 1793. It is known as the Esquiline treasure and most of it is on show in the British Museum. (The Seuso treasure is not on view anywhere since it is still in a legal limbo which may last for some years yet.) The centrepieces of the group are two silver caskets, both covered in raised decoration. The rectangular casket **(54)** gives us a great deal of detail, the main part of which, for the moment, is the inscription which, with a chi-ro and alpha and omega, hopes that Secundus and Proiecta will live in Christ. On the centre of the lid are a man and a woman who are thought to be at their wedding. The second casket is a domed toilet casket with, inside, five silver bottles suitable for oils, perfumes and essences. After this the hoard becomes more diverse with square and rectangular plates with a monogram, a narrow-necked flask, a silver 'saucepan' or handled dish decorated with Venus and waves, and six sets of horse trappings. One extra piece of information may come from the decoration of the rectangular casket in which the bride and groom seem to be guided, with their valuables, to their new house. Clearly there is not enough room for a full catalogue of their worldly goods, but among the objects which are shown several are obviously of metal, and probably silver plate. It might be thought that with an inscription naming man and wife, the owners and date of this treasure should be safely established. Unfortunately, though we know the family involved, there are several possible candidates, at different dates, and it is difficult to improve on the usual date given late in the fourth century.

The assemblage of objects and vessels as it is known today is probably not all that was found in 1793, but there is a distressing tendency for rumours of loss and theft to accumulate round nearly every hoard discovered. What we can say is that the assemblage, even with a few additions, does not make any very good sense in terms of 'family silver'. Since the rectangular casket has several depictions of household scenes and objects on its sides it is tempting to relate what we have to what is shown. The silver flask with its tall thin shape fits well with one shown on the back of the casket, but there is no sign of the mirror shown on the front. One of the servants shown on the back carries a casket on a chain which could be the toilet casket, but the candlestick shown on the lid is missing. The representations also show a handled situla or small bucket, and a handled jug, both of which occur in other assemblages, but there is no sign on the casket of the small rectangular dish with the monogram.

There is no need for all the pieces to have been made at the same time, or to have come into one ownership at one event. Parts of what might have started off as a full set of silver, whatever that might be, could well have followed different paths after the deaths of the first owners. It seems unlikely that the horse trappings were part of a wedding set. They seem to fit better with someone in the family gaining an official position which involved a ceremonial chariot or team of horses. In the same way the small rectangular dish need have no connection with the bridal couple, but might have been a commemorative gift when a relative received state office.

One obvious aspect of the decoration of the rectangular casket and the 'saucepan' is the presence of Venus either attended by cherubs or holding a full marine court. The only point which could cause surprise is the conjunction of these scenes, fully expected at a wedding, with the inscription wishing long life in Christ. The moral, as with the catacombs and the basilica mosaic at Aquileia, is that the imagery is traditional, rather than explicitly religious, and total antagonism between old decoration and the new religion is not to be expected.

One hoard which provokes several different kinds of surprise is the one found at Mildenhall in Suffolk in 1942 and turned into a short story by Roald Dahl shortly after the coroner's inquest in 1946. The complete hoard consists of the large, Oceanus, platter, a large flat plate, a fluted bowl with handles, four bowls, two smaller plates, two goblets, two smaller bowls, a dish cover, eight spoons, five ladle bowls and four ladle handles. What has caused argument is the finding of such luxurious silver in the fenlands of the backwoods of Roman Britain. One school of thought had it that not only was such material obviously imported, for it could not possibly have been made there, it was a modern import, for such material was not even likely to have been owned, used, or buried there. The rumour was that this hoard had been found in North Africa, during the war, and flown in to the American air base near Mildenhall, to be 'found' in more friendly circumstances.

None of this speculation seems either needed or likely to be true. Richard Hobbs's work mentioned earlier, if plotted on a map, shows that the most likely find-spot for a hoard of silver is now East Anglia, the least likely, North Africa or Spain. Rumour never explained why it was better for a foreign team to 'find' a silver treasure which would be very likely declared treasure-trove, in Britain rather than in the chaos of the North African campaigns. And opinion is now beginning to be that silver of a high standard was not only owned in Britain but some of it might well have been made there. The Risley Park lanx

55 *London, British Museum. The Mildenhall silver hoard, the Oceanus plate.*
  Copyright The British Museum

(rectangular platter) with the inscription of the Bishop of Bogio has features which Kenneth Painter has connected with the late pewter industry, heavily concentrated in Britain.

As a set the Mildenhall hoard produces the usual problems. There is the great ornamental plate which has a mask of Oceanus at the centre surrounded by sea nymphs, and in the outer circle a Bacchic dance **(55)**. The two smaller plates have similar decoration, in the classical mode, which go very well with it. The less decorated large plate would act as a serving platter. The handled bowl would act as a serving bowl into the other bowls and dishes, all decorated with classical figures and scenes with animals around the rims, suitable perhaps for four people. The two goblets are unusual as finds, and since they have large flat bases they could equally well be used the other way up as small platters on stands. The ladles with dolphin handles were perhaps a set of six. If so then one is completely lost and one has lost its handle. Then there are the eight spoons which bring a Christian element into what is otherwise a group in conventional classical taste. Three of the spoons are decorated inside the bowl with a leaf pattern, three have simply the chi-ro flanked by alpha and omega, one hopes for long life for Pappitedo (Pappitedo vivas), and the last has the same wish for Pascentia. The Christian spoons fit well in Britain with other finds, sometimes simply a set of spoons but in several cases with Christian inscriptions or monograms.

One further element in the Mildenhall hoard that has to be mentioned is its failure to fit into the general scheme of development of late Roman art which was put forward in the section on Official Sculpture, and general portraiture, aided by the silver Madrid platter, but has taken punishment in all later sections. The Bacchic frenzy on the Great Plate and the revels on the small plates are disturbing not for their subject matter, but the way it is portrayed. True to form there is no background but this, on silver, has always been a matter of taste. There is background in abundance on the hunt plate of the Seuso treasure, which is probably quite close to Mildenhall in date. The figures themselves provide the anomalies. The male figures, mostly naked, are brilliantly portrayed with muscles of almost medical precision. The female figures, though clothed, show through the draperies so that the shape of the body fully determines the disposition of the cloth. There is frenzied movement and full individuality in both pose and features. The plate cannot be far in date from the Madrid plate, which dates to 388, yet they inhabit different worlds of portrayal. It is easy, and convenient, to oppose the demands of official didactic state art and private decoration for the dinner table or the dresser, but nothing could demonstrate more clearly the failure of trying to arrange all late Roman art in a single chronological line of development.

The other East Anglian hoards have much to contribute, but they cannot all be dealt with in detail. Thetford adds gold in reasonable quantities to the lists, not as table ware, or even display plate, but a buckle (**56**), 22 rings, four bracelets, and several chains. There are three silver strainers, an odd implement which is variously referred to in different hoards as an ear pick, a tooth pick or a ritual implement for the Eucharist. The final surprise is the number of spoons — 33. They come in two shapes, with expected long handles and short curled handles. Three have representation of a triton, a panther and a fish, 20 are inscribed with names, and 10 are plain. The names are partly the usual wish for long life for individuals, but some name the god Faunus. The fish has been brought in to add a Christian significance to the find, but this is disputed. If Oceanus can be discounted at Mildenhall, and Venus on the Esquiline, then a single fish need not convert a selection of spoons inscribed for Faunus.

The Hoxne treasure, the most recently discovered, continues the lists of gold jewellery, rings, chains and bracelets. It has four plain cups, large numbers of spoons (75) and ladles (20), and adds to the categories encountered so far statuettes and pepper pots (**57**), and over 500 gold and 14,000 silver coins. Statuettes can be paralleled at Kaiseraugst in Switzerland together with 187 silver coins and medallions and magnificent large plates and sets of bowls and cups.

The ideas of dating of these two hoards are different. At Kaiseraugst the coins are very unusual in that the latest, up to about 350, are seldom found as chance finds or in archaeological contexts. Because they are uncommon in circulation their presence in the hoard ought to be a helpful dating tool and the hoard ought to have been assembled in the years between *c.*350–360. The coins at Hoxne run up to 411, but the problem here is that with very few exceptions coins in general in Britain run up to 411 and then supply stops. To say that many of the coins are not worn does not really help because if coins were no longer coming into Britain in the fifth century coin use presumably stopped, and coins that were held in reserve became stores of bullion rather than objects of daily use.

The scheme of decoration on one dish from Kaiseraugst contrasts with the scheme on a plate from the Seuso hoard. This is not a different way of portraying the same story or person but a different attitude to stories in general. Even that gives a slightly wrong impression, for the two vessels demonstrate two different tendencies at work in late antique representation. The vessel from Kaiseraugst is known as the Achilles dish, that from the Seuso hoard is the Meleager plate. Achilles as a hero of the Trojan war had a claim in the classical world to be partly historical. Meleager was the hero of a story which involved a heroine, Atalante, and the vital moment in the story was the killing of the Calydonian boar. The Meleager plate **(colour plate 21)** has a scene with all the main participants in the central roundel, but the pictures round the rim are from a series of other classical legends and myths. The Achilles dish has not only a major event in the central roundel, but a whole series of supporting scenes from the life of Achilles round the

57 *London, British Museum. The Hoxne gold and silver hoard, the 'empress' pepperpot. Copyright Peter Clayton*

rim. This rather reverses earlier depictions of the two stories. It is quite easy to find full accounts of Meleager and Atalante on mosaic pavements and paintings of earlier times, but if these are followed through time the scenes are drastically cut down until only one remains. This can be so simplified as to leave only a male figure with a spear and a severed animal head at his feet. The story is first edited into separate parts, some parts survive at the expense of others, and finally a single scene is pared down to its bare essentials. On mosaics, while this is happening, the spectator is given some help with written labels added to the design, but this help is never given on silver. It is as if anyone might come into the entrance hall and wonder at your mosaic. It is only kind, in a time a great social change to help those of lesser schooling by labelling the mosaic to tell them what is going on. If, of course, they can read. But few of these unlettered people would be admitted to the family quarters, where visitors would be of the same educational background as the host. The silver does not need to be given textual explanation.

In this series of changes the Achilles plate is clearly going against the grain. The contrast is even stronger than appears at first, for it is difficult, if not impossible, to find earlier representations of an Achilles cycle of stories and events. Accidents of survival may account for part of this difference, but it would be odd if the many single or simple representations of Achilles have survived from the earlier empire when only the cycles have disappeared. One suggestion that has been made is that the classical world needed to bring its theology up to date in order to counterbalance the Christian theology, which had a remarkable coherence and drive. Classical sequences would be needed to show that the old world had more than enough mythology to equal the sequence of the Old and New Testaments, or the life and death of Christ. Achilles might therefore have been chosen as a hero who improved through life, and whose attributes were those that were needed in the world of the fourth century. This might be thought a rather extreme theory to base on the decoration mainly of one dish, but the discovery of a second Achilles plate in the Seuso hoard, a companion to the Meleager plate already mentioned, does help the idea along. On the Seuso Achilles plate there is again a central Achilles roundel, and this time about half of the scenes round the rim are of the Achilles story.

The idea is an interesting one, and has been developed with great detail, but there are problems still to be addressed. There is no such thing on a silver plate as a Christian cycle of stories or events. The nearest we have come to this is the lid of the reliquary box in the Vatican which showed five scenes from the life of Christ. The sequence visible there has been explained as a guide to the main pilgrimage places of the Holy Land. In the catacombs there are indeed scenes from the Old and New testaments, but these seldom lead the viewer through a narrative. They are more often juxtaposed messages representing hope or salvation. The illustrations in manuscripts follow a theme and a pattern, but that is because they are following the text, and it seems very unlikely that adherents of the old religions would either see these, or envy them. Perhaps the most likely site of cycles of Christian paintings would come in the decoration of churches. Surviving examples could be the small panels from the Old Testament at Santa Maria Maggiore in Rome and the New Testament at San Apollinare in Ravenna.

The other problem which affects the theory is the choice of Hero. Here the difference between the great diversity which is called paganism and the laser-sharp concentration which is Christianity breaks out. A town does not have one pagan place of worship to balance the Christian church. It has had for many years a temple to Mercury, a shrine of Minerva, three small temples of local gods and a grove sacred to Apollo. In addition most houses had their own small shrines with a variety of sacred images. While Platonic philosophy was developing through the Roman empire, and that could easily include pagan references, there was nothing that could be identified as pagan theology. Choice of a hero around whom to construct a Heroic Cycle of improving and encouraging nature was therefore extremely difficult. One hero who had shown signs of suitability was Hercules, with his labours, but he never developed in this way. It may be that there were certain aspects of his earlier career that made him unsuitable.

The subject of cycles takes us easily on to the Cyprus treasures. Two separate finds were made, one late in the nineteenth century and the second in 1902. The first find consists of vessels at least some of which can be called by liturgical names, paten, censer, and the whole collection might have belonged to a church. The second find consists of gold jewellery and nine plates which form a matching set with pictures from the life of the

58 Cyprus National Museum. The second Cyprus silver hoard, the wedding plate.
Copyright Peter Clayton

traditional writer of the Psalms, King David. If the pictures are examined one by one they show different aspects of late Roman art. The marriage scene **(58)** is strictly frontally posed with an almost symbolic architectural façade behind. In contrast the plate of David and Goliath shows three parts of the story, one above the other. At the top, on a smaller scale, is the challenge with each hero in front of his respective city. The large scene at the centre shows the fight in progress. The smaller lowest scene shows the end of the fight. There are good ground surfaces, with even some flowers on the turf. There is strong motion and the figures are set in the direction demanded by the action. On the marriage plate all is calm and draperies fall stiffly to the ground, but still with a hint of the figures beneath them. On David, and Goliath especially, the cloaks swirl and billow in frantic action.

Two other plates show David trying on Saul's armour before the fight, and David killing the lion **(59)**. The armour scene is set almost symmetrically, with two people on either side of David in front of the standard architectural background. The lion plate has the lion in a simple landscape, rocks and a stunted tree, and David has one knee on its back, one hand grasps the lion's mane while the other swings a club to finish the attack. A cloak billows out behind David, either showing a strong breeze, or, more likely, the presence of action. The plates are of different sizes with the David and Goliath the largest at 50cm. (20in.); they could probably be set out on display to re-tell the story to anyone who had heard of it.

59 New York, Metropolitan Museum. The second Cyprus silver hoard, the plate showing David and the lion. Copyright Peter Clayton

Nothing has so far been said about dating. Style would suggest different dates perhaps for different plates. David and Goliath with its serial story, its movement, and its avoidance of frontality ought to be earlier; the heavily-posed wedding scene ought to be later, though even here the attendant flute-players are portrayed as fully functional humans. Perhaps a date around that of the *Roman Virgil* would be suitable? In fact this is one of the best dated finds of silver, for the plates have control stamps of the Emperor Heraclius, 610 to 642, distributed between 613 and 630. In some cases the control stamps have been partly obliterated by the process of beating the design, so forming the plates, then stamping them, and then beating the decoration all seem to have happened in a fairly short time interval at the beginning of the seventh century in Constantinople. The sea nymphs and Bacchic revels on the Mildenhall plates should have prepared us for this, but it still comes as a salutary lesson which must be applied to any attempts to force undated objects into a predetermined sequence.

Control marks, like those on the Cyprus plates, can bring us back to Britain, but not to Roman Britain. This will also take us out of the empire and suggest ways in which silver plate survived. The vital site was discovered and excavated at Sutton Hoo in Suffolk just before the Second World War. To most people this is a part of Anglo-Saxon archaeology because it is the burial mound of an Anglo-Saxon leader. The find is dated by coins from Merovingian Gaul to the early 600s. The costliest objects in the grave consist of gold and garnet metalwork, but its interest for us is a collection of late Roman silver of which at least one vessel was over 100 years old at the time of its burial. This is clear because in the case of the large plate the dating is from a control mark of Anastasius (491–518). Other silver from the find includes a fluted dish, ten decorated silver bowls, some plain bowls, a strainer and two spoons. The combination is no stranger than that of many hoards, but is no more informative as to what constitutes 'a set'.

The idea of burying valuables with a dead leader is perfectly normal in the late Roman and post-Roman periods. Burying their silver ware with them is highly unusual, and Sutton Hoo is unique in this. There are signs that the dead person's silver played a part in their burial ritual, but did not end up in the grave. Max Martin has pointed out that it is wrong to say that all the silver found in France, the former Gaul, belongs to the third century. There are at least three large plates, but they have been found in rivers. He also points out that some Germanic burials, perhaps the Burgundians, have a body with many gravegoods but no helmet. On the other hand helmets, but few other personal accoutrements, have been found in rivers. If we take the Sutton Hoo chief as a complete burial, equipment, helmet and silver, then the Burgundians may lack not only their helmets but also their silver, and these, through some different burial rite, were deposited in rivers.

The two spoons at Sutton Hoo (60) join the general discussion over pagan versus Christian which we have met before. Here, however, the argument is in the Germanic sphere and the seventh century. The mild Christian would hardly be buried in full war-like regalia. The convinced pagan might possibly have had ten bowls each decorated with a cross because the design is so basic it need have no direct significance. It is more difficult to uphold convinced paganism when the leader seems to own two spoons, each with a clear cross, and one inscribed Paulos, the other Saulos, in Greek letters. The strong reminder here is of the scourge of Christians Saul, who experienced a dramatic conversion

60 London, British Museum. Sutton Hoo burial, spoons possibly inscribed 'Saulos' and 'Paulos'. Copyright The British Museum

61 St. Petersburg, Hermitage Museum. The Meleager Plate.
   Copyright The State Hermitage Museum

and became the champion of the church Paul. In a burial mound of the seventh century, the time of conversion in Britain, the furnishings of the Sutton Hoo mound are no more surprising than the mixture of paintings in the Via Latina catacomb in Rome.

Some silver went far further afield than post-Roman Britain. The Hermitage museum in Leningrad has one of the best collections of late Roman silver **(61)** not because of modern trade and conquest but because there is a curious concentration of the material in the northern (former) USSR. Some of these deposits have Roman vessels with post-Roman inscriptions, and some also include later vessels from the Sassanian empire centred in Persia. This means that some Roman vessels continued as valued possessions for several hundred years somewhere between Constantinople and the Arctic Circle and were eventually deposited in circumstances totally foreign to their makers.

Other groups of silver were deposited more quickly, but less reverently, chopped up into pieces. One hoard in the Museums of Scotland from Traprain Law, a non-Roman site south of Edinburgh, has parts of some luxurious vessels which bear comparison with many other hoards. It has been claimed that a punch used to decorate one of the Esquiline vessels was also used on a fragment from Traprain, and certainly what is visible of shape and decoration makes this a perfectly good possibility. Commentators determined to promote ancient warfare see the hoard as a smash and grab raid from the Barbarian North on the Roman South. This must remain a possibility, but it seems less likely when it is remembered that outside the empire, and after the empire, silver circulated widely, cut into convenient chunks and parcelled up perhaps by weight. This is really little different from uncultured Roman owners who valued their whole silver vessels by weight and always regarded them as a disposable and easily realisable asset. Roman cash-flow problems must have ended the life of far more silver vessels than all the Barbarians put together.

7. Coins and the economy

I prefer to discuss the economy through the coins and the system of which they were part because that means we can start from fairly firm, known points rather than launching out directly into half-demonstrated generalisations.

In 193, when Septimius Severus started his successful bid for the throne, the coinage in circulation in the western part of the empire would have been completely comprehensible to a citizen born under Augustus, 200 years before. The gold aureus, worth 25 silver denarii, was well struck by well-engraved dies on carefully prepared flans of high quality gold. The Augustan citizen would have had nothing to complain of. Silver was less satisfactory; the silver content had dropped from around 90% to around 75%, the flans were not well prepared, and the end product looked rather scruffy. When the silver content is quoted as 'around' a percentage this does not mean we cannot estimate the silver content of a coin. It means that different coins have different silver contents, which average out at around a given value. So when the silver content dropped some new debased coins were often better than some old coins, but the average fineness had been reduced.

The base metal coins were still headed by the bronze sestertius, at four to the denarius, there was a half sestertius, the dupondius, a quarter, the as, and no doubt in theory there should have been a half and quarter as. I suspect that by 193 the production of the half as cost almost as much as its new face value, so the state had no incentive to strike it. This was a change from the time of Augustus when the smaller denominations did circulate in reasonable numbers, at least in Italy. The disappearance of the half and quarter as suggests that there had been very gentle inflation over the two hundred years between 7 BC–AD 193 in which prices had risen by 4 or 8 times. My reasoning here is that the lowest coin in 7 BC was the quarter as, in AD 193 the as, but they might have been in fairly low production. If we split the difference we can call it a six times price rise, or inflation of 600% over 200 years. This is a cumulative process. At one percent inflation we have a price of 1 denarius in the first year which becomes $1 + 1\%$ of $1 = 1.01$ in the second year. In the third year we have to add on 1% of 1.01, and so on. In 200 years this gets up to a price of about 7 denarii. So a price rise of times 7 over 200 years is a constant rate of 1% inflation per year. To the modern world this is as near to stability as any country would ever hope to get.

By the year 300 the coins had changed out of all recognition and the prices of 193 may have multiplied by as much as 100. In this case, at least in Egypt, we know that the process was not a gentle cumulative rise but a slow rise to about 274 and then a dramatic rise. Again, modern conditions can be compared with ancient, and the clear warning is that fast price rises are not necessarily evidence of total chaos in the economy. A meal in 1998 for

62 Oxford, Ashmolean Museum. Base silver coin with a 'radiate' crown showing the emperor surrounded by the rays of the sun.
Copyright Richard Reece

11 people costing half a million would be evidence of serious evidence of disruption in Britain if expressed in pounds sterling, but has a totally different meaning in Rome in Italian lire. Keeping away, for the moment, from the type of moral economic judgement which regards any change as evidence of failure, what had actually happened?

The first thing was a promise from Severus in the civil wars of 193–7 of a substantial pay rise for his troops if he won. In 194 the silver content of the denarius dropped from values around 75% to values clustered rather more closely round 48%. The pay rise was duly handed out, but the troops could not know, at the time, that though they were given more denarii they were given, in total, less silver. They could not know because unlike the earlier debasement of Nero there was not a clear break in the style of the coinage showing 'before' and 'after'. For Nero that was mainly the addition of a laurel wreath to a bare-headed imperial portrait. Once the information got out anyone could distinguish the poorer coins from the earlier, better coins. The result was that the better coins disappeared from circulation within years, if not months. Severus gave no clear sign, with the result that better and worse coins were not quickly distinguished. Did the coins not look different? The answer is a definite no. The change in silver content left the coinage still bright and silvery.

This method of finding extra money from the same amount of silver coming from the mines is too tempting to forget. We assume that the supply of silver from the mines was roughly constant because at this date we know very little indeed about the output or even the functioning of different mines. The dilution of silver in the coinage by base metal continued through the earlier part of the third century, but not immediately.

In 214 Severus' son Caracalla introduced a new silver coin struck in the same metal as the denarius and which showed the emperor with a crown of the sun's rays which is therefore known as a radiate **(62)**. Opinion is divided on the meaning of this new coin. The older theory is that a radiate crown had been used before to signal the double as, the dupondius, and this is therefore a double denarius. If so, it is well under weight because it is only 1.5 times the weight of the old coin rather than 2. This is taken as a brilliant stroke of policy by which debasement is carried out without adding the extra copper. But a double denarius is only an assumption on a rather frail basis. It is perfectly possible, even likely, that the new coin is a 1.5 denarius. Why strike something between 1 and 2? A rather cheeky suggestion comes from the East, from Antioch, where the drachma had for long been in an uneasy relationship with the denarius. In 214 the western radiate and the Antiochene tetradrachm have about the same amount of silver. The West had at last come in line with the East. We need to know far more about the minting, silver contents and circulation patterns of the two types of coins before we can make a firm judgement.

After 214 the radiate went, came back again, and went again. It finally settled down in production in 238 and from that date the denarius not only went rapidly out of production, but also out of circulation. There was regret. What can the evidence be for such a subjective statement? I take the casting of copies of old, worn, denarii throughout the empire to be clear evidence that the population wished to prolong the waning life of the old coin. The trouble with attempts to interpret this epidemic of casting more fully is that by this time (the 230s–240s) the silver content of the radiate had dropped considerably below the Severan 48% so that every denarius had more silver in than virtually any radiate. We do not know therefore if this is a battle of denominations, an attack of nostalgia, or the simple production of counterfeit denarii to make the bearer believe in a higher silver content.

With the slide of silver content of the radiate between 238–260, from 40% to at best 5% silver, the elements of the coinage system must have been dislocated. One definite result was the disappearance of copper and bronze coins **(63-64)**. It is true that any complete catalogue of Roman coins shows copper issues in the 260s and the 270s but these occur very rarely as archaeological finds. They were issued by the mint in Rome and seem not to have spread much further than Italy. If these are left on one side as token issues for some unknown purpose then the subdivisions of the denarius had ceased to be minted by about 260.

This makes perfectly good sense both in the market place and in a cost-effective mint. When the denarius dropped down to one hundredth of its former silver content it may well have dropped down to the same fraction of its earlier purchasing power. But when a denarius was almost pure silver the smallest fraction available was a quarter of an as, which was a quarter of a sestertius, which was a quarter of a denarius. The fraction was therefore one sixty-fourth, the quadrans, which was a coin of very low purchasing power. The poor widow in the Gospels was able to put that much (dua minuta quod est quadrans) in the charity box. The debased radiate of 270, which might have been two denarii in face value, had less silver in it than one hundredth of an old denarius. Its purchasing power, in terms of silver, was therefore down to the widow's mite, two of which made a quadrans. There was no place in a market system at the time for a coin smaller than that, so the old denarius and all its subdivisions were useless.

63 Oxford, Ashmolean Museum. A worn sestertius with the head of Hadrian (117-138) reused by Postumus (260-268) and overstruck with his radiate portrait. Copyright Richard Reece

64 Oxford, Ashmolean Museum. Reverse of a coin of Postumus (260-8) struck in ?Cologne showing how the figure of Victory has been stylized into a series of lines. Copyright Richard Reece

In a cost-effective mint, without benefit of state subsidies or sophisticated economic theory, the striking of each standard coin needs to make a profit. So the face value of the coin when sent out must be greater than the cost of its production. Since the Roman state seems to have struck standard coinage in order to pay its own state bills it seems very unlikely that the mint ever struck large issues of coins which did not pay for themselves. Small issues of token coins for special social, political or religious purposes could clearly be subsidised by those who needed them.

By 270 the base radiate was the main small value coin in circulation. The only other coin being issued in any numbers was the gold coin, and this in turn caused problems. In the first century it was generally known that 25 denarii were equivalent to a gold coin, an aureus. The likelihood is that this allowed a reasonable margin of profit, or error, between the official exchange rates of bullion gold and silver and their fluctuations, and the relative values of the coined metal. If gold was the standard, then silver might have been one fifteenth of its value, and coins might have been struck and issued to give a relative value of one gold to twenty silver. If the silver to gold ratio fell to 1 to 12 then the state made even more profit than usual. If the ratio rose to 1 to 18 then the profit margin was cut.

But when 100 radiates, perhaps equalling 200 denarii, only made up the silver of one denarius in the old calculations the whole matter of gold and silver ratios must have been in question. On the old system 200 denarii should have been exchanged for 8 gold pieces. A hundred radiates have hardly the intrinsic worth of one old denarius and no-one would have parted with even one gold piece for such meagre return. Of course the state has the theoretical power to decree the face value of coinage. The early Imperial authorities did this by over-valuing the silver in each denarius. The silver was worth x; when coined into a denarius and issued in the state system it circulated at a value of (perhaps) x + 10%. But it seems impossible that any state could over-value supposed bullion coinage by several hundred per cent and still see it commonly used. This could happen in copper, as it happens today in paper, but so far as we know it was not an ancient custom in regard to gold and silver.

This means that somewhere between 215, when we last have any direct evidence, and 270, the lowest depths of the denarius, the relationship between gold and 'silver' must have slipped, changed or dissolved. The fact that gold begins for the first time to vary in both fineness and weight adds to the problems. If 'silver' had a low value, and gold was variable, perhaps needing to be exchanged by weight, and there was no commonly accepted relationship between them, then the difference between the coinage of the mid-first century and that of 270 is probably enough to talk in terms of economic disruption.

The basis of our knowledge of third-century gold coins brings out points of interest. The coins are very rare today and many of the examples were clearly taken out of general circulation. There are hoards of third-century gold coins in Denmark, and there are third-century gold coins set in jewellery. These may not be the majority, but they are certainly a major element in new finds. Coins set in jewellery were clearly not available for further general circulation. The same applies to gold which reached Scandinavia, especially if it was hoarded. There are two possible ways of interpreting the information. In the first, the direct, method these coins are rare, wherever they come from, and if they are rare now they were rare then. Few gold coins were struck in the third century and circulation was probably sluggish. The second method goes further. A substantial proportion of third-century gold to survive was trapped and removed from circulation. The gold that was not trapped has virtually disappeared, for very little of it was hoarded within the empire. This could suggest that, whatever the numbers produced, the circulation and recycling of gold was more frenzied in the third-century than at most other times. What is clearly needed is a count of the dies used to strike the coins. If most of the surviving coins were struck from the same small number of dies then the coinage cannot have been very great. If

65 Oxford, Ashmolean Museum. Coin of Aurelian struck after the reform of 273 when the size, shape and silver content had been improved after the low standards of the middle of the third century.
Copyright Richard Reece

almost every coin was struck from different dies, the coinage was bigger, but there is no way of knowing how big. The true number of dies cut, when every coin surviving comes from a different die, lies somewhere between the number of coins found and infinity.

There were two main attempts to reorganise the coinage in the third century after the all-time-low of 270. In 274 in the reign of the emperor Aurelian the older style of badly made small coins with perhaps 1% of silver in was discontinued. New coins about 5 gm in weight (compared with the old 2 gm) were struck on carefully prepared blanks (quite different from the earlier scrappy blanks) and the silver content was raised from perhaps 1% to over 4% **(65)**. A token issue of bronze was also struck, but this is confined to Italy and it may just have been a subsidised demonstration of the 'return to the old values'. The gradual slide of the old radiate into baseness had dislocated the old coinage system in a slow but steady way. The sudden rise in the purchasing power and face value of the commonly produced basic coin by a factor of at least ten must have been a very large shock to the market system. It is just at this time that in the insulated province of Egypt, a province with its own separate coinage, strong inflation is suddenly seen in the documents.

It seems probable that the base silver radiate circulated in such large numbers because it was a flexible way of buying things in the market place. It was clearly inconvenient for buying milk-cows, or cottages, because of the numbers involved, but for cabbages and herbs it was probably ideal. It may well have been better suited to small-value transactions than almost any earlier coinage system because those always placed the emphasis on high-value denominations. Suddenly to increase the value of the common coin by at least ten would put the whole basic market stall system in turmoil. There is a good case to be made for the idea that it was not the debasement of the coinage which caused problems in the

66 Oxford, Ashmolean Museum. Silver coin of Diocletain c. 300 with a reverse showing the numeral XCVI, or 96 to the pound of silver.
Copyright Richard Reece

third century but the attempts to reverse the process.

The second change in the coinage of the third century bears the name of Diocletian and the date of 294–5. This is a reorganisation quite different both in scope and effect from that of Aurelian. One major difference between the two is the attitude to local coinages. Aurelian seems to have taken little notice of production outside the state mints. City coinages of the Greek East had been hit by the changes in face value of the mid-third century because their coinages were overwhelmingly in bronze. As the purchasing power of all bronze coins dropped with the debasement of silver, so there was less and less point for the city to produce its own bronze coins. Provincial issues dropped both in mints striking and in numbers of coins struck. Aurelian had no direct hand in this. Diocletian, on the other hand, eliminated all surviving coinage struck outside the state mints within two years. The main casualties were Antioch and Alexandria because those were the two main surviving mints of the time. They were both reconstituted as state mints and thenceforward struck mainly the standard issues of Rome. Other mints were reformed, or opened, to provide an empire-wide production system for a very standardised product.

The product of 297 had changed dramatically from the product of 293. Gold had been brought back to uniformity by Aurelian and his successors; Diocletian struck a completely uniform gold piece at the rate of 60 to the Roman pound (about 327 gm) of nearly pure gold. Silver, which had not been seen in any pure form since before 194, returned like the old denarius of Nero at 96 to the pound of good silver. If there are any doubts about why the changes were needed, and what the public wanted, then the fact that some of the silver coins have simply 96 (XCVI) on their reverse gives clear indications **(66)**. The other coins were struck in copper with added silver and so, when they came from the mint with their surfaces enriched, they could pass for silver coins. They were presumably heavily over-valued, but we have little idea by how much. The largest coin was of 10 gm, then one of 5 gm, still radiate, and a small coin of about 2 gm. The largest coin had between 2 and 4%

of silver, the smaller coins had less. If we add to these changes the Maximum Price Edict, and the (changes in) Coinage Edict, of 301, then for the first time in the Roman world we have a body of information which allows us to come close to the coins, their values, their uses and what they could buy.

The silver coin might have been worth 100 denarii, the gold coin about 1200 denarii, the largest base silver 25 and the smaller 5 and 2 denarii. This can be compared with the price for 'one prod or whip, turned' at 5 denarii, or the daily wages of a camel driver or sewer cleaner at 25 denarii. This window of opportunity for study has to be exploited quickly, for within about twenty years the system of coinage was in rapid flux and prices had gone up sharply yet again.

The changes between 294, or 301 and 330 are substantial. Gold had been changed from 60 to the pound to 72 to the pound (the solidus) **(colour plate 22)**. The fineness remained high, and this was the last major change to affect the gold coinage in the next 500 years. Silver, a major plank in the changes of 294, was always rare, had very quickly been debased and had dropped out of sight by about 320. In 327 Constantine brought it back again at a high standard, and presumably a new tariff against gold and copper, but only issued small amounts so far as we know. The large and small silver coin remain an almost theoretical part of the system until later changes in 357. Silvered copper had dropped in size and silver content so that in 330 there was one major denomination whose name and whose relationship to the other coins we can only guess.

The year 357 seems to mark the end of the coinage troubles. Gold was unchanged, silver on a lower weight standard but of excellent fineness, was once more issued in substantial quantities, and copper was freed from its silver content so that certainly by 364 it was once again a low-value copper coin. From that point onwards the changes in the coinage system are slight in comparison to the upheavals of 194 to 364. Gold remained fixed, silver varied only a little, but the volume produced changed from time to time. The copper sank slowly in weight until in 498 the emperor in Constantinople, Anastasius, produced multiples of 40, 20, 10, and five units. These had their values in Greek numerals, alpha = 1, epsilon = 5, iota = 10, kappa = 20, mu = 40, on the reverse as the main information visible.

Throughout the description of the sequence of coinages I have tried to avoid the word which is usually applied to changes in the system that is, reform. My problem with the word is that it has connotations of better and worse, and is almost inevitably involved with state actions. Reform therefore almost declares, each time it is used, 'the state made the coinage better'. Clearly this is a matter of opinion. The state changed the coinage in a direction that it thought was for the better. Or, in less happy circumstances, the state had to change the coinage because of various economic and logistic problems, and it wanted everyone to think that what was dire necessity was really benevolent choice. I strongly suspect that the people in the market place in 274 who were faced with new coins of ten times the value of earlier coins did not think that the change was for the best. But this is to inject into the Roman state something which normally had little place, public opinion below the level of armed revolt. The state produced coinage for its own purposes such as paying state employees and financing state projects. Payment by hundreds of small radiates

*67 Oxford, Ashmolean
Museum. Coin of
Magnentius c. 351 with the
whole reverse taken up by
the Christian sign, the Chi-
Rho — the first two letters of
the name of Christ in
Greek, and the alpha and
omega 'I am the beginning
and the end'.*
Copyright Richard Reece

of uncertain value is clearly worse, and payment in tens of bright new large radiates of settled value is clearly better. From the point of view of the state that was definitely reform.

A second strand in the sequence is the place of gold, silver and copper. It is perhaps no accident that relatively fast, and certainly major changes to the coinage almost all happened between 194–364. The system in AD 190 was as similar to the system in 200 BC as anyone could possibly expect. By 260 the system had gone. In 296 it had changed again. By 364 it was different once more. In 490 the system of 364 was still recognisable. These years of change were the years in which the state, according to one theory, attempted to pass off base coins as silver. All the changes seem to have centred round the problem of how much silver the coin user required in a base coin in order to place confidence in it. There was a constant struggle between the state, which wanted to decrease the amount of silver yet hold the face value constant, and the user, who seems to have dropped the purchasing power towards the intrinsic value. This inevitably had the result of bringing the face value down to the purchasing power, and the cycle started over again. When silver was kept separate, coinage in its own right with an intrinsic value, there was nothing to struggle about.

An alternative theory, which accords with the evidence, but seems unlikely because it requires the state to be beneficent, suggests that the state saw that more people were using more coins and acted accordingly. Copper was no problem, but silver supplies were limited. Up to the years around 200 silver and gold were élite coins. If they spread to the masses they did so purely to bring the masses into range of élite financial dealings. With the debasement forced upon Severus through his wars for the throne, coins sank to a level which brought them close to mass use. Up to this point a market system may well have functioned, but the coins produced did little to help it since they were mainly of too high a value. Now the coins sank towards the level of everyday use and a benevolent state

68 Oxford, Ashmolean Museum. Silver coin (siliqua) of Valens c. 370. The mintmark TRPS includes the name of the mint (TRier) and assures the user that the metal is refined silver (PUSulatum). Copyright Richard Reece

decided to spread the same amount of silver much more widely so that all could share in its use.

Unfortunately, such a move required everyone to rise to the level of sophistication of the policy makers and to accept token coinage. It is not surprising that people newly attracted to real money, which for generations had been above them, responded irresponsibly when they found that what they had been given was not the real thing. Pressures built up and the changes seen in the coinage systems at this time are a result of these pressures. After years of experiment and unsuccessful attempts at coinage for all, the state cut its losses and went back to the system of the first century AD in which pure gold and pure silver were for the top people and the rest were allowed to share in the use of small coppers. In the time of Augustus (27 BC–AD 14) people were in their places and knew what the coin system meant. In the later fourth century the world had gone through radical changes, and inbred knowledge could not be relied on. The gold coins were certified OB, obryzium, pure gold **(colour plate 23)**, and the silver PS pusulatum, pure silver **(68)**. The copper was just copper.

While belief in the state helping to spread the idea of the use of coinage may be difficult we still have to account for the production of small coppers. It is easy to assume that the state would strike small change because in any series of financial transactions small change is obviously needed. Visitors to Italy in the 1970s and early 80s will know that the Italian government of the time apparently saw no point in the production of small change. Supermarkets gave out sweets or chewing gum in change because the small coins were so rare. It was only when many banks started undercutting the government and producing masses of small value notes that officialdom was stung into action. If a modern government can be in this situation it is reasonable to say that the Roman state would probably only produce coins if they were wanted for state purposes.

Gold and silver in the fourth century did filter down the system and move into restricted general use. But metal supplies were limited, state officials, and especially the army, would only accept payment in gold and silver, so how could the gold and silver which had slipped below the government level be recovered and recycled? The answer was to insist that all taxes be paid in gold and silver. People with gold and silver would have to use it to pay their taxes. When a bullion coin slipped into the popular sector there was danger that it might be spent. That could be avoided by making it illegal to use a shop as money-changer by taking in a high value coin and buying a small object. Change for gold and silver was prohibited, so the proud owner of the gold or silver coin which had escaped from state captivity had either uselessly to treasure it or change it at the official money-changers for spendable copper. When those same people came to pay their taxes they could gather together coppers and buy the necessary gold back from the money-changer. And the coin would be whisked away into the tax collector's chest and returned to the mint for recycling. Copper coins of the late fourth century were sent out by the mints as bait to reclaim the gold and silver. This was because the precious metals were almost as sacred as the emperor himself, and in some way a part of him, so they were only on temporary loan to the users. The coinage strongly reinforces the idea of the emperor-centred state.

What we need to know to add detail to the different pictures of coin use set out, and to try to decide between them, is the volume of coinage produced year by year and circulating at any given time. This cannot at present be done with any useful degree of accuracy and there are two views of the problem. One says that error is bad, wrong answers are much worse than no answers, and the whole subject of estimates of ancient coinage must be forbidden territory. This might be called the classical view in which truth is attainable and error is evil. The other attitude holds that no problem was ever solved by forbidding discussion of it. Since error is always with us what we must do is to take note of its existence and whittle it down to acceptable proportions. Investigation of methods for estimation of ancient coinage sizes must continue provided the warning is always given that at present the results are completely speculative, and nothing should be built on them. This seems to me the scientist's way of looking at a problem.

In theory, if every PhD student in the humanities were to be diverted to Roman coinage it might be possible to gain a rough idea of at least the different relative numbers of coins produced at different dates. They would have to gather every known example of every coin from every mint, then compare every example of a given coin, decide if they were struck from the same dies or not, and then add up the numbers of dies for each issue. This would not tell us the actual numbers of coins struck because we do not know how many coins each die could produce. But if dies were used until they broke, it is a fair guess that 2x dies cut to strike one issue in copper compared with x dies for another issue of similar size in the same metal, means that the 2x issue was roughly twice as large as the x issue. The absolute numbers in each issue, rather than the relative size of several issues, depend on the number of coins which any die could, and did, strike. This has been hotly debated, and there is no firm answer in sight. I think it is fair to say that a majority of those interested accept that at present no answer is possible, but that same majority would like to believe in a number between about 10,000 and 30,000 coins per die. This means that a count of 200 dies in a large issue in which the dies were used to breaking point would push the total number of coins produced into the millions.

If we cannot make any progress at the moment on numbers of coins struck we can at least make some headway on numbers of coins used. The discussion so far has assumed that Roman coins exist in the present but has not questioned how they come to survive. Virtually all Roman coins have had a period of disuse if not loss or concealment. It is just possible that there were samples of late Roman gold in chests and jewellery caskets in Constantinople in 1204, and it is possible that some of those coins came back to Venice after the sack of the city. They might then have gone into the chests and jewellery caskets of Venice and several generations later been given to public bodies such as the Universities of Padua or Bologna. These in turn could have filtered through into collections which still survive. If there are coins with such life histories they are in a tiny minority. The great majority of coins that we have now were either lost accidentally or buried intentionally. This means that all Roman coins are either single finds picked up on Roman sites, or from re-discovered hoards.

In setting out the sequence of the later coinage we were using the coins as individual objects without any surrounding information. If we put them back into context we have two new branches of study, that of hoards and sitefinds. Clearly the two give very different information because the sitefinds were casual, accidental, unrecovered losses, while the hoards are the unrecovered examples of coins selected especially for burial. Sitefinds are therefore usually of low value, hoards usually contain coins of higher value. Sitefinds cannot be biased by politics or policy because they are the result of accident. The selection of coins for burial in a hoard can easily be influenced by consideration of which coins could reflect badly on the hoarder, such as forgeries or coins of rebel emperors; or which coins might be affected by public policy such as coins about to be withdrawn or coins which were rarely minted.

Reduced to its simplest form, sitefinds are a sample of what was passing in circulation from hand to hand with a bias towards the lower values, while hoards have always some purpose with a bias towards value. Sitefinds form a reasonably unbiased sample, hoards are a sample with 100% bias. Hoards which were not recovered soon after they were buried bear no knowable relation to the totality of hoards which were buried. This is simply because we know nothing at all about hoards of coins which fulfilled their purposes and were dug up in due course by their buriers. A lot has been written about the reasons for hoards not being recovered in the past but almost all of it is wishful thinking. To start with a cold logical point, it is no good looking at the content of the hoard, in hopes that it could tell you something about the reason for its non-recovery. Putting the hoard together takes place before burial, burial has to come before non-recovery, and I suspect that only a small number of hoards were buried without the intention to recover them. The fact of non-recovery was not known at the time of putting the hoard together and so cannot be read into the composition of the hoard. One school of thought wants the majority of non-recovered hoards to be the result of invasion, war, rape, pillage and plunder. Undoubtedly some were, but the problem comes when undoubted invasions lead to very few coin hoards, and a swarm of coin hoards are seen when there was no known trouble. The connection between hoards buried in the ground and disasters is one that is going out of favour. It has been examined in more detail in the section on silver plate.

Although no hoard has within it the reasons for its non-recovery there is one hoard which through very detailed study has revealed the way in which it was put together. It was discovered at Beaurains near Arras in 1922 and consisted of about 40 gold medallions (multiple values of normal gold coins), about 650 other coins of gold and silver, a candlestick, silver vessels, and jewellery and ornaments. The candlestick survives with some of the jewellery in the British Museum, some parts of the hoard are in the Arras museum, many of the coins and medallions are known, but other parts of the hoard have been dispersed. This is an example in which the finders and later 'agents' purposely spread the rumour of gold and silver being melted down to put investigators off their trail.

The great step forward in understanding the hoard came when Bastien pursued every single coin and medallion he could find (472) and put all the information together. If the coins are put into chronological order they show some very interesting facts. Virtually none of them is worn, and some of the chronological groups include die-linked coins. Both facts strongly suggest that the coins have never been in open circulation, but have been kept together since they were first given out on some special occasion. The face value increases over time from the series of single coins of around 285 to the groups of coins and medallions for the years 296 to about 315. The earliest coins come from eastern mints but by 296, the reconquest of Britain by Constantius I, the emphasis of mint-marks has shifted firmly to the West. The group of 296 includes the great 'Arras' medallion showing a kneeling figure of London, outside the walls of the town, welcoming the official emperor who comes to end a period of rebellion. From an incomplete list the group dated to the Imperial twentieth anniversary (303–4) was worth at least 134 single gold pieces. With about 60 to the pound of gold this means that the owner was given over two pounds of gold.

This takes us on to the means of collecting, and Bastien has constructed a career for the owner of these pieces which moves from a relatively humble position in the court of Diocletian in 285 (eastern mint-marks) to an important post in the court at Trier (Constantius I) and possibly a part in the reconquest of Britain. Hence the campaign medal(lion). By 303 the owner was a high official who had a major share in the yearly hand-outs of gold and silver, but these come to an end about 315. The jewellery includes a ring which has the names Paternus and Valeriana, so if we want we can call the man Paternus. The jewellery of Valeriana (?) shows considerable wealth and sophistication, and the candlestick may be either an official object or part of their home furnishings. The one thing this hoard does not do is give any indication of when or why it was buried. The handouts stop around 315, but that may simply be his retirement date, and there was nothing of such monetary value to add after that date. The Death and Destruction enthusiasts do not take much to this hoard because there is little known trouble around Arras between 310–320 to account for it. One category of find is missing from the hoard which might have been expected after its history had been unravelled. There are no state badges of rank such as the belt fittings and brooches so well known, and so often portrayed later in the fourth century. If we had a picture of Paternus would that mean that he would look like an ordinary upper-class person? And did these badges of rank increase in importance as the fourth century continued?

One other area of hoarding which is of particular interest to the late Roman world, again involves hoards and die studies, but adds the Baltic Sea. Some of the largest hoards of fifth-century gold coins have been found in the islands of the Baltic, especially Gotland, and this needs some sort of explanation. It is important that several coins in these hoards are very often struck from the same dies because this suggests that the coins have never been out in free circulation. Since these coinages are large, and many dies were cut to produce them, the chances of two coins from the same dies meeting up in later circulation are very small indeed. This, in turn, suggests that the coins were put into bags at the mint and were kept together until they were buried. These hoards should therefore represent hoards of bullion rather than hoards of usable coins. The islands of the Baltic were clearly not part of the late Empire, and are not in any obvious direct communication with Constantinople. On the other hand there are records of continual payments of hundreds of pounds of gold to people such as the Goths who were outside the empire and causing authorities much concern. For a time the gold bought off invasions and constant worrying at the frontiers. Why such payments should have ended up in the Baltic must be traced in the movements of the different tribes, but at present these are not well understood.

A different form of coin movement out of the empire into the Barbaricum, the northern and north-eastern fringes outside the empire, has recently been magnificently documented by Alek Bursche. He has gathered together all the late Roman gold coins and medallions from the Barbaricum and brought them together in an illustrated corpus. The most obvious feature of his illustrations is the way that these Roman objects were made Barbarian objects by giving them frames and mountings which range from simple piercing to highly elaborate detail. In every single case the coin or medallion is mounted to show the portrait of the emperor the right way up. The coins were struck with no fixed relation between the head and the tail, so if the head is the right way up the reverse type is usually askew or upside down.

It is the later development of this subject, the multiple gold coin as medallion, as medal, which may bring information back into the Roman empire. The practice of wearing, or at least mounting in a way suitable for wearing, roundels of gold continues in Germanic areas, including Britain, well into the post-Roman period. At first the Roman medallions are imitated **(69)**, and then the designs become more and more disparate. These later 'bracteates' are hammered out of gold sheet rather than struck from dies, but they can be grouped by design and they would fit in with a pattern of distribution from many different centres. At this point the exchange of ideas becomes circular so that bracteates can be discussed as gifts from chiefs to their followers in the way that Barbarian chieftains received diplomatic gifts from Rome: bags of coin for the tribe and a medal for the chief. And the Roman idea receives reinforcement from the later independent practices of the native chieftains.

Individual coins are not as glamorous as hoards because they are mostly copper and usually worn. This means that they have had far less study. Copper coins in the second and third centuries to some extent define the empire. This means that finds of copper coins are usually made within the boundaries of the empire and only infrequently outside. There are exceptions like the fashion around the year 200 of the West Balts around the south-east corner of the Baltic sea (northern Poland and Lithuania) of putting the largest

69 Oxford, Ashmolean Museum. Post Roman gold coin pendant (bracteate) imitating a late Roman medallion. Copyright Ashmolean Museum, Oxford

Roman copper coins, sestertii, in their graves. In general the picture seems to be that token coinage, coinage not worth its weight in the metal of which it is made, is only popular within the area which legally guarantees its purchasing power. A modern parallel would be the old Bank of England pound notes which 'promise to pay the bearer' in gold if paper was not good enough. This worked in England and Wales, and perhaps Scotland, though the Scots had and still have their own note-issuing banks, but there was no point in putting it to the test in modern Antioch. A golden sovereign, however, would have been accepted on the spot. Purchasing sets of postcards in modern Jerusalem, in the absence of Israeli money, is much more easily done in pound coins than in £5 notes.

Maps of the empire cannot be drawn around the distribution of gold coins because they make their way to many different places. Scandinavia, never part of the empire, would come within a gold boundary from the first century AD to the fifth. It would then join the Islamic (gold and silver) empire from the seventh century until the ninth because many hoards of Islamic gold and silver coins are also found there.

Within the empire sitefinds ebb and flow with time. Use and loss of coinage spread with military domination in the early empire, but many areas do not show large-scale coin loss until coins of small value become commonly available in the third century. Almost every site in the empire that has Roman material on it shows the loss of small coppers of the fourth century, but this state of affairs ends shortly after the beginning of the fifth century. Western mints stop production of copper soon after 400 except for Rome, and movement of coins out from the mints for use and loss on sites quickly drops. Rome continues to

143

strike much smaller numbers of copper coins through the fifth century but these hardly circulate in Italy and almost never move in western Europe in general. Silver and gold continues to be struck, but, again, that has little circulation outside Italy. With no new supplies of bullion coin coming in the use of copper becomes risky. If there is no 'promise to pay' in gold then copper coins very quickly lose their token value. It seems likely that common coin using had finished in much of north-west Europe, and certainly Britain, by about 420. Production of copper and gold continued through into the sixth century in most eastern mints but our knowledge of the circulation and use of coinage in the East is at present poor.

With the whole of the Mediterranean in focus at one time, copper coinage can be seen to be in retreat from the West from 400 onwards. It seems to leave Spain in the middle of the century, which is hardly surprising when Spain has fallen into Visigothic hands, and there is little in Malta after about 410. This gives a picture in which the common use of coinage as judged by the loss of copper coin is restricted to the east of Malta and Italy by the middle of the fifth century. The exception is the Vandal state of North Africa which partly spans the dividing line. The Vandals settled down around 430 and seem to have continued to use Roman coinage for some time. Virtually no new Roman coin of the mid-fifth century is found in Carthage itself, but the Roman state would hardly have supplied the enemy with coin. Only by about 470–480 are the first Vandal copper coins issued, and they are very much like the contemporary Roman coins in size and shape.

The reform of Anastasius in Constantinople in 498 was directed mainly at the sad state of copper coins, which had sunk to a very low value. Multiples were introduced to make life simpler. This seems to have had no effect on Carthage, where the basic nummus (plural: nummi) continued until the Byzantine reconquest of 534. Judging by hoards of coins buried or lost in the sixth century, there were still a lot of fourth-century coins available in Carthage even up to about 550. After the reconquest a Byzantine mint took over the Vandal mint and immediately multiple nummi were produced. For some time the one was the main product and loss, but soon the five became common, the ten, and finally the twenty (K = kappa). The information I get from this is rampant inflation resulting from the destruction of the Vandal state by the Byzantine empire. Coin loss on the Danube frontier at this time (Justinian) consisted mainly of 40 nummi pieces, often called folles. Losses in Palestine were also of the higher values. We seem to be able to see here different levels of price structure in different areas of the eastern world. It is unpleasant, but hardly surprising, that the small, efficient, self-contained unit of the Vandals fell to the uncontrolled commercialism of the Empire.

In the successor states of the Roman Empire coinage had different fates. In Britain there was a total gap in any form of coinage from about 420–*c*.650. In Gaul the idea of gold coinage continued, first as imitations of Imperial gold solidi and then the thirds of solidi, tremisses, and then a full Frankish Merovingian coinage started out on its own late in the sixth century. By this time tremisses were the main coin, and it is a purse of these, imported, which dates the Sutton Hoo burial in Suffolk. Different parts of Italy suffered collapse as the Byzantine attempt at reconquest wore the country out and was followed by conquest by the Lombards or Langobards. Rome only seems to start recovering in the mid-700s, but it is important that this is an affair for the City of Rome rather than a helping hand from the Carolingian North. The areas which were taken over by Islam had all joined in the Islamic currency system of gold and silver, but their attitude to copper seems to have varied. Closer inspection might well show that copper coinage was used in parts of the world, which had a good earlier history of the use of copper, such as the Levant.

8. Material

Most excavations on sites which were occupied at the time of the later Roman empire add little to our knowledge of palaces or church plans. Instead they produce town houses or farmsteads. Instead of manuscripts and wall mosaics they produce glass and metalwork. Ivory carvings are replaced by animal bones, and table wares are pottery rather than silver. In other words, just as today, the majority of people lived among ordinary and everyday things rather than the great monuments now visited by the tourist. The different categories of material have completely different information to give which has to be added to the monuments to reach any overall picture of the times.

Animal bones

Bones which form the residue from cooking and eating animals are probably the most common finds, but they are almost impossible to summarise because they vary considerably from place to place and province to province. Modern examples would be the low number of young cattle bones in Britain (veal cutlets) as compared with Italy, or the likely absence of pig bones in the Near and Middle East. Clearly they have information to give, but many provinces lack good reports on large deposits of late animal bones, so making wide comparisons at present very difficult. But there are pointers to ways in which animal bones can be used, and these are extremely important because they show the sceptic the point of not only saving the bones as they are dug up but of paying someone to go through them when the final report is being written to give at least a list of what was found. The cultural and dietary differences already mentioned can be looked for in the past. Did the inhabitants of Italy always favour veal cutlets, have the inhabitants of France always been horse lovers, and so on. Eating preferences will be very difficult to identify as religious prohibitions because the presence or absence of animal bones on a site may be caused by many different factors.

One animal which might repay particular investigation in the later empire is the pig. In the early empire this was a feature of Italian expansion through the beef- and lamb-loving provinces of Gaul and Britain. It features strongly in Latin cookery books, and provided several particular delicacies in the *Maximum Price Edict* of Diocletian. Pork may go up to 12 denarii for an Italian pound while beef may only go up to 8. Sow's udder is set at 20, while liver of swine fed on figs, best quality, is 16. Salted pork is 16, best quality ham 20, and ointment of pork fat 12. Fat fresh pork shows a difference between Latin texts of the edict and Greek. Latin has 12 denarii per pound while Greek has 20. This might suggest that pork is more easily available in the West (Latin speaking) than the East (Greek speaking) if it were not for the fact that all the texts come from the East. It is interesting to know that 'the four feet and the stomach are sold at the same price as the flesh'. Pork sausage is sold by the ounce, 2 denarii, while beef sausage is sold by the pound, 10 denarii. With twelve Roman ounces to the pound this makes pork sausage one of the two most expensive items on the list. In summary, out of sixteen items of meat on the list, twelve come from the pig.

This corresponds well with our written sources, where the *Theodosian law code* has a lot to say about the supply of pigs to Rome. A rescript of 334 points out that 'the guild of swine collectors has dwindled to a few persons' and that since this is a 'compulsory public service' steps must be taken to set things right. The swine collectors presumably set out from Rome to collect swine. Landowners to whom they go 'shall have the freedom of choice as to whether he should pay money to the swine collector. This choice is permitted him so that unrestrained freedom may not be granted to the swine collectors in making their estimates as to the weight of the hogs.' So if the estate owner decides he wants to keep the pigs and pay the money equivalent instead, the swine collector must make a reasonable estimate because otherwise the landowner will simply let the pig go to Rome. Other points at issue are the 'loss which necessarily arises between receipt and distribution'. I assume this is the pig-drop-out-rate on the forced march between collection from the farms and the delivery to Rome. Is this fact or fantasy? One deposit in Rome of the right date, the early fifth century, has a good bone report and that is the site known as the Schola Praeconum. Here over half the identified bone fragments were of pig, and when adjusted for the relative body-weights of the different food animals pig provided over 40% of the meat eaten, with beef coming a close second.

The interesting question concerns the East. In Jewish communities clearly this Italian attraction to pork was absent. When Islam has become organised in the seventh century the same will be true for regions under Islamic control. But how unified were Rome's eastern neighbours before the life of Mohammed bound them into an irresistible force? Material sources could provide a way to answer such questions.

Another aspect of life on which animal bones can comment is organisation. When the family keep a pig in the back garden and slaughter it for their own use at the end of the year all the parts of the skeleton are likely to turn up in the family rubbish pits. This is the scheme which might be expected from self-sufficiency. But if the family were corn producers who relied on a ham industry, a sausage industry and a good pork butcher in the nearest village, pigs would be reared in one place and slaughtered in another, hams would be cured by one farm and sausages made by another. The pork butcher would joint his carcasses and dispose of the less saleable bits, and only the bones from the prime cuts, with the occasional pigs' trotters, would turn up in the corn grower's rubbish.

This may be a material way in to the questions being posed on the nature of towns in the later empire. If all the bone deposits in various sites in a late town are mixed samples covering the whole of the animal skeleton then the community involved has probably not much stake in large-scale food organisations. If the heads and the hooves are represented — to oversimplify — then the animals probably walked to the final destination where they were eaten. If heads and hooves are not in the town then there are signs of a meat industry at work and this in turn suggests at the least merchants specialising in meat provision. There is the division of labour and evidence of specialisation which is the basic building block of the town.

Pottery

After animal bones the next most common category of find is pottery. There are gaps in the record around the empire, but enough has been studied to set out certain ideas. Red-coated pottery is usually quoted as an example of what pottery can tell us. In the early empire of the first century Samian ware with a high gloss and smooth red coat was produced mainly in Italy and the south of Gaul. The material from those production centres is found in Egypt, North Africa, Greece and most of Europe. By the second century Italy had lost its markets as Gaul supplied N Europe, and Spain, North Africa, Egypt, Palestine and the Aegean region all started up their own production. In the third century some of the Gaulish factories closed, others turned to the manufacture of different types of pottery, a few such as those in the Argonne region followed the evolution of red wares. Most of the other areas became self-sufficient in this type of pottery with even Britain producing for itself and North Africa moving to become the main exporter.

The early industry was remarkably standardised in its production. Certain shapes of pot became the norm and variation declined. Even within a given shape the tolerance of dimensions to which individual pots were made can be a matter of millimetres. The later industries, led by the North African producers, took up some of the early forms, which gradually developed and changed with reasonable uniformity between different regions. The combination of uniformity of shapes, gradual change and links between the industries means that red slip ware is the most commonly used means of dating any site in the later empire. This present state of affairs has developed in the past thirty years and is based mainly on the work of John Hayes, who started out to work on the subject in the 1950s. He in turn was helped by the destruction of the centre of Athens by the Goths in 268, and the excavation of those destruction deposits in the Agora by the American School in Athens.

But the subject has continued to grow, and ideas have changed. North Africa, the source of much of this pottery, had few well-dated deposits, so dating depended on the consumers rather than the producers. A few likely historical pieces of information were included in the dating. For example, the fall of Carthage and the surrounding pottery producing area to the Vandals in 430 must have had a major effect on production. If amounts of pottery declined somewhere after 400 then the most likely date for the decline would be 430. But then excavations began at Carthage and the expected Vandal Event was very difficult to see in the archaeology of the town. Doubt has been cast on the devastating effect of the Vandals on the pottery industry, and their arrival in Carthage is no longer taken as a fixed point to date the changes in production.

Other types of pottery are interlinked with other materials. The large oil and wine containers, amphorae, obviously have information to give on the trade in oil and wine, as well as fish sauce, nuts, olives and even nails. Late amphorae have been studied and listed through typologies and the best known and most common types are from North Africa, exporting their surplus of olive oil, and Palestine, exporting both wine and oil. But not only table wares and containers travelled round the Mediterranean. One type of pottery found at Carthage is a type of cooking pot or casserole from the island of Pantelleria. Once identified at Carthage and traced to its source, this ware has been found much further afield.

It may be that the missing link for much study of the movement of pottery is grain. We know virtually nothing about the movement of grain, its source, and its point of consumption from archaeology. Our information comes from texts and inscriptions. But there is a strong view that shiploads of pottery were almost unknown in the Roman Empire except for containers like amphorae. And even there the ship was carrying oil, wine or fish sauce rather than the empty pottery. Table wares and cooking wares are usually assumed to ride on the back of more important items of trade such as corn, so that the almost full hold of the corn ship could well be stuffed with a load of pottery. Alternatively, the grain ship has to find something, preferably heavy, to act as ballast on the return voyage. In this role, pottery is more sellable than rock.

If the general picture of pottery production and the suggestions about connections to other trades are correct then we have in pottery something like the radioactive tracers used to explore blocked pipes in humans and buildings. The pottery may be the guide to much more substantial and complex matters which we cannot see. But to make sense of all this we obviously need a whole series of statements about what late Roman pottery was found where, what its source was, and how the different types change in numbers over time. This is gradually happening as excavations go ahead and, more slowly, are published. Carthage gives an account for Tunisia, Benghazi helps for Cyrenaica, Athens and Corinth give pointers for Greece, and in Beirut major pottery studies are in progress. But the great expatriate archaeological sites of Asia Minor such as Ephesus, Priene, Aphrodisias, Side, Perge and the rest have never produced pottery reports. This should change slowly, but the golden days of site clearance which has left a lot to look at were times when pottery and even coins were not considered of much archaeological use.

Glass

Pottery survives on archaeological sites for two main reasons: it cannot be recycled, and most soil conditions can do little to it once it is buried. This means that most of what was used on a site was broken and then thrown away, and most of what was thrown away is there for us to find. Glass is different in several ways.

In moving from pottery vessels to glass we are moving up the social scale. The effort, technique and knowledge needed to make glass vessels is greater than that for pottery. The raw materials do not occur commonly everywhere, considerable heat is needed to form the molten metal, and blowing glass is a much greater skill than throwing or turning a pot. So while pottery was produced in many parts of the empire within 50 miles of the door of every cottage the production of glass was much more restricted. This meant much greater transport for a much more fragile object, and distance and breakage clearly added to the cost when the survivors of the process were sold in the market. But the cycle did not end there. When the vessel had been used for years, and finally broke, it still had some value, unlike the pot, for if traded in to the glass merchant it could be remelted and used again to make new products. In areas such as Britain where the raw materials were rare, a good trade in broken glass (cullet) could lower, but not eliminate, the need to import the basic ingredients. This means that even if glass vessels in some homes were as common as pottery, this will not be reflected in the finds from an excavation. Broken pot may have been used for hardcore for a garden path, and so is there to be found, but broken glass often left the site for recycling.

Glass fragments from excavations tell us that there are locally produced glass vessels on many sites, but also glass vessels that have travelled hundreds of miles. Fragments from excavation are also often better dated than the complete glass vessels which tend to survive only in graves. Any study of the industry and its development depends on both types of information. There were two great centres of production. One in the west was centred on Cologne and the Rhineland. In the east there seems to have been production in both Syria and Egypt. Production in Cologne certainly went on under post-Roman management. What happened in the East is less well known but glass was certainly produced for Arab customers. In both East and West the new rulers were on the move. Neither had extensive glass making where they came from and continued supply depended on fostering the work of local people who had the specialised skills needed to continue the industry.

In the West the evidence for continuity comes particularly from burials, for example those in the cemetery at Krefeld-Gellep, which span the whole period of change from the Roman Empire to the Merovingian kingdom. Germanic newcomers to the Rhineland found other Germans already settled in the buffer area which late Roman policy had created and those settled Germans had already either taken on, or helped to create, one of several late Roman burial fashions. Glass vessels were put in graves from the third century to the seventh, and the main form used was for drinking. Some of these were simple hemispherical cups that could be comfortably cradled in the palm of the hand, others were tall beakers in the form of slim cones, others are known as claw beakers. These started life in the fourth century as a perfectly respectable Roman fashion. They were simple beakers to which hollow claws have been added, all round, and at different heights **(70)**. This meant that as the beaker was filled with wine the rising liquid continually seemed to spill out into the 'claws', which then filled up while the level in the main body of the beaker stood still. When one tier of claws was full the level in the main body rose until the next tier of claws was reached. Fourth-century forms sometimes make the claws look like miniature dolphins jumping into the side of the beaker, and at the height of glass decoration the claws were decorated with extra frills of different coloured glass.

Moving into the fifth century the vessels of this type became taller, the body became thinner, and the claws formed a greater part of the whole. Development continued until one of the standard Saxon and Anglo-Saxon grave-goods for the wealthy was the Saxon claw beaker.

This Rhineland continuity can be paralleled in the pottery produced in the region of Mayen, around Koblenz, and using as filler local rock from the Eifel mountains; thus Mayen ware or Eifel-Keramik. The jars produced in this ware form an easily recognisable late Roman type in which the rim instead of curving outwards for ease of pouring curves

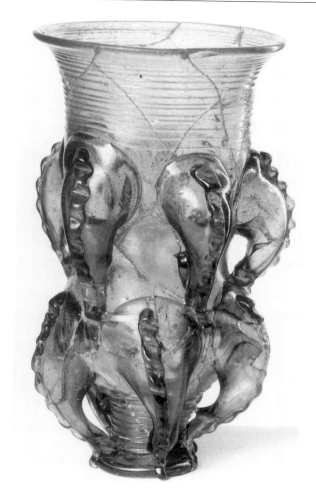

*70 Cologne, Museum. Glass claw
beaker from one of the main
production centres of glass in the
West.
Copyright Römisch-Germanisches
Museum Köln*

back in on itself to give a seat for a lid. The combination of this special form and an easily identified fabric mean that the industry almost defined itself and asked for study. That study has shown a smooth development from third and fourth-century beginnings right through into the seventh and eighth centuries and the revival of long distance trade.

Similar types of continuity are seen in the Levant, where excavators have ceased to draw firm lines between Late Roman / Byzantine and Islamic glass and pottery. They deal instead with rough date brackets such as seventh to ninth century. Historians of the old school might charge the excavators with blurring the picture, but it is becoming more and more obvious that archaeological material refuses to fit into neatly pre-determined historical packages.

At the upper end of the social scale glass is very different, and suggests disruption rather than the continuity shown so clearly by the utilitarian end and the middle of the market. There had been luxury glass vessels from early in the history of glass, and a good if rather isolated example is the Portland vase. It might be fair to say that this glass vessel in two colours, cut to give the impression of cameo, uses glass as a substitute for a semi-precious stone. This is not true of the height of glass luxury in the fourth century when free-blowing, mould-blowing and cutting and engraving had all learned to use this material in its own terms. The most extreme products of the Rhineland glassworks cast doubt on the taste of the Roman customer with money to spend. Perhaps the oddest example is a pair of sandals in clear glass with blue trails which in fact are two flat bottles. The bottles represent the soles of the sandals and the straps are just decorative trails of glass.

As often happens, the more expensive items are less obvious in their attractions and this is the case with the rare cage cups. These have been formed first by blowing a thick colourless vessel and then dipping it to different depths in several other colours of glass. The hollow block produced is then worked with a grinding wheel and the coloured layers are partially cut away, leaving a delicate tracery supported on thin columns left in contact with the central block. The bottom third of the vessel might be coated with blue glass, then this might be covered up to two thirds of the height in red and then finally in green. The upper third will give a green pattern on colourless ground, the middle third can have the green cut completely away to show a red pattern, and the bottom third can have both red and green removed to show a blue pattern. The price here is going to be determined by the work done by the craftsman rather than the basic glass, which is little more costly than the strange pair of sandals, and it may be that the customer has to pay for several months of the craftsman's time. The sandals might have been produced in an afternoon.

A similar type of decoration which I know only as one example in the Schaffhausen museum in Switzerland combines the quite usual decoration of a clear glass bowl by engraving with a grinding wheel, with two colours. Here a clear glass bowl has been dipped in deep red glass and the decoration has been ground through the red. This gives a red background with a design picked out in white.

The Lycurgus cup in the British Museum (71) combines a very rare type of glass with the cutting necessary for the cage cup. Seen in a case with light from the window reflected on it the cup is a strange olive green, rather like a pool of oil spilt on water. If it is illuminated from inside so that the light shines through the glass rather than being reflected off it it shines an intense rose red. This is caused by very small, colloidal, particles of metallic gold throughout the glass. The production of such glass by itself would clearly command a high price, but this vessel has had much more value added by having a design cut in its surface, and undercut, so leaving it standing on thin columns projecting from the centre. The question of how much value a craftsman added to a product in a precious material such as gold, silver or rare glass is hotly disputed, but there is clearly a bill for many hours of craftsman's time to be added to the bill for the specially produced glass.

Most of the luxury items, such as cage cups and two-coloured glass, seem to have ceased production at the end of the fourth century. This is an assumption based on the dates of the graves in which most of them have been found. Fifth-century graves are quite well known in France and Germany, and they sometimes contain glass, but they contain no new types of luxury glass, and very few luxury vessels anyway.

Some vessels which seem to have come down to us direct without ever being buried are now in the treasury of St Mark's in Venice. As Venice hardly existed when fourth-century glass was being made they cannot have a continuous history there. Most of the history of

71 London, British Museum. The Lycurgus Cup, a luxury cut glass vessel in glass which changes colour according to the light. Copyright The British Museum

Venice has been raided from elsewhere: St Mark himself in a smash-and-grab raid on Alexandria, the Patriarchate from Aquileia, and much of the movable decoration of the basilica and contents of the treasury from a crusade in 1204 which diverted to gather goods from Constantinople. A small glass bucket, first recorded in Venice in 1325, seems related to fourth-century products in the West, perhaps Italy. It may have been sent to the East soon after being made, and returned centuries later. The Treasury also contains Byzantine vessels cut from lumps of rock crystal in elaborate gold mountings. At least one commentator would see the cut glass produced both in East and West as the less costly substitute for these, the real things.

Brooches

One of the most obvious forms of later metalwork, visible even on the most exotic of mosaics and paintings, is the brooch. This had changed dramatically since the early Roman period. The early Roman brooch was worn mainly by, or at least buried with,

72 *Trier, Landesmuseum. Crossbow brooch of mid to late fourth century found in Trier. Copyright photographer & Rheinisches Landesmuseum Trier*

women. There is a varied typology, and some of the types are more common in some regions than others. Some of the brooches were decorated with inlaid enamel and this technique is a speciality of north-west Europe. Fourth-century Roman burials show virtually no women with brooches, but they do occur with some men. Typology is now totally restricted to one form which to the English resembles a cross-bow. German speakers see less the overall form than the knobs on the end of the arms and to them it is a Zwiebelknopf Fibeln or an Onionheaded Brooch **(72)**. What you must not do is switch between languages. 'Ein Armbrust Fibeln' is not 'A Crossbow Brooch'. Whatever your dictionary may say, it is something quite different.

There are at least two interesting points here, one of which has been followed and the other has not. The difference is interesting and says quite a lot about the current state of archaeology. When the crossbow brooch has evolved and is turning up in numbers of men's graves from Hungary to Wales and North Italy to Belgium (at least) the obvious thing to do with them is to start a typology. They change over time and several archaeologists have produced very useful ideas on how they change and when. Before the crossbow brooches evolved brooches were mainly women's affairs, and again typologies are called for. But the process of change from the brooch for women to the brooch for men has, so far as I know, hardly been touched on. If this had happened in a prehistoric period there would be numbers of involved studies, one of which would be bound to equate brooches with power in the home. Because it happens in the Roman period when we 'know' what society was like, the matter is hardly noticed.

One recent commentator suggested that it was not in fact Roman for women to wear brooches as essential parts of dress, that they showed the continuation of non-Roman female dress well into the third century. On this line of argument the disappearance of brooches for women is a sign of change in dress fashions, and perhaps a belated move towards Roman fashions. In exactly the same way it could be pointed out that crossbow brooches are certainly not an Italian invention, for they seem to develop in the Danube area. The fact that they seem to become a sign of rank, whether military or civilian, and to spread across the Empire in this way says more about influence and perhaps the homelands of current emperors than anything else.

On this subject some people complain that crossbow brooches are not the sole preserve in death of men. This is true; some graves in which they are found are of women. But these are rare and untypical. Put less combatively, crossbow brooches occur far less frequently in women's graves than in men's, such occurrences are more common at the end of the period than at any other time and should therefore not be used to describe the classic fashion in its prime, and women and crossbow brooches are never linked in any known representation.

When they occur on paintings or mosaics these brooches show that archaeologists for centuries have seen them upside down. The 'foot' of the brooch is always shown in ancient pictures pointing upwards with the three crossbow arms, the 'head' at the bottom. The brooch in fourth and fifth century representations seems to mark out rank and status. The emperor always wears a round brooch set with a large number of precious stones, and the empress, if wearing a brooch, follows the same fashion. The people standing next to the emperor have crossbow brooches, and if this is shown in colour they seem to be of gold. Ecclesiastics do not wear the brooches, nor do the run-of-the-mill soldiers of the bodyguard. They seem to wear gold neck-rings instead. The brooch only seems to be needed to pin the large cloak which covers virtually all clothes worn beneath it. It might be that it is the cloak that represents the position held, or the office in which a particular person is at that moment acting, and the brooch is a secondary adjunct. An archdeacon of the Church of England is entitled to wear gaiters but, of the few who still wear them, I doubt whether any would wear them, as private individuals, to the theatre. On their monuments, raised by grateful church members, they would be more likely to be shown in garb suitable to church services. When we try to interpret representations of crossbow brooches in later Roman scenes we have to try to keep these sorts of factors in our minds.

Brooches do turn up in different metals from plain bronze to gold. Gold brooches are very rare, but within that rarity they have probably been found more often outside Roman contexts and frontiers than within. Silver for some reason is even more rare, but gilded bronze or copper is fairly common. With plain bronze it is difficult to tell, without metal analysis, whether there ever was a precious metal coating, or whether it has been completely eroded. Since the brooches are worn by people shown standing close to emperors it is reasonable to assume that they do signify some sort of position or status. Since they occur in different metals it is reasonable to assume that a particular metal might go with a particular grade. This assumption is supported by the fact that a number of the gold brooches have on them the names of emperors and even in some cases portrait heads. These are presumably imperial gifts.

The point at which disagreement breaks out is over military associations. When a grave is excavated and the anatomically male skeleton has a crossbow brooch on or near the right shoulder, one group of enthusiasts identifies the man as a soldier. Another group of enthusiasts denies the identification. Recourse may be had to mosaics, paintings and metalwork. This does not in fact help because it is the top people, who may or may not be soldiers, close to the emperor who wear the brooches while the carriers of spears and shields do not. It is not an act of desperation to suggest that the problem comes from a misuse of the word soldier. Unless the person is an ecclesiastic who is not allowed to have a second job, status or position, anyone standing near the emperor is by definition a state servant. Some state servants fight with weapons or military tactics, and so fulfil our requirements of a soldier. Others ensure supplies, to military and civilian alike, and these a modern mind might class as civil servants. The point is that all upper-grade late Roman civil servants, state servants, were just as much officers of the emperor as any platoon commander. To that extent the later Empire is a military state.

Bracelets

While brooches changed from mainly female to mainly male ornaments in the later empire, bracelets to some extent took their place, together with beads. These were the expected decoration of the body in the grave, and they are seen on representations in painting and sculpture. The change that happens in the later empire is that bracelets become more commonly found, while individual examples become more mass-produced and, presumably, cheaper. The early bracelet in the grave may be in silver, cast bronze, jet, bone, shale or glass. Each one of these needs a certain amount of craftsmanship and time for production. The bracelet, quite often more than one, in the late grave is a simple affair of twisted bronze strands or cast band with engraved designs.

It may seem unfortunate to concentrate on the grave, but there is a problem here in that we cannot be sure whether the changes seen in museum collections come from changes in life fashion or burial fashion. Objects from graves are usually recovered efficiently if the grave has been recognised as such. The numbers of whole vessels of glass and pottery in museums testify to this, for whole vessels are rarely found in any archaeological context other than a grave. A tray of bracelets in a museum may have a strong 'grave' element even if this is not recorded, so that changes noticed may be heavily influenced by what was put into the grave rather than what was worn. Apart from cemeteries the other type of site which often yields numbers of bracelets is the temple. Here again, we are dealing not with what is being worn but what is being offered to the gods. If coin offerings at temples are anything to go by then it is not the single precious item, the proud possession of the household, which is offered, but the doubtful coins of lesser value. Thus the bracelets of which we have so many fourth-century examples may be mass-produced types for funerary or devotional offerings. Fortunately they also occur quite commonly on occupation sites, the rubbish pits of farms, villas and town houses, so there is hope that the phenomenon is a real change in fashion.

The people who excel in bracelet use are the women and girls of Pannonia, the area of modern Hungary inside the Danube bend. Giles Clarke, who dug and published the Lankhills cemetery at Winchester, pointed this out when he was looking for parallels to some of his graves in which some female skeletons had up to 13 bracelets usually concentrated on the left arm. His best parallels came from Pannonia and that suggested to him that the idea of such a burial rite came from that area. Ellen Swift has pointed out that both in Pannonia and the few graves at Lankhills it is the girls who are buried with this rite. To me this strengthens the connections suggested.

A particularly interesting aspect of Ellen Swift's work is the type of bracelet found in different areas of the Empire. She shows that some types are widely distributed while others have a regional distribution. A point which connects with the Lankhills study is that the bracelets made of twisted strands are different in Britain and in Hungary, but they meet at the great cemetery of Krefeld-Gellep just North of Düsseldorf. This is almost cheating because the cemetery is at such a cross-roads of east and west, north and south, even Roman and German, that its thousands of graves are bound to contain between them most available rituals and objects.

As an aside it is worth pointing out that Krefeld-Gellep may be the cross-roads for an area comprising Britain, Germany, Gaul, Poland and Hungary, but that hardly coincides with the Roman empire. In fact it is as much outside the empire as in. The cemetery is less than 50 miles from Aachen, the Roman spa town which Charlemagne made his capital, and it could be seen as a fourth-century hint to where the future lay.

Beads

When objects such as beads have such a strong conventional association with 'the natives' it is very tempting to push the evidence, which is only just being collected, to show that the Barbarians produced by far the best beads and gave them to the Romans in exchange for useful things like gold, spices and weapons. Early Roman beads are either rather dull, uniform types like the blue frit melon bead or polished pieces of precious and semi-precious stones. It is in the later empire that the great variety of glass beads of many different colours, combinations and composition become common **(colour plate 24)**. These were accompanied by cut precious stones such as the cornelian beads from around the Hungarian Danube which, again, turned up at Lankhills. Emeralds were always popular, but some necklaces seem to include them almost as 'nice green stones' rather than anything precious.

Garnets, the red transparent stone with more depth and colour than rubies, are used by the Romans throughout the empire, but usually as polished lumps of stone. It was not until the Germanic, or Asian, fashion of cutting garnets to use their flat planes to reflect and scatter the light that their beauty could really be seen. In the fifth century some jewellery combines the Roman and the Germanic techniques to very good effect.

For many beads in the fourth century the centre of gravity of a plotted distribution of finds may lie outside the empire, or on the borders. In a similar way many types of beads disregard the chronological boundaries of the Roman empire to flourish both before and after its dismemberment. It is with these types of evidence in mind that I like to think of the sturdy farmers and traders outside the frontiers, to whom the future belonged, stocking up with beads when going to trade with the effete Roman natives.

Belts

There are at least three aspects of the belt. One is practical, to hold up trousers or to gather in a full tunic at the waist. A second is linked, by which the belt becomes an essential part of a uniform. The third grows out of this when the belt becomes a symbol of office in its own right.

For information on the practical aspects we depend on representations in different forms of art. While many tunics are clearly caught in by some binding at the waist, because the part which covers the chest often forms a fold over the waist, it is rare to see the belt itself. This applies as much to the pruners and ploughmen as to the wealthy members of the hunting party. The emperor, when in military dress, often has a cord round the waist, but it seems little more than that, and it ends simply tied up in a knot.

Trousers are a sadly undervalued aspect of the Roman empire. What is needed is a very careful and close study of representations from the second century to the sixth to try to sort out the occurrence of these garments. The remarks here can only be anecdotal and have no claim to authority. But some statement is needed because the spread of trousers is presumably associated with the increase in belts. There is a further complication which is partly to do with words, but has practical importance as well. When are trousers different from tights? Is the only difference between them the provision of feet on tights, but not on trousers? If tights always have feet — and many of the representations of late Roman art strongly suggest a foot and leg covering combined — which seems to extend up to the waist, how is wear avoided?

The type of representation which strongly suggests the wearing of tights is that of the state servants capturing and transporting animals on the Piazza Armerina mosaics, and the Justinian panel at San Vitale in Ravenna. In most of these cases the white leg covering, which is worn under the loose tunic, shows on the feet black lines especially around the toes and heels. These suggest a leather sole, not usually visible, which can be slipped on over the tights. The exceptions are of two forms. Simon James pointed out to me that those in authority at Piazza Armerina are the ones to wear the tights, while those doing the work, and sometimes being berated for it, have tunics and sometimes leggings. This dress is shared by the young men who are presumably sons of the owners, who sacrifice at an altar to Diana before setting out on their (private) hunting expedition. They wear the loose tunic, not even belted, with leggings closely laced up to just under the knee. The servant holding the horse has the same dress but with a much simpler white tunic. All this suggests that the distinction is not a matter of class, but of official or private rôle.

The second exception, seen at San Vitale is the emperor Justinian. He wears red shoes which came to him presumably because earlier emperors appropriated the title of Pontifex Maximus or chief priest whose prerogative they were. They descended from the Roman emperor to the bishop of Rome who still wears them as Pope.

The problem which has to be faced is that tights are only portrayed disappearing under full official cloaks as with Justinian's companions, or under full tunics. Fortunately there is one exception which comes from the decoration of a tomb at Silistra near the Danube in Bulgaria (**73**). The tomb is covered with painted decoration on the inside, even for the whole of the vault. Round the wall are panels with representations of people. At one end stand a couple, presumably man and wife, owners, builders or occupiers of the tomb. He stands draped in full-length cloak caught on the shoulder with a crossbow brooch. In his hands is a rolled document, and it is very tempting to put the cloak, crossbow brooch and scroll together as symbols of office.

On the opposite end of the tomb are pictures of two candelabra. The couple are flanked by two servants, and the side walls each show three servants. Each servant carries

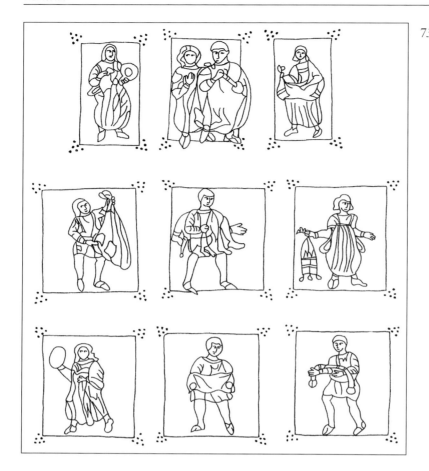

73 Silistra, N. Bulgaria. Wall paintings of an underground burial chamber showing the owners with some of their servants and belongings. Copyright Ellen Swift after D. & C. Jusaulori /L. Schneider

something which seems to be appropriate either to the master or the mistress. It would be satisfying if the eight servants were divided equally. Of the four servants nearest the couple it is easy to see a jug and dish, a mirror and a toilet casket on a chain, and all of these can also be seen carried by the servants who escort the newly-married couple on the Esquiline casket. The fourth of these servants carries a cloak, perhaps with a pin, or a cloth with a design. The four further servants carry things clearly meant for the master. There are his tights, with clearly portrayed feet and a small belt loose in its loops around the top of the tights, his tunic with the two large circles on the front, his heavy belt with a large ornamental buckle, and finally his overall cloak with its crossbow brooch already in place. There have been several studies of this tomb decoration but I can see nothing which prevents the simplest possible interpretation. The wife has the symbols of her domestic rôle brought to her; the man has the symbols of his military rôle brought to him. It is also simplest to assume that he is in fact dressed in all the garments. Certainly we can see the feet of the tights and the overall cloak with the crossbow brooch. The question which cannot at present be answered is whether he has the tunic and the heavy belt on underneath. I prefer to think that these are alternative forms of dress, but I may well be wrong.

The main piece of evidence which supports me is a particular late Roman burial rite which the research of Nick Cooke has shown to be spread through much of the empire. It is also one of the very few rites which crosses regional boundaries and inserts itself into fairly well-defined local customs. In this rite the male skeleton has the crossbow brooch on or near the right shoulder and the man seems therefore to be buried wearing his crossbow brooch, and perhaps the cloak which it pins. Sometimes such a burial is accompanied by a belt set. That is, the metal components of, and fixtures on, a leather belt but this is virtually never worn. It is usually rolled up on one side of the grave, or near the shoulder or the feet, or even set over his legs. This suggests to me full dress and working dress. For a soldier, among the different types of state servant who might have these objects, dress uniform and battledress. In this case the cloak and the crossbow form the dress uniform and the belt is part of battledress.

We are left with the thin belt, with a buckle, threaded through the loops of the tights. This is quite different from the large heavy ornate belt that is being carried to the Silistra man as a separate piece of equipment. In this way we could separate out thin belts which hold up tights and trousers, and thick belts which are more for show. This would make sense of the archaeological finds, for belt buckles do in fact come in two sizes and shapes. One of these is clearly set on a narrow belt, the other is made for a belt of much wider form.

As a postscript to both brooches and belts it is interesting that Ellen Swift has found the latest, and most exalted, brooches in NW Europe to move back from the frontiers into the more settled regions of Gaul. Could we have here the dislocation of the different forms of dress, the honorific and the practical, so that fighting is left to the thin belts without crossbow brooches on the frontiers while high office holders enjoy their large salaries and their badges of office in the safety of the Gallic countryside?

Trousers have been pushed out of mind. In earlier Roman art they are associated with horse-riding Persians, as on mosaics which show the battle between Alexander and the Persians. They are associated with the curly cap which always seems to denote the easterner. In later art this dress, with trousers and cap, is always used for the Three Magi who come from the East to present gifts to the baby Jesus. This is particularly pointed at Ravenna, where the Justinian panel in San Vitale suggests tights for military and ecclesiastics while the Three Wise Men panel at San Apollinare Nuovo shows trousers coming down over different coloured shoes. As in all subjects where certainty is lacking 'a detailed study is urgently needed'.

9. A brief historical summary

The chronology of the Roman republic was based on the consuls, elected each year in pairs. The basic method of dating was therefore to say 'In the year of X and Y, being consuls'. A second strand was to reckon from 762 BC, the founding of the City of Rome; in Latin, Ab Urbe Condita, or AUC. With the transformation into empire these methods of dating continued, but the regnal years of the emperor gradually grew in importance; for example 'in the third year of Constantine'. It was only in the sixth century that the idea of dating from the birth of Christ was devised by Dionysius, a Scythian monk living in Rome who died about 550. He took the birth of Christ to be in AUC 753 and worked on from there. The one thing that is now agreed is that he was wrong, but, however contradictory it may sound the birth of Christ is now put by various factions somewhere between 6 BC–AD 6. It is worth noting that the last year Before Christ, 1 BC, was immediately followed by the first year of Our Lord, Anno Domini, AD 1, so there is no room for the year 0 beloved of makers of tables and summarisers of evidence.

The empire, in a sense, 'happened', rather than 'was constructed'. The method of succession from one emperor to another was never set out or agreed and this must be held responsible for some of the major troubles of the empire. By the second century AD the family principle of the first Emperor Augustus (27 BC–AD 14) had given way to a principle of adoption. This, by tradition, gave the empire its Golden Age, and a series of emperors, Trajan (98–117), Hadrian (117–138), Antoninus Pius (138–161), Marcus Aurelius (161–180), whose substantial reigns at least ensured stability. The dynastic principle wormed its way back into the system with the marriage of Marcus Aurelius to the daughter of Antoninus Pius, Faustina II. The dynastic principle immediately demonstrated its faults when their son, Commodus (180–192) proclaimed himself as the re-incarnation of Hercules. One of his main claims to fame was the refounding of the city of Rome as Colonia Herculiana, and coins duly show the emperor ploughing the ritual furrow round the 'new' territory.

After the murder of Commodus the imperial (Praetorian) guard, perhaps in sheer desperation, put the empire up for auction and the highest promise of money for the guard gave the empire to Pertinax. Civil war broke out in 193 from which emerged Septimius Severus as sole emperor in 197. He had some mopping up of rivals to do, and the scars which this action left on many parts of the empire that had backed the wrong candidate remained for a long time.

Septimius Severus came from Africa, from Lepcis Magna in modern Libya. His coin portraits do not give any help to those who want to proclaim him as the first black emperor; he looks Caucasian. He was linked by marriage to Syria, and a rather complicated family tree provided emperors until 235. The banner headlines came from Antoninus, high priest of the god Elagabal, represented by a black stone in the temple at Emesa (Homs in modern Syria). He was popularly known after his god as Elagabalus, and his main claim to fame was the simple proposition that since the new emperor represented the sun god, the best of the East, it would appropriately symbolise the fusion of East and West if he were to marry the chief priestess of the West, the chief Vestal Virgin. Those who like their dose of scandal, whether now or in the past, need to remember that being a Vestal Virgin was not a life-long vocation, it was a twenty-year stint, after which a good marriage was quite appropriate, perhaps almost expected. It was little more than insensitive of the new emperor not to give her time to retire.

This odd detail is given to show the problems and cross-currents which had developed at the centre of the empire so quickly after the four great adoptive reigns from 98–180. Peter Brown put this period of frantic change in the third century in an interesting perspective when he asked whether the crevasse of the inner life had not been opening up unseen during the century of unnatural stability. Change is inevitable, and to hang on to stability and batten down the hatches can lead to fast and furious action when the time is right. Civil war from 193–197, factions within the empire, provinces fighting other provinces, the army separated out into different sides, was bad enough, and was partly repaired by Severus. But a succession of weak rulers after him may have given too much opportunity for change.

Any ancient history course that reaches Severus tends to do so with relief that here is a well-documented reign at which things can be brought to a close. To go on into the third century is to investigate chaos, the inevitable result of an absence of good written sources.

After the Severan dynasty had died out there was a series of problems from peoples outside both the eastern and western frontiers. These problems demanded strong military leaders, and those were found. The internal problem came when an emperor needed either to change or be changed. If he was killed in action against the enemy, which was very unusual, then his second in command could be proclaimed, and battles could be fought with any other candidates. Other candidates are referred to as usurpers after we know which candidate won. This is true even within a reign, for a new candidate putting himself forward against a sitting tenant is transformed from potential usurper to new emperor simply by winning. By definition you cannot have a successful usurper; he is the new emperor and his success legitimises his challenge. This is a distinctly wasteful method of succession which diverts attention from the main problem, the enemy outside. Those who want to make sense of the third-century emperors should go to Sir Ronald Syme's *Emperors and Biography* in which he tries to assemble what is known about the long list of Imperial lives. His main opponent is a fourth-century schoolmaster, possible author of the *Historia Augusta*, once thought to be our one good guide to the third century. The pedantic hand, which used some original sources and then added considerable embroidery, is known by librarians as a book to keep off shelves which can be reached by children. Unfortunately this is incorrect. The author is a fascinating inventor of false information about coins, but very weak on sex.

The false trails of the *Historia Augusta* end at the same time as the disorganisation of the third century. By accident or design the accession of Diocletian in 284 marks the beginning of a new phase in Roman history. The early empire up to the third century is known as the Principate, the rule of the princeps, who in the best conditions was a first among equals. The later empire, after Diocletian, is known as the Dominate, the rule of the Dominus, who is always Lord of all he surveys.

Because Diocletian was the first well-recorded emperor for some time, there is a danger that he gets the credit for all sorts of changes that had actually been going on during the third century despite its turmoil. Diocletian may well get the credit for the codification and making explicit of many changes which gradual evolution and usage had begun. He was said to be a former slave, Diocles, who had made his way up through the army. One source has him as a contender for the throne against the ruler Carus. Carus won the battle and thereby made Diocles a usurper. One of Carus' captains stabbed the emperor, making the usurper the obvious ruler. That was 284 and any betting person, relying on imperial form through the third century, would not have given good odds that Diocletian would still be emperor in 290. In 305 Diocletian, senior of four emperors, under the particular care of Jupiter made the highly unexpected and unprecedented move of abdicating. He had established the tetrarchy (rule by four) and shown it how to continue: the two assistant emperors would become the seniors and would in turn each appoint an assistant. He had been extremely ill in 303, a complete mental and physical breakdown, and wanted some peace. He had built for himself a little retirement villa, which later housed the whole medieval town of Split, near Salona in Croatia, and he retired there, so all our modern commentators say, to grow cabbages.

His plans were no doubt perfect, it was the people involved who would not follow them. By 308 there were eight people claiming to be one of the two senior emperors. Diocletian was called out of retirement to a conference at Carnuntum, between Vienna and the Hungarian border, but this failed, and he moved back into total obscurity. Meanwhile the son of one of Diocletian's assistants, Constantine son of Constantius, was clearing away the brushwood of opposition left by the tetrarchy. He completed his clearing up when the last rival, Licinius, was killed in 324.

In the meanwhile Christianity had first been outlawed under Diocletian (303), churches pulled down, scriptures confiscated and burnt, and a great boost given to the young and vigorous church by selective martyrdom. Constantius was later known as one emperor who had at least been temperate in his administration of anti-Christian laws. Whether this was a later myth to glorify his all-powerful son, or whether it was his real attitude we can probably never know. Certainly the best place for martyrdom seems to have been outside Constantius's sphere of influence, which was Britain and Gaul. By 311 one of Constantine's last rivals, Galerius, was gravely ill, and he lifted the total ban on Christianity provided the Christians would pray for his health. Their prayers did not prove very effective, and he died shortly after. In 312 Constantine evicted the emperor in Rome, Maxentius, after a dream or vision, in which he had been promised victory under the sign of the first two letters of the name of Christ in Greek, XP, superimposed. In *hoc signo vinces*, or *hoc signo victor eris*: in this sign you will conquer or by this sign you will win. The edict of toleration followed in 313, and soon after that it was probably less trouble to be a Christian than to be a pagan.

Christianity was not made the state or official religion of the empire by Constantine. That should probably be set in 383 when the altar of Victory was removed from the Senate House in Rome. But by 383 the Senate and Rome were no longer the centre of worldly power and authority. The bishop of Rome was to be built up by St Augustine, shortly after that, into a powerful position which later developed into the papacy, but worldly power had moved with Constantine to his new city, Constantinopolis. The promontory, sticking out from Europe towards Asia across the narrow straights which drained the Black Sea into the Mediterranean, had a small city on it which had been there for perhaps a thousand years, Byzantion. It had been fairly affluent in the early empire but had backed the wrong side in the civil wars of 193–197 and had sunk into obscurity. It seems a powerful vindication of Constantine's choice for a new capital that the thriving city of Constantinople continued till the sack by the Venetians in 1204, survived the Ottoman conquest of 1453, and was still the main mint city of the Ottoman empire, as Kustatineyah, till 1918. Today it continues as Istanbul, which seems to be a Turkish form of the Greek for 'to the city', as our grandparents went 'up to town' (on the 'up' line) for special occasions.

Perhaps we ought to mention here that Rome could not feel surprised at its desertion by Constantine however upset it was at the loss of Imperial status. Diocletian had visited Rome perhaps twice in his reign, since he spent most of his time where he was needed to fight and to administer. And he was not needed in a rather drowsy backwater halfway down the Italian peninsula overrun by old families who still thought they counted. His visit in 303, to mark the beginning of his twentieth anniversary celebrations, was presumably the time when his great baths were inaugurated, so there was still something which bound the Roman emperor to Rome. When Constantine moved to the east there was still need for an imperial outpost in the west and later emperors in the west used Milan as a capital, then Ravenna.

With Constantine, and Christianity, the dynastic principle returned after an absence of some time. As 'Emperor' became more a position and status, rather than a vehicle for the capabilities of an exceptional soldier, and as his person became sacra, set aside, sacred, so there was a non-physical power which needed to be handed on from generation to generation. If the link between the last of the family of Constantine and that of Valentinian is correct, then there is a family chain stretching from the 290s–450s. Some links in the chain were very weak, for we know little more of the person of the Emperor Honorius than that he kept geese; but there was continuity.

The male line of Constantine died out with his great step-nephew Julian (355–361) whose cold Christian upbringing in the court of Constantine made him a confirmed pagan as soon as it was safe for him to express his preference. He seems to have been a very able administrator who by forcibly collecting taxes only needed to collect one third of the amount theoretically due, but he was hardly a realist in hoping to reverse the Christian revolution. It was not so much the strength of the Christians and their ideology, as the weakness of the pagans and the almost total rundown of what ideology they had ever had. His three years from 361–363 as sole emperor made little difference in fact to the general trends of the time.

The house of Valentinian (364 onwards) set to work to reorder an empire under external attack. Valentinian died in 375, of apoplexy brought on by the manners of barbarian ambassadors, and his brother Valens died in the battle of Adrianople, in the marshes near the Danube mouth, against Gothic armies possibly assisted by Hunnic extras. It is doubtful whether this was seen, at the time, as more than a reverse to be countered. To later commentators it is the beginning of the end. Such an end has to be mainly concerned with the West, if it is not to be drawn out till 1453, a West which Constantine had left some time before. Slowly the western provinces changed as independent kingdoms of German descent started up. The main folk movement started on the last night of 406 when the Rhine froze over and entrance to the empire became easy. The Visigoths eventually settled in Spain and southern France with a capital at Toulouse. The Vandals moved over to Africa and settled in Carthage. The Anglo-Saxons settled in Britain, Burgundians were centred on Worms, the Franks remained by the Rhine. By 440 the western provinces of Africa, the Germanies the Britains and the Gauls were separate kingdoms and by 500 Italy and the Danube provinces had followed. The western empire had fallen, if that is the alternative terminology you prefer, but the eastern empire continued.

There are dates to which people cling in their dissection of the end of the western empire but no one is definitive. After the death of Theodosius the Great in 395 the throne belonged to two children, Arcadius and Honorius, aged 12 and 8. The commander in chief, Stilicho, claimed that Theodosius, in his last breath, had made him guardian to the boys and so regent. Arcadius took the East and based himself at Constantinople and was old enough, or had good enough advisers, to dismiss the claim. Honorius was left in the West with Stilicho and submitted. To some people this is the division of the empires, East and West, even the start of the Byzantine empire, but most would agree that this is to rate the separation too highly.

A favourite date for The End is 410, August to be precise, when Alaric the Visigoth, who had besieged Rome in two earlier years, 408 and 409, finally sacked the city. While it seems a pity to spoil a good story — and rape, sack and pillage always rate highly — there are severe problems. Constantinople was totally unaffected by this end. The emperor Honorius, who had moved his court from the city on the plains, Milan, to the city in the marshes, Ravenna, in 408, was safe and well. He was indeed worried when the Goths proclaimed a puppet emperor, Priscus Attalus, and marched out to evict a pretender. But it seems to have been the challenge to his authority rather than the safety of the Eternal City which called for action. The archaeology of Rome in the fourth and fifth centuries is at present very thin, but there is at least one pointer to Alaric's actions. The Basilica Aemilia was burnt down at some time in the later empire, as large lumps of charcoal fused by molten bronze on to chips of marble clearly show. In the debris was a bag of coins. The bag was burned and the linen threads replaced with metal salts as the coins corroded. When the clump of coins was separated in 1980 the latest coin was one of 409 struck in Rome, so it would be over-critical to object to this as one example of Alaric's work.

The main problem with such a thin archaeological record is not the need for supporting evidence for the event but the fact that there is virtually no evidence as to what happened immediately afterwards. Since churches were built, and food was consumed, and rubbish was deposited less than ten years after The End we probably have to assume that the shock value was more than the physical disruption. No doubt portable valuables were taken, and certainly some major buildings were fired, but the tidying up operation must have been brisk and effective, and life clearly went on. Letters from people who were there, Pelagius, or heard about it from elsewhere, Jerome in Bethlehem, regard it as an epoch-making event and reckoned events before the sack, or after, but Augustine in North Africa seems to be more concerned with the settling of refugees from Italy. In fact his joy that the emperor had at last moved to make a law penalising heretics in the week after the sack rather overshadows his grief at the fall of the city. Since citizenship is to be based in heaven it is difficult to be too sorry about the sack of a city in which there remain an unhealthy number of influential pagans.

Later in the same century, in 475, the emperor recognised by Constantinople, Julius Nepos, was replaced in Rome by a youth called Romulus, son of the Patrician Orestes. In 476 Orestes was killed by the head of the Germanic part of the army (Odovacar) and Romulus was deposed, but given a pension of 6000 gold pieces (solidi) a year. While this sounds an enormous sum, for two noughts would have to be added if it were turned into modern pounds sterling, we have to remember that the greatest families of the time measured their yearly income in hundreds of pounds of gold. Each pound of gold produced 72 solidi, so Romulus's pension was not even 100 pounds of gold.

His name has proved too good to miss so that Rome can begin and end with a Romulus. It is true that no later emperor was proclaimed in the West, but to make him the last emperor is to miss the point that Julius Nepos, the properly constituted emperor, was still alive and well in Dalmatia (modern Croatia) till he was murdered in 480. The end of the last western emperor is therefore 480. At his death Odovacar, in control of Italy, wrote to the remaining emperor in Constantinople suggesting that there should be a replacement, but Leo saw no need for that since in him the whole Roman empire had sufficient emperor. Germanic feuding led to the establishment of the Ostrogothic kingdom of Theoderic (died 526). He seems to have governed his own people as King, and the Romans of Italy as Viceroy or Imperial deputy. He struck bronze coinage of his own, and a small amount of silver. His mint at Ravenna also struck gold, but that was always in the name of the emperor in Constantinople. Imperial authority was therefore to some extent recognised, but perhaps it has to be added that this depended on the good sense of Constantinople in not interfering.

In the fifth century the emperors were seldom memorable. To some extent it is a time when the women make a greater impression than the men. Chief amongst these must be the redoubtable Galla Placidia. She was daughter of Theodosius the Great and half-sister of Arcadius and Honorius. She was captured by Alaric as a hostage in 410 and carried off to Gaul, where her wedding to Alaric's brother Athaulf was celebrated in full Roman style. The marriage speech was declaimed by the puppet emperor Priscus Attalus, whose elevation had goaded Honorius to action. Naturally his place was with the Goths rather than the Romans. Galla Placidia seems to have left behind a high-ranking officer, Constantius, who was to rise further on her return. By 415 she had buried Athaulf, after converting him, and returned to Ravenna to marry Constantius, who later became emperor as Constantius III. Their child became the emperor Valentinian III.

She is perhaps best known through the building in Ravenna known today as the mausoleum 'of' Galla Placidia in the sense of 'built by' rather than 'buried in'. In fact she was buried in a round mausoleum added to the south-east corner of Old St Peter's in Rome where she died. Her gold coins, which are relatively common, show a rather schematic portrait decked out in full jewelled regalia. Above her head the hand of God is often shown with a wreath, perhaps to still any doubts about her authority.

The best-known empresses of the fifth century in the East were the sister of Theodosius II, son of Arcadius, and later on his wife, Eudocia. Pulcheria was the power behind the eastern throne early in the reign, but having chosen a wife for her brother (421) she eventually left the court. Eudocia travelled to Jerusalem after she had seen her daughter Eudoxia married to the emperor in Ravenna Valentinian III son of Galla Placidia. As she passed through Antioch she made a speech which was very well received, but, while she was away from Constantinople her position was undermined and she in turn left Constantinople permanently in 441.

Theodosius II died in 450 having, as AHM Jones puts it, 'reigned rather than ruled', and his sister Pulcheria seems to have accepted the nomination of the powerful army forces, Marcian. She crowned him herself and perhaps sealed his position with a nominal marriage. In a sense there is transmission of authority through the female line. A male needs to be there but, provided he is looked after by a competent female — mother, sister or later wife — he can be either a six-year-old boy (Valentinian III) or a complete nonentity. At this time the army, though extremely powerful, ran a course parallel to that of the emperor. The seat of power in the army, Aspar, could not aim at the throne himself because he was both Barbarian and Arian, so there had to be an imperial nominee. Marcian was safe since although he had been in the army he had never attained high rank. When Marcian died in 457 another obscure soldier named Leo was chosen. This perhaps marks a turning point.

Leo seems to have had some ideas of his own, and to have acted on several occasions against Aspar's advice. Matters came to a head when a highlander from central Anatolia called Tarasicodissa provided evidence that Aspar's son had dealings with the Persian enemy, and the balance began to change. Tarasicodissa was rewarded, changed his name to Zeno and married Leo's daughter Ariadne. Aspar was finally eliminated, together with other Germanic commanders, and the army to that extent was brought under imperial control. But mixed up in all these machinations were the Ostrogoths who had been harassing the eastern European frontiers under their king Theoderic Strabo (not he of Ravenna, Theoderic the Great). The Ostrogoths were in a sense bought off with military salaries and sent off to worry the West, where they were soon established in Italy. This leaves out of account the Huns, a collection of tribes who most untypically had banded together under one leader, Attila. The Huns were for much of this time a disturbing force further from the Empire than the Goths, but they did spend some time in Gaul, and when in North Italy caused major destruction and threatened to march south on Rome. They fell apart on the death of Attila in 453.

Such summaries conceal a whole world of intrigue and diplomacy in which the opposing sides of Romans and barbarians become almost blurred. The 'barbarian' Theoderic Strabo went off to Italy with the Roman title equivalent to Commander of the Forces and the appropriate salary. Hunnic soldiers had been used by the Romans in Gaul, with Attila's permission, to settle military problems there. Attila had a succession of Latin secretaries to help in the dealings with the Empire and one of these, a Pannonian, was Orestes. He later became Commander in Italy in 474, and made his son Romulus emperor in 475. The Byzantine court sent envoys to Attila in 448 at his court, which seems to have been somewhere in the east of modern Hungary, and Priscus the historian who went with the party has left a fascinating and rather complimentary account of what they found. If Priscus had been returned to earth around AD 1100 when the first crusades passed through Constantinople, or 1204 when the Venetians sacked the city, my feeling is that he would have judged the Huns the rather more civilised. That is not to ignore the destruction which the Huns did wreak on Aquileia, or on the Danube frontier, but to point out that their professions and their actions were rather more consistent than those of Holy Warriors who considered themselves civilised.

On Zeno's death his wife Ariadne, daughter of Leo, chose as successor Anastasius and later married him. Power had once again been passed through the female Imperial line from one male appointee to another. Leo's reign brought in the question of ethnicity, germanicness and hunnicness. Anastasius's reign starts with a religious problem which, as always, centred on 'straight thinking' or orthodoxy and (wrong) 'choice' or heresy. Anastasius is variously described as a convinced Monophysite, and as having an Arian mother, and a Manichaean uncle (see glossary). All these groups were wrong choices, heresies, and the Patriarch of Constantinople objected to a person with such connections and views becoming emperor. Matters were settled by requiring the new emperor to make a profession of orthodoxy before he was installed.

After Anastasius came Justin I and he was joined as emperor by his nephew Justinian, who became sole emperor in 527. He directed the empire forcefully, not alone but with Theodora since 'we have taken as partner in our counsels our most pious consort given to us by God' (introduction to Novel (= law) 8). Theodora was clearly a remarkable woman, and she has the distinction of being the first person for about two hundred years about whom a detailed piece of sexual scandal is recorded. The fact that it is probably imaginary, and reflects more on the writer than the subject, only strengthens the claim that sex, having left the Roman empire under Constantine, only returned under Justinian.

Justinian, perhaps like Diocletian, owes his fame to his survival. A reign from 527-565 ensured that many things are attributed to him. There are credits and debits; the Ravenna mosaics in San Vitale could not happen without the reconquest of Italy from the Ostrogoths, but that disrupted and impoverished the whole country. The great church of Hagia Sophia in Constantinople should ensure him a place as one of the best emperors. But he left an empire heavily overstretched, both in military and financial terms, because of the grandiose visions of reconquest of 'the remaining countries which the ancient Romans possessed to the limits of both oceans' (Novel 30).

The aftermath of Justinian's reconquests merge in with major problems on the Persian front early in the 600s and then the rise of Islam in the middle of the century to remove large sections of the Byzantine empire. A much smaller and more compact state continued round the Aegean, sometimes shrinking and sometimes expanding again, till the 1400s. On Christmas Day 1400 the emperor Manuel II, Basileos ton Romaion, king of the Romans, was the guest of King Henry IV of England at a banquet where Manuel was asking for help against the Turks on behalf of an enclave around his capital city. Little help was given and at sunset on Monday, May 28th 1453, the final Turkish attack was launched and by noon the next day Rome had finally fallen.

Glossary of Early Christian terms and ideas.

A glossary is usually arranged like a dictionary with isolated terms expanded to give a brief definition. In this case that would lead to so many circular references that a continuous narrative has been preferred with the more unusual terms and names printed in bold.

The Christian religion centred on the life and death of a historical person, Jesus, who is known outside the purely Christian writings. This would now be generally agreed; what has always been at issue is the meaning invested in the life and death of this historical person. Jesus himself was a Jew and grew up in the Jewish tradition based on the books of the **Law** and the books of the **Prophets**. Out of the life of Jesus grew more books, the four **Gospels**, which gave an account of His life and its meaning, the **Epistles**, letters which several elders of the church and especially St Paul wrote to different communities spread round the Mediterranean world to help them over points of understanding, order and governance. There was also a book of **Revelation**, a mystical account of the church and its relationship to God. For Christians, the Law and the Prophets form the **Old Testament**, the Gospels, Epistles and Revelation form the **New Testament**.

The Old Testament is the 'Evidence up to the time of Jesus'; the New Testament takes things on from there. Many aspects of the OT were taken both by congregations and writers to point to aspects of the NT. This accounts for the large number of OT stories and personages illustrated in Christian contexts.

In the first book of the Law, **Genesis** or Beginnings, God created Heaven and Earth. First man was made, **Adam**, and then a woman, his wife **Eve**. They lived in the garden of **Eden**, innocent and happy, forbidden only to eat the fruit of the tree of knowledge of good and evil. The **serpent**, embodiment of evil, which is separation from God, persuaded Eve that the fruit was good to eat, she persuaded Adam to eat it as well, and that was the end of innocence. Adam and Eve had to clothe themselves because they suddenly realised they were naked, first with fig leaves, then with skins. They were evicted from the garden by an **Angel with a flaming sword** and went out to make their own way in the world. Since their lives now had a fixed term, children had to be born to replace them, hence **Cain and Abel**. The nomadic herdsman Abel and the settled farmer Cain brought **thankofferings** to God. This is usually shown as Abel holding out a lamb (San Vitale). God accepted Abel's offering but not Cain's, whereupon Cain killed Abel. (Via Latina Catacomb, Vienna Genesis)

Things went from bad to worse over many generations until the time of **Noah**. He and his family were the only good people on the earth, so they were warned to build an **Ark** and to gather into it two of everything living while God prepared continuous rain which flooded the earth and killed off everyone and everything outside the ark. The ark in early

Christian times is more like a large brass-bound box on short legs than the boat with roof and curly ends familiar today. (Via Latina, Vienna Genesis)

Life returned to normal, over many generations, and **Abraham** lived in Ur in Mesopotamia. Abraham and his family set out for Canaan, which was to become the homeland of the Jews. On the journey Abraham was met by **Melchizedek**, king of Salem and a priest. Melchizedek gave Abraham **bread and wine** which NT writers take to be a prefiguring of the **Eucharist** (San Vitale). Later, **Abraham and his wife Sarah** were met by **three men, angels**, who told the old couple that they would have a child (San Vitale). The son **Isaac** was born, but then God commanded Abraham to **sacrifice Isaac** to him. Abraham obeyed, but at the last moment God stopped him, and instead provided for sacrifice a **ram caught in a thicket** (San Vitale, Via Latina). Abraham sent out a servant to find a wife for Isaac, and the **servant, with ten camels** found **Rebecca at the well.** She gave him and his camels water to drink (Vienna Genesis). Isaac had two sons, **Jacob and Esau**, and Jacob had a son called **Joseph**. Joseph's coat of many colours made his brothers jealous; he was sold as a slave and ended up in **Egypt.** There he prospered and became a high official. His brothers came to Egypt in search of food without knowing that he was there. He helped them, and the family were reconciled (Vienna Genesis, Via Latina). With Jacob's death we have reached the end of the first book of the OT, but have accounted for well over half the OT scenes commonly represented in the early Christian world.

The second book, Exodus, opens in Egypt with the Jews in captivity. Jewish boys were supposed to be killed at birth, so when **Moses** was born his mother put him in a **basket floated in the river** (Via Latina). **Pharaoh's daughter** discovered the boy, brought him up, and eventually Moses led the Jews out of captivity from Egypt. They had to **cross the Red Sea**, but when Moses commanded, the **sea parted** and the Jews walked through to the other side. The **Egyptian army** pursuing them was caught as the sea rolled back into place (Via Latina). For good governance Moses was given by God the **Ten Commandments engraved on tablets of stone** (Tours Pentateuch, Via Latina). The tablets were set in the **Ark of the Covenant**, which the Israelites carried round with them on their travels.

At this point representations used by the early Christians become much more selective, and the narrative story is more or less abandoned. While some books of the OT are mainly rules and regulations and clearly do not lend themselves to illustration, the concentration on Genesis and Exodus seems consistent in the different types of representation. Three further figures who have been mentioned in the text are **Daniel, Jonah** and **Balaam**.

Balaam appears in the book of Numbers, the fourth book of the OT. The circumstances of his work as a prophet and contact with Balak, King of the Moabites, is seldom referred to. What matters is the fact that he set off on an ass on a journey of which God disapproved. An **angel with a flaming sword** therefore blocked his way where the road was narrow. The ass sensed the angel and refused to go on, **Balaam beat her**, and this happened three times. Finally God allowed Balaam to see the angel and Balaam realised that he had been going against the wishes of God and had very narrowly escaped destruction.

Daniel was a prophet in captivity with the Jews at the court of Darius, King of the Persians Informers told the king that Daniel prayed three times a day to his God, and as punishment Daniel was put in the **lions' den**. After a night he was let out unharmed. He was replaced in the den by the informers with their wives and children and 'the lions had mastery of them, and brake all their bones in pieces or ever they came to the bottom of the den' (Via Latina, and many burials).

Jonah was a prophet who was told by God to go from his homeland to preach at Nineveh, to the east. He was reluctant, went to the coast, **took ship** and went the other way. The **ship ran into a storm**, the **crew threw Jonah overboard** because he was going against God's call, and all was well for them. **Jonah was swallowed by a great fish** and stayed in its belly for three days. He repented, **the fish vomited him up**, and he went home. A second call came, and this time Jonah went obediently to Nineveh and declared that the city was doomed. The citizens took heed and reformed and God forgave them. Jonah was furious and after giving the Lord a piece of his mind he settled down outside the city wall in a shack he made himself to watch what happened. God made a **gourd grow over the shack** to give him shade (Via Latina), then, destroyed it and Jonah got sunstroke. He was sad for the destroyed gourd, then realised why God had allowed Nineveh to survive.

Most of the OT scenes that have been mentioned and described in the text were used to reinforce points of doctrine by the early Christian community and it is that to which we can now turn.

Christianity was based on the life, death and resurrection of Jesus. The first Christians knew about this for themselves; later generations had to get the knowledge either as handed down through oral tradition or through reading or hearing the approved accounts. People who could be relied upon for information were the **twelve companions of Jesus, the Apostles**. When the information came to be written down and codified the best accounts were clearly those of the Apostles themselves or, failing that, their disciples and companions in turn. Of the many accounts which circulated, four crystallised out as definitive and to two of these the names of the Apostles **John** and **Matthew** were attached. The other two accounts had the names of younger writers, **Mark and Luke**. The writer of Luke continued the account of the life of Jesus into the life of the early church, and this was the **Acts of the Apostles**. The writers of the four gospels were proclaiming the good news and so were called **Evangelists**. In the mysterious **Revelation of St John** there are **four beasts** in front of the Throne of God and these have been related to the writers of the four Gospels. One was like a **lion, St Mark**, the second like a **calf, St Luke**, the third beast had a **face as a man, St Matthew**, and the fourth beast was like a **flying eagle, St John**. One man had not been with Jesus in his life, but became an equal of the Apostles later on. This was **Saul of Tarsus**, originally scourge of the Christians and then, after a conversion on his way to Damascus, **St Paul**, pillar of the church.

The life of Jesus as related by the four **canonical gospels**, those that establish the **rule** of the Christian faith, and by some other texts, was divided into scenes convenient for painting, mosaic or sculpture. The **birth of Jesus, the Nativity**, at Bethlehem was seldom shown in the way that we think of it on Christmas cards, with the family grouped around the cradle in a draughty stable. One of the clearest depictions, on the Vatican reliquary lid, shows this scene backed by the **Ox and the Ass**. This picture goes outside the four main gospels, where you will search for the Ox and the Ass without success, and uses for inspiration the non-selected writings, the **Apocrypha**. The **baptism** of Jesus by his cousin, **John the Baptist**, presents few problems except for the fact that this is one of the few occasions on which **God the Father** is heard to speak in the presence of **God the Son**. The appearance at this time of the **Spirit of God** descending like a **dove** completes the **Holy Trinity of God the Father, God the Son, and God the Holy Spirit**. Depictions of the Baptism show the Son and the dove; the Father might be shown by a **hand in the sky**.

After the Baptism the life of Jesus consists mainly of acts, **miracles** and addresses. During these events, the Gospels say, Jesus was recognised by some as the chosen, or **anointed one**, and so was sometimes known as the **Christ**. Some commentators see this as later interpretation. The (traditionally) three years of preaching and miracles lead to the **entry to Jerusalem** with Jesus riding on a colt, the foal of an Ass, with crowds lining the route. A meal was taken in the evening by Jesus and the Disciples and it is this which is the pattern for the central cult service of the church. The scene soon changed to arrest in the garden of Gethsemane after one of the original twelve, **Judas Iscariot**, has betrayed Jesus to the Jewish authorities. Judas was paid for his information, but in remorse he took the **money** back and then hanged himself. The **Passion** narrative moved on with a **trial** before the **Roman governor**, **Pontius Pilate**, who at first refused to condemn Jesus because of lack of evidence. Later he was persuaded and Jesus was condemned to be **crucified** at the same time as two genuine criminals. Depiction of the crucifixion is unknown in the fourth century and still rare in the fifth. Constantine abolished crucifixion as a standard penalty, but examples later than his reign are known. Only when it ceased to identify the centre of the religion with common criminals was this scene commonly depicted.

But, in a sense, this is the start of the story rather than the end. Death was followed by **three days in the tomb** and then the **tomb was empty**. Even the most progressive of commentators agree on a bottom line which is that while the process of the **resurrection** cannot be proved, demonstrated or disproved, what is beyond argument is the effect that the finding of the empty tomb had on the disciples. Some would add, 'and that is what matters'. After the resurrection, or return, of Jesus comes the **Ascension** when his form rose into the clouds leaving footprints behind in the turf. After a short pause of **fifty days (=) Pentecost** followed when the disciples found they could speak all languages. The promise of Jesus to send a **comforter** was shown by **tongues of flame** that came down on the heads of the disciples and demonstrated that they were the recipients of the **Holy Spirit**.

Many pictures of Jesus involve the miracles he did or the occasions when he preached. Full details of these can obviously be found in the NT. Many are linked with OT scenes and the linking brings out points on both sides. In Via Latina the **crossing of the Red Sea** is set on two occasions opposite the **raising of Lazarus**. In the first case the Israelites are saved from slavery in Egypt by Moses. In the second case Jesus brought back to life a friend who had died. Jesus is therefore the sequel to Moses in that He saves the believer from the slavery of Sin and Death. It is safe to assume that there is probably no such thing as a scene in Early Christian art which is purely decorative and devoid of any interpretative meaning. This may be true of all art, but here we risk being embroiled in circular definition, for decoration may be art which has no interpretative meaning. The example of the Raising of Lazarus must stand for the many other examples which are depicted in early Christian art.

The last meal of Jesus with his disciples is capitalised as The Last Supper, and this became a focal point of the church's action with names ranging from a **Commemoration of the Lord's Supper** to a **Communion Service** or a **Eucharist** (= thanksgiving). The name **Mass** seems to be quite basically associated with the words in Latin which end the service '**Ite, missa est**' which in English involve **Going Out**, being **dismissed** back into the world. This avoids a whole world of modern interpretations in collision, some of which were present even in the early Church.

The word Church suggests a body of people, while church suggests the building in which they meet together at regular intervals. This building, when it developed as a purpose-built structure, needed a **table** on which the **common meal**, or token meal of **bread and wine**, could be placed and round which prayers could be said. The word **altar**, with connotations of stone or marble, could be taken over without difficulty from the Jewish tradition, though there, as with Greeks or Romans, the idea of a location for a **sacrifice** must be present. This does not seem to have provoked major problems until the Reformation, when the whole idea of **sacrifice** as attached to the **Lord's Supper** became **Anathema** (literally **things hung up**, by extension, in pagan temples, and therefore **utterly abominable**).

One member of the congregation presided at each service, soon marked out as **priest**, or even **bishop**, and the **altar end** of the church was organised so that he had a seat behind the altar, usually in an **apse**, or **semicircular extension in the end wall**. The **congregation** who had already been through the process of **baptism** would stand in the main body of the church, the **nave** (derivation uncertain), others might be allowed in the side areas, or **aisles (wings)**, suitably curtained off from the happenings. Some early churches had galleries above the aisles (St Demetrios in Thessalonika, though rebuilt, gives a good idea of this arrangement).

Just as different church plans evolved in different areas of the Empire, so did different theologies. Some Jews became Christians, as did some who believed in Greek philosophy, and others who had leanings towards the secret knowledge of the East. There was therefore the Church in Jerusalem, with a claim to established authority, since that is where it had all happened, and where most of the first witnesses remained. The Hellenistic (Greek-speaking) Church grew up in many places in many forms as people like St Paul travelled widely spreading the news. People in Corinth, or even Rome, to whom Paul and his disciples wrote firm, helpful, but sometimes extremely complicated, letters had a different experience from the people in Jerusalem, so it was to be expected that differences of opinion and emphasis would emerge. This was enshrined in the NT with the inclusion of St John's Gospel and several letters of St Paul which sometimes differ in their interpretations or even write in entirely different ways about the same basic things. This in the worst circumstances led to **choice** of **faction** to follow, and both choice and faction are included in the word **heresy**. To start with, to have a choice is not necessarily wrong, though the existence of factions sounds dangerous. When '**What is**

Right' has been decided once and for all, then by definition choice of alternatives is impossible. Those who believe 'What is right' call it **Orthodoxy**, or right thinking, and the right believers are described as the **Catholic** Church

If choice exists it is between right and wrong, and that which gives the alternative, the **Not Right**, is damned as a heresy. This soon comes to mean an important deviation in belief from what is Right. Such deviation has within it danger of **Eternal Damnation**, but the **Heretics** should at least have their **errors** pointed out to them. If they realise their error they may be saved; if they persists it may be kinder to kill them so that they do not infect others. The church soon learnt to get the secular state to execute heretics who they always hoped, up to the last moment, would realise their errors.

This may be the point at which to provide a menu of **choices**. It would be good to preface it with an eternal health warning as to what must be believed, but a creed which pleased the Church of England would hurt Coptic and Ethiopian Christians, and a creed approved by the Orthodox churches is not acceptable to Rome.

The doctrine which has caused most difference of opinion is that of the **Trinity**. Most of the older churches would accept the view of the Trinity outlined under the **Baptism of Jesus**. **God the Father** is unseen in the Heavens, He is seen on Earth in the life of **God the Son**, and after the Ascension of the Son, **God the Holy Spirit** comes to the world as a continual presence.

The problems start when people discuss what is the relationship of these three **Persons**. Who started things off? Does God exist first as One, and then **create** the Son, and do they both **give rise to** the Spirit? To answer these questions without offending anyone is impossible. Is Jesus a **creation** of the Father? The **Arian heretic** would say Yes. First was the Father, then the Son was created as part of the general process of creation, and His dignity as Son was a gift and not an **intrinsic** part of His nature. Does the **Holy Spirit proceed from the Father and the Son**? Yes say the West; very firmly NO say the East.

If **Right Belief** says that the **three persons of the Trinity are One God**, existing **co-eternally** for ever, being at all times **the same substance without any difference or inequality**, then what was the **nature of Jesus**? The **Nestorian heretic** would say that there were **two separate persons** in the one body, one divine and one human. The **Monophysite heretic** would say there was only **one single nature, and that divine**. This causes anguish amongst Right Believers because it seems to mean that the person who went through the life, and particularly death, of Jesus was not really a man, but **seemed like one**. Yet others would say that a **single nature** must be right because otherwise we are talking of a split personality. Yes, mono, one, physis, nature, but **compounded of the human and the divine**.

Arianism was so named after the priest **Arius** who died about 336 and around whom the controversy centred. It has been mentioned mainly in relation to the **Goths** because when they settled in Italy one of the most obvious differences between them and the Romans was their Arian deviation from Italian Orthodoxy. This was because bishop **Wulfila, or Ulphilas**, who converted them from the 350s onwards, had grown up in Arian surroundings and was even consecrated bishop by **Eusebius of Nicomedia**, a friend of Arius. Eusebius's importance at the court of **Constantine** the Great and his son **Constantius II** meant that at times both Emperor and many in the court and church in the capital were Arian. At times Arianism was Right Thinking, with the result that everything else was, by definition, heresy.

Nestorianism may be named after **Nestorius**, whose teachings may have set out the main lines of the heresy. **Monophysitism** comes from the basic definition of the heresy: **mono = one, physis = nature**.

These heresies, and many others, which could be quoted, have one obvious thing in common. They all flourished in the eastern part of the empire and in the **Greek** language. When translated into **Latin** or English they seem to become more leaden, explicit and quibbling.

There were major arguments in the West, but these were rather different in nature. **Donatism** caused major disruptions in the first half of the fourth century, particularly in **North Africa**, and lingered on until the seventh century, but this was a **schism** (a **tear** as in cloth) rather than a **heresy**. It meant that your opponents believed much the same as you did on most important points of doctrine, but their practices were different. In this case, the dispute centred on the correct attitude to those weaker ministers and members of the congregation who had given in to the persecution which broke out around 303 and given in the scriptures to be burned. Bishop **Donatus** led the party, which said that these people were so far in the wrong that the ministers no longer had valid powers and the people should never again be admitted to worship in the church. The opposing party said that no sin was too great for **forgiveness** provided the sinner repented. The erring minister, if he repented, could still officiate at services because he was the bodily representative of Jesus. The repentant people in general should be re-admitted to the fellowship after a suitable lapse of time. This led to total division and to some extent the division reflected city and country, Romanised and indigenous, with the former taking the harder line. It has been seen as a politically fired disagreement, but this is strongly contested.

Another western disagreement which took place mainly in Latin was this time about fundamental points of doctrine and was therefore a heresy. It centred on **Pelagius**, a man born in Britain but polished in Rome, so that no one ever accused him of being a rustic. His opponents such as **St Augustine, Bishop of Hippo** in North Africa, and **St Jerome** accused him of being almost everything else and the whole controversy was so bitter that the reputation of everyone involved in it seems diminished as a result. This heresy rumbles on still today because to the person in the church pew, or even in the market place, it sounds as if it matters. Reduced to an insensitive minimum the question is whether you can be **saved through your own efforts**, (error attributed to Pelagius), or whether, however strenuous and good you are, you need the **benefits built up for you through the life and death of Jesus**, (Orthodoxy). We have to rely for the point of view of the **Pelagians** on a few letters which have survived, and the replies by their opponents to their main campaign statements which have all been eliminated. Both sides get deep into quibbles and perhaps both have an interest in not sticking to the main points, for that would end in a simple Yes versus No shouting match. I hope it is fair to say that **St Augustine**, as the champion of **Orthodoxy**, thought he had to hold out because any concession towards the enemy would be to undermine the whole purpose of the **Incarnation: the arrival of God in the human world**. If we could have put ourselves right, we did not need beyond-human help.

Gnosticism and Manichaeism have been left till last because they are somehow always on the edge. If included in any discussion of Christian problems they need to be qualified by the adjective Christian because there are aspects of both which go well outside this area. The Gnostics claimed **gnosis (=) knowledge**. A fundamental part of that knowledge was the distinction between two equal and opposing powers, **Good and Evil**, which are often described as Light and Dark. This admission that the **two powers are equal and opposite** is often shortened to **Dualism**. The person who set out the **Gnostic** case most clearly was **Mani** who was born in **Mesopotamia** in the early third century. **St Paul**, in the Christian tradition, had been influenced by the Gnostic tradition, and Mani is said to be influenced by the writings of St Paul and his followers. St Augustine of Hippo was a **Manichee** for nine years before he was converted to Orthodox Christianity, and after that he was highly sensitive on the subject and devastating in his attacks on the sect. But he never joined in the general moral smear campaigns which attributed to the **Manichees** nearly every abominable practice possible.

One aspect of the doctrine is that there is **powerful Good**, and each person has some **imprisoned** in the **body** which is generally **Evil**. Life is for saving and promoting the Good against the tangible world and the body, both of which belong mainly to Evil. Early Christians, and some later ones, who read the letters of St Paul and his followers without due care and attention were attracted to the challenge of Dualism. They needed to compare this with the Gospel of St John, where the struggle is proclaimed as over if only the reader will believe the fact. But as always those who want to live by the text have to do so very selectively, and ignore all that conflicts with their needs.

While the problems of **Bishop Donatus** in North Africa, who felt that **traditores,** those who had handed over the Gospels, could never be valid priests or full members of the church again, or the ideas of **Pelagius** on **free will and self help**, may generate some discussion today, the Greek problems on the **nature of Jesus** and the **internal architecture of the Trinity** often raise the question 'does it matter'. Here there are really two questions. Did it matter at the time, and can it matter now?

At the time that these questions were in open discussion there can be no doubt at all that they mattered. If nothing else they caused many riots and large numbers of deaths. It may well be that theological questions were argued about superficially by people whose main interest was a punch-up, and there is no doubt that in the more extreme riots mobs were rented by both sides. But the main heresies outlined here were all capable of being reduced to slogans which could inflame and enthuse crowds, and to that extent they were extremely important facts of life.

Whether they can matter today again divides into two parts. Even knowledgable Christians rarely lose sleep over doctrines of the Trinity, but it does matter to some whether Jesus was a troubled person like themselves, or just a visiting deity temporarily inconvenienced by a human body. To the many who are not Christians 'matter' will mean something different. Perhaps it depends on whether they are willing to enter into the spirit and concerns of an age in order to understand it better, or whether an age of superstition and religious quibbling must be judged uninteresting. If the people of the later Roman empire interest us, then their beliefs and concerns, however odd, must 'matter' to us today.

Further reading

Introduction

There are not many books which take the later Empire, or Late Antiquity, as a period to be understood in its own right. Probably the best is *The World of Late Antiquity*, Peter Brown, Thames and Hudson, 1971. More recent, and more historical, are the two books by Averil Cameron, *The Later Roman Empire (284–430)*, Fontana, 1993, and *The Mediterranean World in Late Antiquity (395–600)*, Routledge, 1993.

Some subjects are not developed in later chapters so they need mention here. A useful set of information on separate cities can be found in *The City in Late Antiquity*, edited by John Rich, Routledge 1992, and there is an excellent survey of ideas on the late city in Italy by Bryan Ward-Perkins *in Continuists, Catastrophists, and the Towns of post-Roman Northern Italy*, Papers of the British School at Rome, vol 65, pp 157 to 176 (1997). Three particular cities, Rome, Milan and Constantinople are brilliantly treated by R Krautheimer, *Three Christian Capitals: topography and politics*, Los Angeles/London, 1983. More abstract aspects of life in late antiquity have been dealt with in three books by Peter Brown, *Power and Persuasion in Late Antiquity*, University of Wisconsin Press, 1992, *The Body and Society*, Columbia University Press, 1988, and *The Rise of Western Christendom: triumph and adversity AD 200–1000*, Blackwell, 1996.

History

This comes in two classic forms sober and totally authoritative or gossipy and sometimes unreliable. The standard work is *The Later Roman Empire 284 to 602*, by A.H.M. Jones, Blackwell, 1964. This is the book to go to for almost any historical aspect of the later empire as a starting point. It summarises virtually all the original, primary sources but does not list all the modern sources. After 1964, probably the best way of finding later authoritative works, and what someone thinks of them, is to go through the review section of the Journal of Roman Studies from 1960 onwards, and from 1988 the Journal of Roman Archaeology. Jones more often deflates quotable judgements than makes them, so if you want to know who the Good Things and the Bad People of the later empire are you should read *The history of the later Roman Empire 395 to 565*, by JB Bury. This was republished in two paperback volumes by Dover Books in 1958. I suspect that most of the criticisms levelled against it are caused by the fact that he believes many of his ancient sources and quotes them as if they were all fact. But this in turn is an asset because he does give long quotations from sources which are otherwise difficult to find.

Sculpture, painting and mosaics

The vital point here is extensive illustration but unfortunately most books are selective. The fashion for substantial illustration of important monuments, in their own right, which flourished in the 1970s, especially through Thames and Hudson, seems to have faded out, so that a majority of more recent books show you only what they feel is more important for the exposition of some particular case study in ideas. *The Pelican History of Art* remains a basic starting point with *Roman Art*, by Donald Strong, revised by Roger Ling, 1995, *Early Christian and Byzantine Architecture by R Krautheimer*, revised by him and by S.Curcic, 1986, and *Early Christian and Byzantine Art*, by John Beckwith, 1970. The pictures in all three are very useful indeed. The texts of Strong and Krautheimer are some of the best summaries that can be found.

Four Thames and Hudson classic volumes provide a very good coverage of all the monuments mentioned in this book. After Strong, by far the best commentator is R Bianchi Bandinelli; *Rome the centre of power to AD 300* (1970), and *Rome the Later Empire 200–400* (1971). Here the quality of the excellent plates is balanced by an incisive and tough text. Two books on the Christian aspects of the same time scale by André Grabar: *The beginnings of Christian Art 200 to 395* (1967) and *Byzantium 395 to 565* (1966) have excellent pictures but a waffly text which never really gets anywhere.

More recent works include *Age of Spirituality*, edited by K Weitzmann, New York 1979; *Byzantium: treasures of Byzantine art and culture*, edited by D Buckton, London 1994; Lyn Rodley, *Byzantine art and architecture*, Cambridge 1994.

An even more extensive collection of pictures, many not repeated in the other books comes in *Late Roman Painting* by Wladimiro Dorigo, JM Dent, 1971. In this case the text is so highly atmospheric that summary or note-taking is almost impossible. S Walker and M Bierbrier, *Ancient Faces: mummy portraits from Roman Egypt*, London 1997, gives a thorough account of these paintings with lots of pictures.

Manuscripts, silver and other materials

There is one approachable book on illuminated manuscripts which in 127 pages and 48 superb colour plates gives an authoritative survey: *Late Antique and Early Christian book illumination*, by Kurt Weitzmann, Chatto and Windus, 1977. Silver still relies on the excellent survey by Donald Strong, *Greek and Roman gold and silver plate*, Methuen, 1966. After that there is the British Museum catalogue of the exhibition: *Wealth of the Roman world*, by JPC Kent and K Painter. Detailed publications tend to be very detailed, and in the language of the country to which the find belongs. One report in English is *The Seuso Treasure* by M Mango and A Bennett, Journal of Roman Archaeology supplementary series 12, 1994.

Many different aspects of material are discussed in very approachable terms in *Roman Crafts*, edited by Donald Strong and David Brown, Duckworth, 1976. This includes chapters on silver, bronze, enamelling, jewellery, minting of coins, pottery, lamps, terracottas, glass, iron making and smithing, woodwork, textiles, leatherwork, marble carving, stucco work, wall painting, and mosaics on walls and floors. Many new ideas, and much more evidence, have come up since 1976, and it would be very useful indeed to have that information gathered together once more as a starting point for further reading and investigation.

Coins and the economy divide into two parts. The coins as struck are now fully covered up to 491 in the various volumes of *Roman Imperial Coinage*. The editors have changed through the fifty years that it has taken to complete the survey, but they started off with Mattingly and Sydenham and ended up with Carson, Kent and Burnett. Volume 6 starts with the reform of Diocletian in 294 to 296 and volume 10 ends with the accession of Anastasius. After 491 detail is best pursued in *Byzantine coins in the Dumbarton Oaks collection*, vol 1 by AR Bellinger and vol 2 by P Grierson, Washington 1968. For coins as found it is more difficult to find a general survey. I suggest my own *Coinage in Roman Britain*, Seaby, 1987, only because it outlines some of the methods which can be used anywhere, and because there is not at present any wider survey. The economy has many aspects that cannot all be followed. Pottery and its economic meaning in the later empire is discussed in detail in *Trade in the W. Mediterranean 400–700*, by Paul Reynolds, British Archaeological Reports International Series 604, 1995. At the other end of the scale on the more historical side is *The economy of the Roman Empire* by R Duncan-Jones, Cambridge 1974.

Churches and religion

Church architecture is fully covered in Krautheimer's great work mentioned above. Church archaeology is much more difficult to track down, but there are a series of early reports on work at Lyon, Grenoble and Vienne, very well illustrated and in fairly basic French, in *Guides Archéologiques de la France* numbers 9 (Grenoble), 10 (Lyon), and 11 (Vienne). Similar volumes were written for Geneva and Aosta and are well worth trying to find, but publication details are elusive because they were first produced for the International Congress of Christian Archaeology.

For the change from a majority of pagans to a majority of Christians there are many useful texts and ideas in R Lane Fox, *Pagans and Christians*, Penguin Books, 1986. *The Rise of Christianity* has to be followed in the block-buster of that title by WHC Frend, London, 1984. *The Early Church* by Henry Chadwick, Penguin Books, 1992 gives a very thoughtful account of the expansion of Christianity. Any reader who wants to get behind the Gospel narratives to find out what was going on at the time the Gospels were being written has to start with the brilliantly incisive commentary by DE Nineham, St Mark, *Penguin New Testament Commentaries*, 1963. It might be fair to warn some people that this theological study might conflict with their Religion.

Virtually anything you want to know about the Christian church, whether totally metaphysical or practical, ancient or modern, is summarised with high authority in the *Oxford Dictionary of the Christian Church*. This is revised at regular intervals and it is always worth consulting the latest edition.

What's new?

The way to answer this question, year by year, is to look at the review section of the *Journal of Roman Archaeology* which started with volume 1 in 1988 . Works in all languages are reviewed, in several different languages, and range from general surveys to the most intricate detail. If you want only a general background you can often get that from the review because reviewers are encouraged to write around the actual books in question, and often to bring in other information as well. Both the *Journal of Roman Archaeology* and the *Journal of Roman Studies* have review-articles which give very wide surveys of particular topics.

Text illustrations

35   Vienna, National Library. Vienna Genesis, Rebecca at the well. Österreichische Nationalbibliothek, Wien
36   Rossano, S. Italy. Rossano Gospels, Christ before Pilate. Copyright Hirmer
37   Cambridge, Corpus Christi College. St. Augustine Gospels, portrait of St. Luke. Copyright The Master and Fellows of Corpus Christi College, Cambridge
38   Paris, Bibliothèque Nationale. Tours Pentateuch, Moses receiving the Ten Commandments. Cliché Bibliothèque nationale de France, Paris.
39   Rome, Church of SS Giovanni e Paolo. Exterior view. Copyright Richard Reece
40   Geneva, Church of la Madeleine. Plan of the sequence of church buildings. Copyright Ellen Swift after C.H. Bonnet/Service cantonal d'archeologie, in Bonnet 1986.
41   Rome, St. John Lateran. Exterior view of the baptistry. Copyright Nicholas Vella
42   Rome, Church of Santa Sabina. Interior view. Copyright Nicholas Vella
43   Rome, Church of Santa Sabina. Interior view showing the nave arcade. Copyright Nicholas Vella
44   Grado, N. Italy, Church of S Maria delle Grazie. View of the west end of the church of the 7th–9th century. Copyright Richard Reece
45   Vaison-la-Romaine, S. France. 5th century epitaph now in the cloisters of the cathedral. Copyright Richard Reece
46   Rome, Church of Santa Costanza. View of the ambulatory. Copyright Nicholas Vella
47   Ravenna, Mausoleum of Theoderic. View of the exterior. Copyright Peter Clayton
48   Ravenna, Mausoleum of Theoderic. Detail of carving round the capstone. Copyright Richard Reece
49   Constantinople, Church of Hagia Sophia. The ground plan. Copyright Ellen Swift after E.H. Swift/P. Lampl, in Krautheimer 1965.
50   Constantinople, Church of Hagia Sophia. Interior view from west to east. Copyright Peter Clayton
51   Ravenna, Church of San Vitale. View of the exterior. Copyright Peter Clayton
52-53 Augst, Museum. The KaiserAugst silver hoard. Copyright Humbert & Vogt, Römermuseum Augst.
54   London, British Museum. The Esquiline silver hoard from Rome, the marriage casket. Copyright The British Museum
55   London, British Museum. The Mildenhall silver hoard, the Oceanus plate. Copyright The British Museum
56   London, British Museum. The Thetford gold and silver hoard, the gold buckle. Copyright Peter Clayton
57   London, British Museum. The Hoxne gold and silver hoard, the 'empress' pepperpot. Copyright Peter Clayton
58   Cyprus National Museum. The second Cyprus silver hoard, the wedding plate. Copyright Peter Clayton
59   New York, Metropolitan Museum. The second Cyprus silver hoard, the plate showing David and the lion. Copyright Peter Clayton
60   London, British Museum. Sutton Hoo burial, spoons possibly inscribed 'Saulos' and 'Paulos'. Copyright The British Museum
61   St. Petersburg, Hermitage Museum. The Meleager Plate. Copyright The State Hermitage Museum
62   Oxford, Ashmolean Museum. Base silver coin with a 'radiate' crown. Copyright Richard Reece
63   Oxford, Ashmolean Museum. A worn sestertius with the head of Hadrian (117–138) reused by Postumus (260–268) and overstruck with his radiate portrait. Copyright Richard Reece
64   Oxford, Ashmolean Museum. Reverse of a coin of Postumus (260–8) showing the figure of Victory. Copyright Richard Reece
65   Oxford, Ashmolean Museum. Coin of Aurelian struck after the reform of 273. Copyright Richard Reece
66   Oxford, Ashmolean Museum. Silver coin of Diocletain c. 300 with a reverse showing the numeral XCVI. Copyright Richard Reece
67   Oxford, Ashmolean Museum. Coin of Magnentius c. 351 with a reverse showing the Chi-Rho. Copyright Richard Reece

68 Oxford, Ashmolean Museum. Silver coin (siliqua) of Valens c. 370. Copyright Richard Reece
69 Oxford, Ashmolean Museum. Post Roman gold coin pendant (bracteate) imitating a late Roman medallion. Copyright Ashmolean Museum, Oxford
70 Cologne, Museum. Glass claw beaker. Copyright Römisch-Germanisches Museum Köln
71 London, British Museum. The Lycurgus Cup. Copyright The British Museum
72 Trier, Landesmuseum. Crossbow brooch of mid to late fourth century found in Trier. Copyright photographer & Rheinisches Landesmuseum Trier
73 Silistra, N. Bulgaria. Wall paintings of an underground burial chamber. Copyright Ellen Swift after D. & C. Jusaulori

Colour illustrations

1 Oxford, Ashmolean Museum. Coin portraits of the emperors Marcus Aurelius, Gallienus, Postumus and Diocletian. Copyright Richard Reece
2 Oxford, Ashmolean Museum. Coin portraits of the emperors Constantine the Great, Constans, Valens and Theodosius II. Copyright Richard Reece
3 Cherchell, Algeria. Mosaic of the agricultural work of the different seasons. Copyright Cherchell Archaeological Museum. every effort has been made to contact the owners of the Copyright. Reproduction rights will be willingly paid for should they contact the publishers.
4 Piazza Armerina, Sicily. Mosaic of animal hunts, the capture of the bison. Copyright Mary Sullivan, Bluffton College
5 Ravenna, Mausoleum of Galla Placidia. Interior mosaics.Copyright Peter Clayton
6 Ravenna, Orthodox Baptistry. Baptism of Christ.Copyright Peter Clayton
7 Ravenna, Arian Baptistry. The dome mosaic.Copyright Peter Clayton
8 Ravenna, Arian Baptistry. Baptism of Christ. Copyright Peter Clayton
9 Ravenna, Church of San Apollinare Nuovo. Christ Enthroned. Copyright Peter Clayton
10 Ravenna, Church of San Apollinare Nuovo. The palace of Theoderic. Copyright Peter Clayton
11 Ravenna, Church of San Apollinare Nuovo. Mosaic panel with an imperial portrait, perhaps of Justinian. Copyright Peter Clayton
12 Ravenna, Church of San Vitale. Apse mosaic with the empress Theodora and her court. Copyright Peter Clayton
13 Ravenna, Church of San Vitale. The offerings of Abel and Melchisidec. Copyright Peter Clayton
14 Constantinople, Imperial Palace. Mosaic of boys riding on a camel. Copyright Artephot/A. Held
15 Rome, Vatican library. The Vatican Virgil, the death of Dido. Copyright Biblioteca Apostolica Vaticana
16 Rome, Vatican library. The Roman virgil, Dido & Aeneas sheltering in a cave. Copyright Biblioteca Apostolica Vaticana
17 Florence, Laurentian Library. Rabbula Gospels, the Ascension. Copyright Firenze, Biblioteca Medicea Laurenziana, Ms. Laur. Plut. 1.56, c. 13v
18 Paris, Bibliothèque Nationale. Tours Pentateuch, The Flood. Cliché Bibliothèque nationale de France, Paris
19 Rome, San Paolo flm. Interior view of the nave. Copyright Nicholas Vella
20 London, British Museum. The Water Newton Hoard silver hoard, the Innocentia bowl. Copyright Peter Clayton
21 The Seuso Hoard. The Meleager plate.Copyright Peter Clayton
22 Oxford, Ashmolean Museum. Two gold coins, an aureus of Maximian c.300, and a solidus of Constantius II c. 358. Copyright Richard Reece
23 Oxford, Ashmolean Museum. Gold coin, solidus, of Magnus Maximus c. 383.Copyright Richard Reece
24 Wörms, Museum. Glass beads from a typical late Roman necklace, found in Wörms. Copyright Museum in Andreasstift, Stadtverwaltung Wörms

Index